# Dagoes Read

## Tradition and
## the Italian/American Writer

Essay Series 25

Fred L. Gardaphé

# Dagoes Read

## Tradition and
## the Italian/American Writer

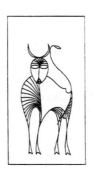

**Guernica**
Toronto / New York / Lancaster
1996

Antonio D'Alfonso, Editor
Guernica Editions Inc.
P.O. Box 117, Station P, Toronto (Ontario), Canada M5S 2S6
250 Sonwil Drive, Buffalo, N.Y., 14225 U.S.A.
Gazelle, Falcon House, Queen Square, Lancaster LR1 1RN U.K.

Typeset by Betta Della Rosa, York

Legal Deposit — Third Quarter
National Library of Canada

Library of Congress Catalog Card Number: 94-74402

Canadian Cataloguing in Publication Data
Main entry under title:
Dagoes read: tradition and the Italian/American writer
(Essay series ; 25)
ISBN 1-55071-031-1
1. Canadian literature — Italian-Canadian authors — history and criticism
2. American literature — Italian-American authors — history and criticism
3. Canadian literature — 20th century — history and criticism.
I. Gardaphé, Fred L. II. Series: Essays series (Toronto, Ont.) ; 25.
PS153.I8D34 1996   C810.9'851   C95-900062-3

# *Table of Contents*

In memory of my grandparents Fred, Isabella, Michele, Paolina, and Donata, my father Fred, and in honor of the lives of my mother Anna, and my family Susan, Frederico, and Marianna.

# Acknowledgments

This book would not have been possible without Father Armando Pierini who had the vision to forsee a community united by the printed word, Father Lawrence Cozzi who enabled the tradition not only to continue, but to thrive, Dominic Candeloro, whose work on the *Italians in Chicago Project*, made me realize that there was a need for writing. The editors, Emil Stubitz, Jim Ylisela, Jr., Joe Cosentino, and Paul Basile who helped my words reach readers. I owe a great debt to my family, especially to my Uncle Pasquale Rotolo, who gave me a copy of Luigi Barzini's *The Italians* the year my father died, to my Mother who bought me books, to my grandparents and the rest who kept the oral tradition alive long enough to give me something to write about.

# Dagoes Read

$\mathscr{I}$suppose I owe some explanation of why the word *dagoes* appears on the cover of a book by an Italian American. I know the word attracts, upsets and even has caused emotional harm to many. However, for the least accepting of you I offer the following. The first epigraph above was offered to me by my mother as an example of what she would do when someone called her a *dago*. She did not have the power to write books which would help others understand who she was. But whatever her limitations, she didn't back down. She confronted her taunters with poetry right out of the oral tradition.

When Italian/American writers began to write, they were facing incredible odds in terms of being accepted as human beings, let alone as intellectuals. There exists very little criticism of their work and very few of them ever made it into the standard literary histories. What criticism that does exist is more like those criminals in a *Columbo* episode; they think Columbo is a stupid pest and in the end find out that they have, like the Fielding Chase quote, been outwitted by him because they misread him. This is to say that people don't expect much from a dago and when they get anything, they're more likely than not to misread it.

Italian/American literature began the moment an Italian immigrant wrote in reaction to life in America. For many, it begins when that immigrant learned to read and write the English language, but those are people

9

who wish to avoid what was and is produced in the Italian language, perhaps because they cannot read Italian, but more likely because Italian has become, for them, a foreign language. While we may never know for sure who that first immigrant was, we have good reason to suggest a candidate because of an early essay by Frank Lentricchia which can document Luigi Ventura's *Peppino* as perhaps the first Italian/American novel. But Ventura's work is held prisoner in few American libraries. The majority of readers don't even know he exists.[1] Italian/American literature then is the result of what happened when those *dagoes* began to read. And finally the necessary criticism and histories will appear only when dagoes read other dagoes.

This collection brings together a number of articles, interviews, and reviews which I contributed to the *Fra Noi*, between the years 1984 and 1994, but the story of those contributions goes back before then. In 1978 I began studying Italian with the idea of traveling to Italy and perhaps meeting up with our family there. I was the first to return to Italy. Upon my return from a life-changing trip, I wanted to continue studying Italian and for the first time since I was seventeen, I felt compelled to write. I began writing about that trip and had no idea where to send the writing. I remembered the *Fra Noi* as a local newsletter which on occasion I would read to my grandpa. I got hold of a copy at my grandma's house and sent off a few pieces of writing. Nothing, no response for months. I then decided that if Italian/American culture wouldn't come to me that I would go in search of it. The story is long, and meeting people like Father Lawrence Cozzi, whom I had known since I was a kid, and Dominic Candeloro helped me understand that there were people who believed that doing cultural work was important, but the key was meeting Anthony Sorrentino, then Executive-director of the Joint Civic Committee of Italian Americans. He took me out to lunch, actually read a few of my essays and the next thing I knew I "Picking *Cicoria*" was published in May of 1984. My first criticism came from the founder/publisher, Father Armando Pierini, who told me that when the dandelions are in bloom the weeds are not good for eating. I seemed to remember fields full of yellow plants. Father Pierini then filled me in on stories about my grandfather that I had never heard. Staying close to him brought me closer to Italian culture and to a past I craved; conversations over sambucca-laced espresso helped.

I contributed only a few pieces that year, but in the spring of 1985 Jim Ylisela became editor and found a file full of my previous submissions. He called me up and thus began my regular appearance in the paper as well as a reluctant apprenticeship as a reporter. In April of 1985 we started the paper's first Arts Section and thus began the renaissance of the *Fra Noi*. Started by Father Pierini in the 1960s as a community newsletter designed to unite and rally Italian Americans around the building of the Villa Scalabrini, the newspaper became a real voice for Italian/American culture. It was then that I was able to put my years of reading Italian/American writers to practical use. While I wrote I began to understand that my audience was not only those who read the papers at the time, but those who who were yet to be born. Often other writers would ask me if I thought what we were doing made a difference and I told them we were producing messages in bottles that would someday wash up on others' shores. Writing for the future became my motivation. And now, the past's future is here. At the urging of Antonio D'Alfonso, I have gathered those messages and placed them in a larger container. Like the fine red wine, called dago red, that was produced in Italian/American basements throughout the U.S.A. and Canada, these writings were produced mostly in the basements of my life. I offer them to you now with the traditional *Saluti*! And with the hopes that they help you understand more about Italian/American culture and the literary tradition created by its individual writers.

## Note

1. See Frank Lentricchia's "Luigi Ventura and the Origins of Italian-American Fiction," *Italian Americana*, 1.2 (Spring 1975): 189-195.

# *Tradition and the Individual Italian*

## Creating an Italian/American Literary Tradition

> *Tradition. . . cannot be inherited, and if uuo want*
> *it you must obtain it by great labour.*
>
> T.S. Eliot,
> "Tradition and the Individual Talent"

*A*s a community, Italian Americans are just beginning to understand the value of the written word. For years publishers have been saying that the Italian American is not the target audience for most books — they don't buy books because they don't read. However, there is something happening to Italian/American culture that is changing this stereotypic notion. This "something" emerges as Italian Americans transfer dependence on oral tradition to one of a written tradition.

I am often approached by people who have asked me to write their life-stories. Why, all of a sudden, do these Italian Americans begin searching for writers? I believe this is caused by the disintegration of the traditional Italian/American community and the dissemination of Italian individuals into American society. The life stories of our ancestors were part of the common knowledge of those who lived communal lives. In small villages, where contact with others was almost daily, the topics of conversations could be expanded to include history. And history, in terms of origin stories, was kept alive from generation to generation by memory and word of mouth. The past was always a part of the present. This method was sufficient as long as a family did not move away from its place of origins. Even today, all you need to do to learn about your ancestral past is to spend some time in the *piazze* of the southern Italian villages amidst the old pensioners. However things began to change even though Italian immigrants settled in areas called Little Italies.

In these "old" neighborhoods, the oral traditions were kept alive through the constant interaction among families and friends. Even though my father died when I was young, there was never a lack of people in my neighborhood who, over a beef sandwich, a bag of cecci or some home-made wine, could tell me stories that made my father live. This oral transmission system worked because of the continuous contact we had with the extended family and *paesani*. And as long as the oral system operated the need for reading and writing was limited to the demands of social and economic factors of the larger society. There was little need to record history as history lived in the minds and words of those who surrounded our lives. But as the old neighborhoods dissolved with migration to multicultural settings and to the far-away places where jobs had taken us, that everyday contact with the past gave way to occasional encounters in which, at best, only a small number of stories could get passed on. One result of this communal disintegration was the loss of an access to a past that could not only inform but enhance the present. This lost surfaced in questions that need to be answered and an emptiness that needs to be filled.

All good writing begins with good questions; and all great writers begin by filling the great voids in their lives. There is no doubt that for Italian Americans the number of questions and the size of the voids are growing. This is especially true as the original pioneers disappear without having been listened to. This is precisely why we are coming into a time in which our writers will be recognized. Their recognition will be due to their ability to listen and to respond to what's heard by creating literature.

It is typical of any advanced literate society to depend less and less on its elders. After all, the past is recorded in books, in films, on tapes; dependence on the elder's memory is exchanged for dependence on the expert. The problem with Italian Americans is that we have yet to understand this function of a print-oriented society, a society that separates past from present. As we advance, we exchange our personal histories for a public history that has distorted our communal presence through the presentation and preservation of stereotypes.

In short, as we move into the fourth and fifth generation we find that, in spite of the predominance of mass media, we are depending more and more on the written word for the recording of our history and common institutions beyond the family for dissemination of that history. The evolution of Italian/American culture depends very much on our ability to produce our history. And if we do not write our own history, we will find that future Italian

Americans will, in spite of the best intentions of individual family influence, lose control of their identities. No matter the occasion, whenever a speaker is called upon to address an Italian/American issue, he or she inevitably points to an illustrious past filled with great works of art. But Renaissance painters are not directly related to the Italian experiences that form bases for Italian/American culture. Only when the present interacts with the past, can we say that a tradition is being created. The stories of our past, especially when told by our elders, have been the major vehicle by which our heritage is transmitted from generation to generation. But this process became endangered when Italians migrated to America. Loss of shared primary languages, lack of shared environments (as children leave not only the homes, but the neighborhoods and often the states of their upbringing), impedes the development of a sense of tradition. As T.S. Eliot knew, the task of organizing a literary tradition belongs to the literary critics and historians, but the task of recognizing one belongs to the individual reader and writer.

# Italian/American Poetry Deserves Better

## Ferdinando Alfonsi

*W*hile recent attempts to refigure the American literary canon have recognized texts produced by minority cultures, they have all failed remarkably to include contributions by Italian/American writers in their refigurations. This literature has been relegated to the *vicoli* of literary discourse. Not recognized as being Italian or American, abandoned, if you will, by its two parent cultures, this orphaned literature has had to depend primarily upon its creators for serious critical attention.

This has been the case with nearly all other ethnic/American literature: a significant cultural presence is strengthened by the development of the critical voice which is able to enter into a dialogue with the critics of the dominant culture. In the case of Italian/American literature, such a dialogue is necessary on two cultural fronts: Italy and America. The development of this dialogue is a collective project that requires the participation of three groups of intellectuals: Italianists, Americanists and the newly developing Italian/Americanists; cooperation, and in many cases collaboration, of all three groups is essential for the creation of a discourse that centers on the work of Italian/American writers.

Dr. Ferdinando Alfonsi is an Italianist who has devoted much of his recent energy to developing this important dialogue. These efforts have resulted in the bilingual anthology *Italo-American Poets* (Antonio Carello Editore, 1985) and his *Dictionary of Italo-American Poets* (Peter Lang, 1989). In his latest contribution to this project, the bilingual *Italian American Poetry: Essays and Texts*, Alfonsi begins the work of examining the hundreds of poets found in his *Dictionary*. Alfonsi says this study of five poets (plus himself) is the first of twenty projected volumes that will focus on themes, symbols, and the language of the poetry produced by American writers of Italian descent.

*Essays and Texts* is divided into five sections: first are general essays which examine the following questions: What is Italian/American poetry? Why is Italian/American literature behind other ethnic/ American literature? Is there a language peculiar to Italian/American poetry? And what are the images of Italy that are found in this poetry? The second section is devoted to the examination of individual authors: Ferdinando Alfonsi, Arthur Clements, Celestino De Juliis, Maria Mazziotti Gillan, Joseph Greco, and Joseph Tuccio. A third section presents five poems (in English and Italian) by each of the writers examined. These are followed by a brief bibliography, and finally an Appendix, which contains a supplement to Alfonsi's 1989 *Dictionary*.

In part one, Alfonsi republishes "Italian American Poetry: In Search of a Definition," which served as an introduction to his earlier *Dictionary*. The problems with this essay, that is Alfonsi reads ethnicity as not a social construction, but as an element that "manifests itself in the somatic structure" (26), have been sufficiently addressed in earlier critiques by Professors Justin Vitiello (*Italica*, 68.1 (Spring 1991): 60-62) and Anthony J. Tamburri (*Voices in Italian Americana*, 2.1 (Spring 1991): 135-37). Suffice it to add that while Alfonsi asks all the right questions, his answers leave much to be desired.

In trying to come to terms with why Italian Americans are "at least two generations behind if we consider what has already been accomplished by other ethnic groups" (41), Alfonsi offers a weak attempt at an answer. First of all, cultural development can not and should not be likened to a foot race. Secondly, Alfonsi would do well to expand his exposure to contemporary theorists in the field of ethnicity, women's studies, and Italian/American studies: *Arba Sicula, Italian Americana*, and *Voices in Italian Americana*. While there is no single answer there, the tools to approach the answers are certainly available. In addition, he might try reading some Vico, whose theory of cultural evolution better fits Alfonsi's need to chart the development of Italian/American poetry in relation to other American ethnic groups. This essay could better develop Italian/American discourse by considering such vital contributions as *The Dream Book: Writings by Italian American Women* (1987) and *From the Margin: Writings in Italian Americana* (1991).

Alfonsi's third chapter on the language of Italian/American culture, is perhaps this book's most valid contribution to the study of Italian/American literature. It is a fine survey of this linguistic phenomenon and is a welcomed addition to the earlier linguistic studies by Luigi Ballerini and Fredi Chiapelli, the late Robert J. Di Pietro, and Michael La Sorte. The next chapter, "Italy in Italo-American Poetry," introduces what is perhaps the most problematic element of this study: Alfonsi's need to include his own poetry (111-12). If the reader has yet to suspect Alfonsi's analysis, this chapter and the following should leave no doubt that Alfonsi's agenda is questionable. Chapter V, "The Poetry of Ferdinando Alfonsi," written by the professor's wife, throws the entire work into question. One can only ask why Alfonsi has decided that out of the hundreds of Italian/American poets he has documented in his dictionary, he had to include himself, and place this essay before the others. Even if Alfonsi's work was better known, the essay assumes an unearned familiarity with poems that are not included in the "Texts" section. The major question raised here is can we take this work seriously? Aside from this, there is the question of why Alfonsi includes such poetasters as Joseph Tuccio with legitimate poets as Arthur Clements and Maria Gillan. The problem with Alfonsi's tired and dated way of reading of all the poets for symbols, themes, and diction, is that while he rightly searches out Italian connections to Dante and Moravia, he ignores the obvious American and English influences. Can we read Maria Gillan without recognizing the influences of the other poets of Paterson such as William Carlos Williams and Allen Ginsberg, or sister poets such as Denise Levertov and Diane di Prima? While such an approach might work for lesser poets such as Tuccio, the more talented Gillan, Clements, and De Juliis certainly deserve better. Italian/American literature is more complex than Alfonsi's interpretations lead us to believe. While he has certainly contributed to the project of Italian/American criticism, the question remains, has this contribution added to the reasons why it can continue to be ignored?

# *Poetry Helps Ancona Live in Two Worlds*

## Vincenzo Ancona

## 1

At seventy-six years of age, poet and folk artist Vincenzo Ancona speaks of his life in the plural. "I'm a very lucky man," he says, "I have two lives. One in Sicily and one here in America." For the past ten years, Ancona has been able to spend time in both places. "I can't leave America because I have created a family here and I am satisfied here; but also I can't leave Sicily, so much of what I am is there as well."

In Sicily, Ancona's life followed the flow of nature. Born to a family of farmers and fishermen, his life shifted between the two occupations as the seasons dictated. Ancona tells of the songs that accompanied work in Sicily. "Men and women sung while they worked. It helped to create a rhythm and a sense of doing things together. It also helped to take our minds off the incredible physical demands the worked made on our bodies." This singing, the tales his grandmother and parents used to tell, and exposure to the many poets of his hometown, introduced Ancona to the rich oral traditions of Sicilian culture sparking a desire to write. "When I was little I heard poetry and we would have to memorize it. I had no idea of developing my own poetry, but as I grew older it just came out. I knew the work of many Sicilian poets, but I never thought of myself as one of them. I always wanted to write poetry and though I only went to school for a short while, before my father needed me in the fields and boats, I never lost that desire to write."

## Poetry Helps Ancona Live in Two Worlds

It was the experience of immigration that would trigger his writing. Born in 1915 in Castellammare del Golfo, Trapani Sicily, Ancona emigrated to America in 1956 and settled into a factory worker's life in New York's Bensonhurst. Although the experience removed him from the more natural flow of rural Sicilian life, there was something about the American experience that caused him to begin writing. In America, Ancona worked days in a broom factory and composed his verses at night, an experience reminiscent of turn-of-the-century immigrant, Pascal D'Angelo, a prizewinning poet and author of the autobiography *Son of Italy*. Ancona began composing devotional poetry commemorating the saints and *La Madonna del Soccorso*, his town's patroness. He also wrote strong reminiscences of life in Sicily.

One of his earliest poetic successes was "Senza Pane," a parody of a popular sentimental Neapolitan hit song, "Senza Rose." Inspired by the hard times under Mussolini's rule, "Senza Pane" spoke to hundreds of thousands who had shared the same experience. It became a popular poem both in Sicily and in America. Ancona became so popular in Sicily that when he returned in 1968, for the first time since his emigration, he received a hero's welcome which he recounts in an interview published in his new book. "I believed in my heart that no one would be at the airport. . . Yet everybody was waiting for me. They called me The Poet." Seven years later Ancona met folklorist Joseph Sciorra, who together with anthropologist Anna Chairetakis began recording his work. Working with Gaetano Cipolla, a professor of Italian, founder of Legas Press and president of *Arba Sicula*, they were able to publish *Malidittu la lingua (Damned Language)*. To preserve the experience of the oral tradition, they included cassette recordings of Ancona reciting his songs and poems in the Sicilian dialect. "This whole project is our attempt to keep the language alive. When you lose the language, you lose the culture. For centuries, poetry like mine lived in the ears of everyone who heard it, now, I don't know if it will last, that's why I did this book. I want this book to reach as many Sicilian Americans as possible; it is their culture that is celebrated in my work. And to abandon the language is to lose the culture." Unlike many other Sicilian immigrants, Ancona never faced the threat of losing the language. Since coming to America he has lived and worked exclusively among and with Sicilians. "If I needed anything, food, home repairs, lawyers, anything, it could all be found and dealt with by speaking Sicilian. I never learned English well enough, so I stay out of that tongue whenever possible." Ancona is a popular performer in New York social clubs and cafes. Since retiring in 1979, he spends half the year in America and half in Sicily. And with each trip, he enriches both of his lives.

## 2

*T*he publication of *Malidittu la lingua (Damned Language): Poetry and Miniatures of Vincenzo Ancona* represents a major contribution to Sicilian and Sicilian/American culture. It is the result of the combined efforts of Gaetano Cipolla (professor of Italian), Joseph Sciorra (folklorist) Anna L. Chairetakis (anthropologist) and Ancona, a natural poet and storyteller. Sciorra and Chairetakis collected Ancona's work and recorded it; Cipolla, editor and founder of Legas Press, translated Ancona's Sicilian into English.

Two cassette tapes accompany the book and capture the music of Ancona's voice enabling the non-Sicilian to participate in the oral tradition it represents. *Malidittu la lingua* is as educational as it is entertaining. Two well written essays serve as excellent antipasti to stimulate our appetite for Ancona's poetry. Luisa Del Giudice's informative essay on Sicilian oral and literary traditions sets Ancona's work in the context of centuries of Sicilian poetry and folk culture. The essay situates Ancona as an intermediary between Sicilian and American, oral and written, urban and rural cultures. "Vincenzo Ancona: Poet of Two Worlds," a biographical essay about Ancona written by Chairetakis and Sciorra, provides an informative historical sketch of the Sicilian and American lives of Ancona the son of Sicilian farmers and fishermen. Fifteen illustrations capture the images of Ancona the man and his work, both his poetry and wire weaving.

Ancona's work is presented in four sections: "The American Experience," "Life in Sicily," "Anecdotes," and "Tales." The first section features the immigrant's response to life in a new world. It opens with the poem from which this collection takes its title. "Malidittu la lingua" humorously recounts Ancona's problems in adapting to life according to the English language in which meters become feet.

> Isn't the meter good geometry? Americans create obscurity when they
> insist on measuring with their feet.

"Amerisicula" describes the effect of the mingling of Sicilian and American cultures while it portrays life in Bensonhurst's little Sicily where one can live a good life without learning the English language. Many of the poems in this section deal with the desire to return to Sicily and contain beautiful reminiscences of life in the immigrant's homeland. But all is not nostalgic nor humorous in this section. "Lament of an American Senior Citizen" is a biting critique of the way America treats its elders.

There are tangles of deceit.

> Those who work pay all the taxes.
> When it's time for their retirement,
> after paying for a lifetime,
> when they're worn out, sick and old,
> they are left without a cent.
> This is truly a rich land.
> It takes much and gives back less!

This "Life I Lead" is a telling account of how the author's learning to weave figures out of wire led him away from a depressed retirement and into self-expression through art. The final poem in this segment is the wonderful "Contrasto: Dialogue between Husband and Wife," which, as Sciorra and Chairetakis point out, enables conflicting points of view on a subject to be discussed. In this poem, the conflict concerns life in American versus life in Sicily. The husband advocates the couple's return against his wife's witty defense of the life they've made in America.

The most telling selection in the "Life in Sicily" section is the epic "Bread from Wheat," which describes the process from plowing the fields to bagging the grain which becomes the staple of the Sicilian farmer's diet. "The Olive Tree" is an ode to the tree as a symbol of eternal life. "Dialogue on Divorce," a fiery contrasto between Ancona and fellow poet Nino Provenzano, delves into the viability of old world notions in contemporary America.

The final two sections contain both short poems and longer ballads which reflect a combination of natural wit and wisdom that will make you nod your head and wish you had said it. They contain stories, which once read, are certain to become part of your own storytelling repertoire, which is, after all, the whole point of oral tradition. This volume is an important addition to Sicilian/American culture and establishes Vincenzo Ancona as one of this culture's most eloquent *cantastorie*.

*August 1991*

# Ardizzone Captures Awards

## Tony Ardizzone

*T*he years 1985 and 1986 have been storybook years for the young Chicago-born author Tony Ardizzone. In 1985, the National Endowment for the Arts awarded him a fellowship for fiction writing, based on the submission of the fifty pages of the third draft of the novel, *Heart of the Order*. In June of the same year, Henry Holt and Company accepted *Heart* for publication. His manuscript was singled out from several hundred submissions for the 1985 Virginia Prize for Fiction. Also in that year, *The Evening News*, his first story collection, received a prestigious Flannery O'Connor Award for short fiction. And now, those books are ready for the public. Last month, Tony returned to Chicago, sponsored by *Fra Noi* and the English Department of Columbia College, to read from his work. One of the readings, sponsored by Guild Books, took place just a few blocks from the Chicago neighborhood where he grew up.

## A Writer's Roots

Tony has a strong sense of his family's background. His father's father was born in Agrigento, Sicily, and left Sicily to avoid military conscription. Ironically he ended up fighting in the First World War for America and was honorably discharged. "My grandfather died of tuberculosis before my parents were married," says Tony, "so I only have stories of him. He did factory work, and near the end of his life took care of the bocce courts in the old Sicilian neighborhood near St. Philip Benizi Church. My grandmother was the oldest of nine children. Her family emigrated from Sicily to

22

Louisiana. My grandparents met in Chicago. With a name like Anthony Vito Ardizzone, people never ask about my other half. My mother's family came from Alsace Lorraine and Lichtenstein."

Tony was born in Columbus Hospital. His parents had a basement flat on Webster Street. A few years later they moved to the corner of Fullerton and Southport. They moved one more time, north to near Bryn Mawr and Clark Streets where they reside today, so that their youngest daughter could attend a special grammar school for the deaf.

## Chicago Boy

Tony's writing is filled with scenes set in Chicago. His first novel, *In the Name of the Father*, contains scenes at Wrigley Field. He claims allegiance to the Cubs, no matter how they fare in the league standings.

"There was never any choice, I guess. I just followed in my father's footsteps. He is a big Cub's fan. When I was seven, he said it was time I went to a baseball game."

Tony remembers the day vividly. "My father was always very busy. When he took out time for us it was a big deal. We paid fifty cents each to sit in the bleachers. As soon as we hit the ramps he told me to close my eyes. So I did. It was amazing. I could hear the sounds echoing all around me. He put his hands on the back of my shoulders (I can still feel that hand) and led me up the ramp, all the way to center field; then he faced me toward home plate.

"When he told me to open my eyes I saw the expanse of the field — the Cubs were taking batting practice, pitchers were doing windsprints and stretching out — I looked around the stands and then behind him was that huge scoreboard."

## The Birth of Heart

Though he never played organized baseball, he's a veteran of street ball. The scenes of games in Chicago alleys in *Heart of the Order* attest to his expertise. "We used to play until our arms fell out of our sockets. Baseball was always a safe topic for discussion. I could always speak more honestly about my feelings to my mother, but I could always talk to my father about what the Cubs did that day."

*Heart of the Order* is the story of Danny Bacigalupo, a kid from northside Chicago who is haunted by the accidental death of one of his street ball playing friends. Bacigalupo struggles through the minor league system of the Denver Dynos to find himself as a ball player and as a human being. He began writing the novel when his son, Nick, was six months old — he's now nearly five. "I wanted to work with the idea of a father telling his child something. Then I began to write about baseball. It took me eight months to get a good first draft. My agent showed it to some houses and they felt it wasn't ready yet. So I rewrote it completely. There were four good drafts prior to the book that is now in the readers' hands.

"Several publishing houses saw it. Some had praise, but none had the excitement of Holt. Jack Macrae, the senior editor at Holt, wanted me to work it more. He helped me to deliver it, and now they are very enthusiastic about it. That's what a writer needs — a house that's excited about his work." The people at Holt aren't the only ones excited about this novel. *USA Today* called it "great baseball fiction." And the novel has some producers interested in the film rights.

## Family Centered

In all of Tony's writing, family plays a major role. He devotes much time to the interaction of family members. He and his wife, Diane Kondrat, are expecting their second child. Although his family is smaller than his parents', it's still very important to him. Though there are obvious differences, he feels that his own family shares the key that makes families work — love and respect.

"My family has more schooling. And we're more fortunate in that we have more money than our parents did when they were starting out. My wife has her own career as an actress and director in theatre. But we always try to do things together as a family." Both Tony and Diane have demanding careers. She acts and directs theater; together they share the responsibilities of raising Nick. Tony works in the day and Diane gets the evenings.

Tony has two brothers and two sisters and says they're pretty much separated. His younger brother lives in Phoenix, his two sisters and youngest brother live in the Chicago area. He lives in Virginia. "It's a different world now," he says. "You've got to go where the jobs are. You can't keep together like we used to. Nick won't have the same sense of his aunts and uncles as I did. Nor will he experience the repetition of celebrating family rituals.

"In our big family it seemed that every two weeks there was a birthday party. And on Sunday nights, when Ed Sullivan would be on, the men would be in the living room, the women in the dining room drinking coffee and talking and the kids would play at everyone's feet. Nick and the new child aren't going to have that."

Tony's father supported his family since he was eight years old because his father suffered from tuberculosis. "My father always had two jobs. He sold newspapers in Grant Park and downtown near Union Station. When I was very young he had weekend stands near State and Lake. That was when people used to come downtown on Friday and Saturday nights to go to the theaters.

"Once, when I was eight, one of his helpers got sick in the middle of winter and he said he needed me. My mother said, 'No, he's too young to go. Something might happen.' My father won. They put so many clothes on me I could hardly move my arms.

"My father told me to think fast, make the correct change, and if somebody tried to rob me, I should give them the money. It was a nice night, the snow was falling, and people were charmed. I made a lot of tips that night.

"During the week he had stands near Union Station. Throughout grammar and high school I would take the El down there as quickly as I could and sold papers. That was back when the afternoon papers, the *Daily News* and the *Chicago American* were seven cents each."

## College Bound

Tony attended St. Jehosophat's and St. Gregory's grammar school. "At one of those parent-teacher conferences one of my English teachers, at St. Gregory's, Miss Bagnola, really encouraged my parents to support my education. She said I could really work. So my parents did all they could to send me to good schools." Tony says he wanted to go to De Paul High School in the city. He and his father visited DePaul, St. George's in Evanston and Loyola out in Wilmette. "My father thought it would be better if I went to Loyola; I wanted DePaul. So the compromise was St. George's. Later I realized that he really wanted me to attend St. George's, but he knew if he pushed for Loyola, I'd settle for St. George."

"In high school the big push was science, so I took four years of math and science and was involved in a number of science projects. I took Advance Placement physics and calculus." One teacher encouraged him to write stories and poetry. Then he began to read novels and was drawn into literature. "I think I'm a writer because when I was sixteen I read novels and poems that were just wonderful. We used to knock around Old Town. One day we discovered Barbara's Book store and I picked up a copy of Lawrence Ferlinghetti's *Coney Island of the Mind*. I bought it, read it, and said, 'My god this is poetry? I want to be a writer if it means I can write like this.' I had never read anything that contemporary, that wild. It was like jazz.

"In some ways it gave me the courage to write, but more it showed me the possibilities of writing. And that was the first time I had that idea."

Upon graduation from St. George's, Tony went on to the University of Illinois in Champaign. There was never any doubt that he would go to college. His father wanted him to study business in college — to be practical. But Tony didn't want that. He studied Arts and Letters and finally declared a major in English. "I took some writing classes and enjoyed them. And then got the idea that I wanted to be a writer so I began to act like a writer.

"I had a girlfriend who supported my writing. I'd call her up, read her my stories in the lobby of her dorm, and then go for long walks. It was very romantic and during the late 1960s a very fitting thing to do."

## One of the Champaign 39

Tony attended college during a period when students were questioning their values. "Students weren't going into things that were commercial. We were all talking about more lofty ideals — and mine was to make art.

His father wasn't very excited about the idea, but at some point resigned himself, believing he had done what he could.

"I have two other brothers and he was working on them. My younger brother, Bob, went into engineering; my youngest brother Jim went into business and earned his CPA."

One of his stories, "Intersection" portrays collegians during the protest period of the 1960s. "I was somewhat politically involved. When I was a senior in college, 10,000 students were arrested during the 1971 moratorium march on Washington. They overfilled the jail and then they filled the coliseum. There was lots of tear gas and many kids were hurt.

"Our idea was that if the government's not going to stop the war then we're going to stop the government."

Tony was arrested later that term during a peaceful sit-in in the student union while protesting the presence of Marine recruiters. Their argument was that the Union was paid for by student dues and the Marines were there without a student invitation.

"Technically we were arrested for interfering with the ingress and egress to this public facility. Then the school made a big deal of it and called us the Champaign 39." There were hearings and the administration expelled the protesters. Because he was a senior, Tony didn't suffer as much as those juniors or sophomores who lost their financial aid. Faculty members who had participated were dismissed. Tony's diploma was held up, but finally the law under which they were arrested was overturned and he was awarded his degree with honors. "I was not some kind of ranting radical. I believed that what was important to me were the values that I could and wanted to live by. During that period of my life the world expanded five times."

## Life after College

Tony made it through college by working as a waiter in fraternities — "a meal job," as he puts it. He also had an Illinois Guaranteed loan that had to be repaid. So after graduation he returned to Chicago and got a teaching job at St. Mary's Center for Learning — at Taylor and Crenshaw. At the time the school was a mixture of Black, Hispanic, Italian, and Polish American students. It was a "free school." He was content to stay there a few years before he realized that teaching high school wasn't what he wanted to be doing. During that time he was taking writing classes at Circle Campus. He studied with Michael Anania, John Nims, Eugene Wildman, Ralph Mills, Jr. and was hanging around poets involved in a series of readings at the Blue Door Antique Store.

"The place was located on a side street off Lincoln Avenue in a basement. It was lit by candles on the tables. People passed around bottles in paper bags while local poets read from their work. I felt I was a part of the writing scene."

He started applying to graduate schools and right about that time got a call from the editor of the *Chicago Review*, who had decided to publish a small piece of his first novel, *In the Name of the Father*. Tony calls it encouragement at the right time. "A few years earlier, in 1969, while a sophomore in college, one of my stories was accepted by the *Carolina Quarterly*. After that, and especially after the *Chicago Review*. I had the idea that this writing business must be easy. But then came hundreds of rejections." His next acceptance would be years away.

## First Novel

Tony attended graduate school at Bowling Green State University in Ohio where he was offered free tuition and a teaching assistantship. He received his M.F.A. in Creative Writing in 1975. Three years later Doubleday published his first novel, *In the Name of the Father* a story of a fatherless boy named Tonto Schwartz, who struggles into manhood and understanding the father who died before he could know him. For a first novel it was quite successful, receiving good reviews in many papers, including *The New York Times*. Tony says it was a very straight forward story and very traditional compared to his latest venture.

## Oral Traditions

During the past eight years, Ardizzone's been working on short stories, many of which appear in *The Evening News* and from time to time on another novel he calls *Chicago Boy* which continues the story of one of the characters from his first novel, Vito Scaparelli, who dies in Vietnam. "I was working on a scene in which a mother is telling a story. About that time Calvino's book, *Italian Folktales*, came out and I realized that other people tell stories too. I was after the sense of the oral story and the way that aunts and uncles, don't tell you literally what happens; they relate it metaphorically and leave it to you to read between the lines. "I would like to write the whole novel as a series of folk tales."

Tony says he owes some of his interest in storytelling to his mother, who loves to spin tales. " 'My Mother's Story,' in *The Evening News* is about as autobiographical a piece as I've ever written," he says. "I even used my own name in that story. I tried to tell all truth, though my mother now tells me I got many details wrong." Tony was an avid reader even though there weren't many books around the house as he was growing up. "My parents basically read the newspapers. And when I was young I liked to read books about dinosaurs, science, and geology.

"There was a mobile library set up at Clark and Petersen, and on Saturdays I'd walk up there, get an armful and bring them back the next week. His home in Virginia is now filled with books.

## Academics and Writing

Tony finds that teaching college and writing can be a good mixture of work. He separates the two activities by writing early in the day. In the afternoon he heads off to Old Dominion University, where he received tenure in 1984, to teach courses in fiction and composition. He works in his home, in a back room upstairs, and says he doesn't feel the need to go away to a writer's retreat. "I get up early, before Diane and Nick are awake and work for two or three hours. Diane is great about it. She doesn't look at me and try to figure out if I had a good day or a lousy day. Nick gets to knock on the door when he gets up, and I open it, give him a kiss and a hug. He usually tries to sneak past, trying to play with me. "It gets to the point where if I finish early one day and come downstairs, Nick sometimes wisecracks, 'It's too early for you, Papa; go back upstairs and keep working.' "

Working in academics can limit the experiences a writer needs to stimulate imagination and creativity, and Tony is aware of this danger. "I don't want to start writing about a man who is a writer in a school, so I have to do other things." Other things for Tony include going to ball games (the Met's have a minor league team in town) and playing on a softball team. He also has a backyard garden that contains all the basics — tomatoes, peppers and basil. "You can never have too much basil," he says. "I make a great pesto sauce. I make it with garlic and olive oil and freeze it for the days when fresh basil is scarce." Another stimulation good for writing is travel, and recently Tony has started to do more of it.

Old Dominion has an exchange program with a University in Rabat, the capital of Morocco. Last year he spent two months teaching in three Moroccan universities — Casablanca, Rabat, and Fez. "I was able to travel around the country and now I have friends there. I'd like to go back. In fact, I'm working on a book of stories set in Morocco." He hopes to someday do what he feels he must eventually do — travel to Sicily. "I've been to Europe and traveled around on a student Eurail pass, but I knew I wasn't going to be able to do justice to Italy or Sicily, so I saved those for a later time.

"I need to find the village that my grandparents' families came from. I'd also like to improve my Italian. Since my mother doesn't speak it, the only time I used to hear it was when my father was with Nonna and his sisters. I know some words, but they're mostly the bad words."

## A Pennant Winner

"*In bocca al lupo*," Italians say when they are wishing someone good luck before going off to an exam, a contest or other adventure, and it means, "In the mouth of the wolf." The response is "*Crepi il lupo*" (May the wolf die).

A second novel requires all the luck that legend says a phrase like that can bring. For Tony Ardizzone, the wolf did die for he has succeeded in bringing us a wonderful tale of hope and finding one's place in life. And luck has nothing to do with it all.

What we could very well have in *Heart of the Order* is the Italian/American answer to Salinger's *Catcher in the Rye*, Twain's, *Huckleberry Finn*, and Malamud's *The Natural* rolled into one fine novel. Ardizzone has managed a triple play. His creation of an exciting voice (taking the form of a father to son monologue), a story that keeps pages turning and indelible imagery combine all the ingredients of excellent storytelling.

Protagonist Danilo Bacigalupo, son of Italian immigrants, brother of many, grows up on Chicago's northside. In a game of alley baseball he hits a line drive that changes his life. The shot results in Mickey Meenan's death and the adoption of Mickey's spirit by Danny. The post World War II Chicago street life is beautifully described. The wisdom of parents wonderfully portrayed. Adolescence is hard to live through and even harder to write about, yet Ardizzone keeps us thinking of our own and laughing all the way. The rise and fall of a ballplayer is done in a way that has never seen print. There are enough twists and turns in the plot to keep you wondering what will happen next — a trick only a good novelist can keep fresh. There is also a continual breath of magical realism, that sustains the dream state that good fiction must create. This is done most masterfully through the right amount of exaggeration and experimentation.

Ardizzone gives us passionate characters who are realistically motivated to surreal heights. *In the Name of the Father*, his first novel, was just warm up tosses compared to the force behind his latest work. Worthy of large audiences, this year's most valuable player in the novel arena could very well be Tony Ardizzone. *Bravissimo*.

## This Writer's Stories Make News

Winner of the prestigious Flannery O'Connor Award for short fiction, this collection of short stories is the author's first and is published in what can only be called, Tony's year. In the past year, this young man's writing has earned a $20,000 fellowship from the National Endowment for the Arts, the Virginia Prize for Fiction for his second novel *Heart of the Order* and now the prestigious Flannery O'Connor award. *The Evening News* contains eleven short stories that vary in style and voice — so much so that it's hard to believe one writer has produced them all.

Just like television news, this collection is filled with politics, war, human interest, and sports stories. The author is at home in any point of view, be it the Italian grandmother in "Nonna;" the adolescent girl in "The Daughter and the Tradesman;" or a teenaged boy in "Idling." Ardizzone takes Italian/American characters and gives any audience a reason to read all about them. They are accessible and speak for all people — something that until recently publishers believed few Italian/American writers could do.

"The Transplant" tells the tale of a yuppie who moves to Chicago, leaves his wife and finds himself deep in the shallow end of change. "The Intersection," is one of the few stories of 1960s anti-war activities that speaks interesting truths about events peculiar to that era. It lacks the sentimentality that has destroyed the attempts of many other writers to capture the reasoning and the feeling behind those events. The story from which this collection takes its title is a tale of the hope and desperation of a suburban young couple, soon to be parents, as seen through their television viewing habits. "So Paul and Maria watch the evening news because it seldom fails to reaffirm their separate beliefs. Paul turns up the volume, adjusts the color, then settles on the couch. The best minds of the sixties had foreseen all of this, he thinks. But being right gives him little solace. He hopes the world can resolve its problems. He is tired and wants to grow old in relative stability and peace . . . Everything makes her think of the fate of her coming baby. The face of the Argentine widow staring grimly at the flag-draped coffin. The Irish children throwing back canisters of tear gas in the Ulster Streets. Women wearing babushkas in foodlines in Poland. The crack of automatic rifles in El Salvador. The very worst are the pictures of the starving children in Africa. Arms like wooden spoons, distended stomachs, flies crawling on their nostrils and open lips. Why can't the news limit itself to the weather? she thinks."

How many of us plan meals and bedtime to coincide with the evening news. How much the world has changed because of what has been brought into our homes by that tireless tube has yet to be documented, but Ardizzone gives us all the research we need in the story of Paul and Maria.

Through this collection, Ardizzone has established himself as a fine short story writer. He is craftsman and experimenter extraordinaire. And because he knows his trade, his experiments in such stories as "My Father's Laugh," and "The Walk-On" come off as cleanly and effectively as his more traditional tales: "World Without End," "My Mother's Stories," and "The Eyes of Children."

What will certainly be a favorite to Italian/American readers is the gem, "Nonna." We have here the story of an old Italian grandmother who heads out of her home to shop. As she walks through the Taylor Street neighborhood we are given the history of this once thriving Little Italy, through the eyes of a survivor. She is confused and the changes in the neighborhood are explained through the filter of her mind. "Nonna" is certainly a masterpiece of Italian/American fiction.

There is plenty of excellent reading here. There are wonderful stories and most of all there is thought in this writing. Unlike television, this *Evening News* will make you remember that life is more than headlines and eye catching photos.

# Closer to Home

While Chicago-born writer Tony Ardizzone has yet to visit the Sicilian homeland of his father's parents, he's never come closer to it than he has in his latest writing. *Larabi's Ox*, Ardizzone's fourth book and his second collection of stories, explores Arabian notions of destiny, oral tradition and the struggle between ancient and modern culture through a cycle of fourteen stories which follow the lives of three Americans who visit Morocco for the first time.

The book was selected by novelist Gloria Naylor as winner of the 1992 Milkweed National Fiction Prize. In her "Foreword" to *Larabi's Ox*, Naylor writes that this collection:

> breathes with its artistry, and more importantly through its artistry . . . offer[s] what the best of fiction does: the felt human landscape with its terrifying heights and abysses; its oddly shaped and jarring strangeness; the awed realization on your part that, against all rhythm and reason, the artist has taken you home.

Ardizzone's earlier writing has been awarded two National Endowment for the Arts fellowships, quite an accomplishment as there's a limit of three during one's life. His first collection of stories, *The Evening News*, won the 1986 Flannery O'Connor Award for Short Fiction, and portions of his second novel, *Heart of the Order*, won the Virginia Prize for fiction. In spite of this track record, none of his earlier work comes close to the power we find in these set in Morocco. What's remarkable about *Larabi's Ox* is the way Ardizzone blends and bridges each story with knowledge of the Koran, folktales, and history. While he familiarizes us with the sights, sounds, tastes, and smells of this exotic location, he never allows us to forget that for those raised in America, life in Morocco could never be home.

The main characters are Peter Corvino, a recently divorced college professor who's all but given up on academia, Henry Goodson, a wealthy chemotherapy patient in search of a good place to die, and Sarah Rosen, a Rogers Park woman who travels alone to Morocco because she was told she shouldn't. While the three never meet, they share the same bus from the airport as recounted in the opening and title story.

*Larabi's Ox* serves as an orientation to the contrasts of contemporary Arab culture, where modernization is strapped on the back of ancient tradition ruled by Allah's will. In "The Beggars" Peter Corvino meets veterans of life in Morocco. A seasoned French traveler warns him to avoid the swarm of beggars that surround foreign visitors:

> Walk right past them. When they come up to you, just push the dirty
> fleas out of your way . . . You must learn how to handle these people if
> you expect to stay here and work. It's not like they're people.

Peter's sensitivity won't allow him to heed such racist advice and consequently he is drawn deep into the center of the culture of Arab poverty. Peter's experiences take and change him through "Exchange" in which he comes to understand the life of a married Moroccan couple, through "The Surrender" in which he follows two beggar boys home to an urban nightmare and "The Baraka of Beggars and Kings" in which he bargains for a carpet that takes him for a ride deeper into Arab culture. Through "The Unfinished Minaret," "Sons of Adam," "Postcard from Ouarzazate," and "Valley of the Draa" Henry Goodson develops from the typical fat, khaki-clad, camera-necked tourist, who constantly compares Arab to American culture and whose goal is to make Moroccan life into souvenirs, into a character right out of Arabian Nights. Perhaps the finest story of this nearly flawless collection is "The Whore of Fez el Bali" in which Sarah Rosen, a beautiful redhead is accused of buying a child. A tribunal of native passers-by stop to pass judgment, and the whole experience makes Sarah realize how little control she really has over her life. Sarah comes to terms with her life in "In the Garden of the Djinn," through which we learn her background, and "Expatriates," in which she meets an American alcoholic widow expatriate who can not return to life in America. Sarah has an affair with a native in "The Hand of Fatima" and finally in "The Fire-eater" she learns that she can do anything:

Whether it was travel or break off an affair with a man or ease a fiery torch down her throat and live to spit out the flame.

With *Larabi's Ox* Ardizzone has matured as a storyteller and has earned his place in the ranks of America's best contemporary writers.

*September-October 1986/ September 1992*

# Dreams Come True

## Helen Barolini

*Chiacchiera*, the men used to call it. "Chatter." At family gatherings, after the meals and clean up, the women would gather at one table, kick off their shoes and talk, always shooing away any kid old enough to understand what they were saying. I always wondered what they talked about. I used to think that *chiacchiera* meant something I wasn't supposed to listen to. *The Dream Book* is the first I heard of what goes on at the women's table.

This collection of fifty-six Italian/American women writers is the first of its kind: a major anthology of Italian/American writing. It is a "must buy" for anyone who has a sister, a mother, an aunt, a cousin or a *paesana* who you always loved to listen to. They are here and they are speaking. You need but to read to listen. And if you listen you will learn.

Don't skip the introduction; in it, Ms. Barolini not only displays her fine talent for writing prose, but also her vast knowledge of the literature of the world. She creates as brilliant an essay on Italian/American literature and the Italian/American woman as has ever seen the ink of print. If you have never read a novel, a play, a poem, an essay by an Italian American, her introduction will tell you why you haven't and why you should. "Emerging from the powerful fortress called Family, Italian Americans are understandably reluctant to share with outsiders, to make their lives accessible and knowable; there is a strong cultural bias against looking to closely at 'secrets.' It is not difficult to find the parallel with Italian/American women writers: the necessary distancing from family that writing demands sets up intolerable conflicts within women who have been reared in the cultural tradition of *omertà* — the conspiracy of silence which sees nothing, hears nothing, tells nothing and thus betrays nothing. Writing is an act of assertiveness and Italian/American women, with few exceptions, have not been reared for public assertion" (23).

This book is filled with strong writers: the established known such as Diane Di Prima, Dorothy Bryant, and Frances Winwar and the previously unknown voices which includes most of the rest. I especially enjoyed Lynette Iezzoni's short story "Window Seat" and the excerpt from Chicago writer Tina DeRosa's novel *Paper Fish*. The writing in this anthology speaks of and to all generations and the combination makes this book a pleasure to read and a treasure to own. The nonfiction includes literary as well as personal essays and immigrant recollections. Each excerpt from a novel will tease you into purchasing the whole, that is if you can find it. There is also a wonderful play by Michele Linfante's entitled *Pizza* which is printed in its entirety. The problem with this book is one peculiar to anthologies. There is not enough space. Who knows how much more there is out there? How many more anthologies could be filled? There has to be more. This is only a taste, and editor Barolini has prepared an antipasto here, unlike any you have ever tasted, one that you will come back to as long as you own the book. *The Dream Book* is an event, it is as though the Italian/American women have turned from talking to each other at the table, rose up in unison and started talking to the world. And it is not *chiacchiera*.

*September 1985*

# The Immigrant Lives

## Adria Bernardi

$\mathcal{I}$t is now over one-hundred years since the large waves of Italian immigrants swept onto American shores. Three, sometimes four and five generations have spawned from those turn-of-the-century immigrants, and during this growth, from generation to generation, so much has changed for the American of Italian descent; so much change, so little of it recorded . . . until now. Adria Bernardi, a third-generation American of Italian descent, is one grandchild of immigrant Italians who, for the past five years, has kept one eye on the future as she turned her other towards the past. In her collection of personal essays and oral histories of Italian immigrants of Highwood Bernardi stops time long enough to capture the stories that have filled the minutes, days and years of over forty Italian immigrants. She captures the story of others as only an entranced listener can; she relates the story of self, as can only the gifted writer.

In the opening, title essay, "Houses with Names," Bernardi reminds us that history lives in names, and names are powerful storytelling tools. Bernardi knows that history is made more interesting through dialogue, and she is especially adept at presenting the dialogue between young and old. With Bernardi as our guide we follow youth in its quest for knowledge and meaning, a quest that takes us into the oral tradition of questions asked and the answers that often use questions as cues to relate good stories. Bernardi's skill as a writer is obvious not only in the words she spreads across pages as smoothly as the best, but in the interweaving of hers and the words of her subjects. Typical oral histories present each subject in his or her own chapter, tie them together with a few editorial comments, and send it all to the reader. Bernardi, being anything but the typical historian, builds a narrative, from beginning to end that reads part mystery, part history, part autobiography, all rendered in a most careful and poetic prose. Bernardi becomes the invisible protagonist who appears periodically throughout the book to remind us that we are reading and not actually listening to the lives of her informants. The collection ends with a an essay that pairs nicely with the opening. "As long as I can recall, there was the explaining of names," she tells us in "The Burden of a Name." And by ending in this fashion, she reveals that all the while she was listening to the people she has presented to us, and all the while we were listening to them, Bernardi has been busy crafting a tale of her own, a tale that turns lives into literature, a tale that brings literature to life.

Though dealing with immigrants settled in a specific place, Bernardi's writing and the stories she records belong to all places and all people. *Houses with Names* transcends its north shore location, as well as its Italian/American subject, as it reveals the place we are all most familiar with, the place of the self in a world of friends and strangers, a world where each name is the house of many stories in which the true storyteller is always ready for company, a world in which the listener will always feel at home.

*January 1990*

# Today's Women

## Lucia Chiavola Birnbaum

This is a most important book for all of us — men and women alike. In *Liberazione della donna*, Dr. Birnbaum reaches back into the folklore of the mediterranean earthmother to provide a context for the rich history of women in Italy and in doing so reminds all of us that this story is bigger than Italy. She gives the first comprehensive account of women's history in Italy and presents the materials chronologically. This book is all about connections and Birnbaum provides us with an intricate step-by-step progression of early women's power to the loss of that power and to the struggle to regain that power. She connects present to past, stereotype to its origins, and history to herstory.

This book sheds light on a struggle that has remained in the darker pages of history. Birnbaum has gathered materials from a variety of sources, both direct (personal experiences in Italy and Sicily) and indirect (civil records and cultural literature), and through a careful examination of this written and spoken evidence, she documents the Italian woman's struggle for self-definition, self-direction and self-rule in a way that has never before reached readers of English.

Birnbaum presents the results of rich historical research in a style of writing that keeps us turning pages. More than informing us, Birnbaum reminds us of what women have been doing for thousands of years — protesting the male's use of injustice to dominate and his preoccupation with violence. She has compiled a bibliographical essay that will save months of tedious research, hopefully encouraging scholars to continue in this underdeveloped history of Italian culture. Birnbaum examines the roles of women in all levels of Italian society from the nuns to the prostitutes, from the activists to the followers, and provides us with an account of their work that most of us have never before considered.

*Today's Women*

This book speaks to women and men of all countries. From yesterday's protests of Fascism to the present demonstrations against NATO missile bases in Comisole, Sicily, Birnbaum tells the story of those who would die to preserve life, of those women who gave birth to us all. And for this wonderful work we must reply — *Bravissima!*

❀

How much do we really know about pre-christian and pre-roman Italy? How much of what happened back then was destroyed or lost over the centuries? How much has survived intact, in disguise? What's behind the Italian fascination with the madonna? And how might the answers to these questions affect our attempts to make this world a better place to live? These questions and more drive Lucia Chiavola Birnbaum's latest investigation into the relationship of the past to the future.

# Yesterday's Women

*Black Madonnas: feminism, religion and politics in Italy* (Northeastern University Press) is the result of Chiavola Birnbaum's more than twenty years of investigation into the cultures of Italy. Her first response to that experience came in *Liberazione della donna,* the American Book Award winning study. *Black Madonnas* is a continuation of what she began in the earlier book, but it does more than document the rise of the Italian women's movement; it is a strong, though at times somewhat rambling argument for us to look to the past, to the way it continues to live in submerged cultures and rituals, for a way to redirect our thinking of the future.

Birnbaum considers Black Madonnas as "a metaphor for a memory of the time when the earth was believed to be the body of a woman and all creatures were equal." Her two-hundred page study is a steady stream of evidence to support this notion of the past and a tireless attempt to make that past speak to the present in hopes of effecting sane social change. Through an analysis of language, art, myths, and folklore, Birnbaum uncovers the pre-christian base for much of Christian culture. Her efforts help to explain why there are so many madonne in Italian, African and Asian cultures. She offers us a way of connecting them all into a multicultural mosaic that reflects a basic unity that lies beneath the superficial diversity of the world.

What she brings together in one book is an amazing achievement. Through library research, site visits, interviews and explication of folktales, Birnbaum compiles an unprecedented amount of evidence in one volume. At times, there's so much to say that important information and speculations are just dropped in without analysis, leaving the connections to be made by the reader. For those familiar with Gramsci, Marx, and feminist history and theory this will be less of a problem than for those non-academics, the ones to whom this book really speaks. And this book truly speaks of a popular culture, a people's culture that once was guided by women. Birnbaum has found the Achilles heel of a patriarchal society and holds it up for all to see.

Punctuated with twenty classic illustrations and contemporary photographs, her argument makes a strong case for the importance of Italian peasant culture's ability to reconnect us all to a past that can redirect ways we envision the future. This is revisionary history at its best and avoids the "academic only" trap by including travelogue-like sections that bring the research alive. By interviewing local venerators, historians, and artists she provides a cacophony of voices that enliven the text while providing a variety of perspectives that both support and challenge her theories.

This is a most important book, a must for those who plan to interpret Italian and Italian/American culture and for all those who are looking for alternatives to the direction the way the world is now headed. Chiavola Birnbaum connects St. Francis of Assisi with the Flower Children of the 1960s and the mythical Isis and Cybele with the many madonne found in eastern as well as western cultures. She redeems heretics such as Joachim of Fiore from the 12th century, and Guglielma, daughter of Queen Constance of Hungary, who was burned at the stake for her teachings that the Holy Spirit of the trinity was a woman.

By offering explanations of how and why female figures of veneration were replaced with males she creates new interpretations of such popular cultural mainstays as Santa Claus who entered our cultural imagination through San Nicola and his destruction of the temple of Artemis.

For a culture in decay, *Black Madonnas* is a sweet antidote and a sober testament to the ways of enacting cultural renewal. In a world wounded by militant defense of difference, *Black Madonnas* points the way for the healing that is long overdue if we expect to effect a sane survival into the next millennium. *Black Madonnas* is a rich well from which a world dehydrated by division can quench a terrible thirst for peace.

*January 1987 / May 1993*

# *Bona Fortuna*

## Mary Jo Bona

### 1

> *In our ears,*
> *a voice,*
> *connected to us like a cord,*
> *whispers*
> *you aren't really very much*
> *you guinea, you wop,*
> *so we struggle*
> *to blot out the sound of the crow*

Maria Gillan,
"The Crow"

$\mathcal{T}$he job of developing a literature is a tough one and requires dedication, hard work and a trained sensibility. There is no one better prepared to do this work than Mary Jo Bona. A native of Chicago with a Ph. D. In American literature from the University of Wisconsin, Bona has edited *The Voices We Carry*, an anthology of contemporary Italian/American women's fiction. This collection represents a major step in the development of Italian/American literature.

Bona, a professor of English at Gonzaga University, has become one of the leading voices in Italian/American cultural studies After completing her dissertation on Italian/American women's writing she began giving talks and publishing articles on the writings of Italian/American women. A few years ago she sent a book proposal off to a publisher. The publisher suggested that before she publish a critical study, she do an anthology of creative writing by Italian/American women. So she sent invitations out to twenty-five women, fourteen responded. Guernica Editions heard about the project and wanted it.

*The Voices We Carry* is the first anthology dedicated to fiction by Italian/American women. Unlike Helen Barolini's *Dream Book*, this collection focuses on fourteen women whose work take on new dimensions when placed with each other's in this anthology. Bona arranged the selections into four thematic sections dealing with history, new encounters with Italy, the family, and the end of a generation. Her introduction is a fine essay which places the writers into American literary history.

The strength of the volume comes from the work by veteran writers such as Dorothy Bryant, Diana Cavallo, Mary Bush, and Susan Leonardi. The selections of novels-in-progress by Daniela Gioseffi, Rachel Guido DeVries, Lynn Vanucci, tell us there's a lot to look forward to in terms of Italian/American women's fiction.

Much of the writing in this collection deals with the family. But beyond the stereotypical depictions of the warm supportive family, selections present what it feels like for an Italian/American women who may or may not be married, who may or may not be different because of class, religion, ethnicity, family upbringing, and lifestyle choices. They also speak to the feeling of losing a home and the subsequent search for it.

Bona attributes her interest in Italian/American women's writing as coming from her mother, who in 1985 found Helen Barolini's *Dream Book*, and showed it to her daughter. Bona then shifted her attention from 19th century American writers, such as Henry James, toward the handful of Italian/American women writers. She is responsible for establishing the idea that there is a tradition of Italian/American women's writing and that, it is one that differs from Italian/American male writers.

"The women," she says, "talk about how it was harsher to be a girl; boys were to be educated and the girls were expected to get married and marry within the same ethnic group. It wasn't assumed that they would write."

"To choose to write about the family is to choose to be a traitor of sorts," says Bona. "Becoming writers expands their horizons and enables them to deal with those voices that Maria Gillan's poem talks about. These stories let us know what is it like deal with a crow on your shoulder telling you that you are nothing, that you are a wop. Because some of those voices belong to our Italian ancestors, it is no wonder that we too have internal negative self images. In some ways we have become our own worst enemies.

I want to try to dismantle that whole notion which comes from the larger culture that is sexist and racist."

Bona believes that this publication can help change not only the image of Italian/American women, but also the stereotypes about the Italian/American as a reader and consumer of books. "In the American publishing world," she says, "there are certain cultural groups that have more effective advocacy. Italian America is behind when it comes to work in academia and publishing. We're not helped by writers such as Gay Talese, who write about Italian Americans as being non-readers. I understand historically why he said that, but it does us no good now. Besides, it goes against all the contrary evidence that shows that we do read."

But knowing this and proving it are two different things. In order to get the word out about this book Bona plans to do readings at large bookstores in Chicago and other major cities.

## 2

*The Voices We Carry* takes its title from a line of a powerful poem by Maria Mazziotti Gillan. In her poem "The Crow," Gillan writes:

> We are driven women
> and we'll never escape
> the voices we carry within us.

And the women in this collection are certainly driven. The variety of stories and the styles through which they are presented range, from the nicely nostalgic to the outright anti-sentimental.

By dividing the collection into four thematic sections, Bona has structured our reception of these diverse writers so that their stories interact with each other. I recommend reading them in the order they appear. In this way, you'll better understand why Lynn Vannucci's "An Accidental Murder" is an appropriate ending to this important anthology.

The first section, "The Recreation of Historical Lives," opens with, "Planting," a long awaited glimpse into Mary Bush's latest work. For the first time, we gain access to the world of the indentured Italians who fled southern Italy only to find themselves in similar straights in America's postbellum South. Much of what happens comes to us through Amalia, the matriarch of this transplanted family, and Bush's keen sensibilities create a dynamic world in which no burden goes unborne and no hope is too small to grasp.

In "The Lost Era of Frank Sinatra," Rachel Guido deVries, recreates her parents' generation in a manner reminiscent of Delmore Schwartz's powerful "In Dreams Begin Responsibilities." Like Schwartz, de Vries captures a courtship in cinematic detail, but deVries uses an ironic sense of humor that relieves the tragic development of what will certainly become a prototype for the dysfunctional family.

Daniela Gioseffi's excerpts from "Americans: One Minute to Midnight," juxtapose perspectives of a daughter of the 1960s generation with that of an her immigrant father to create a wild read. Dorissa's experience in jail, after her boyfriend takes the Washington monument hostage, is psychologically similar to Donatuccio's experience in trans-Atlantic steerage.

The "Juniper Street Sketches" of Diana Cavallo capture in incredible detail and sensitivity the rituals, both transplanted and invented, which helped to define Italian/American culture. Cavallo is unmatched in her ability to make scenes shimmer through words, to turn memories into meaning for even the most detached reader.

Part Two, "The Intersection Between America and L'Italia," includes Lisa Ruffolo's "Southern Italy," a transformation of Black Capri into an ancient Italian through her interaction with friends, an Italian lover and the enchanting sea and landscape of Italy's south; Laura Marello's "Claiming Kin" deals with family on both sides of the Atlantic; and Dodici Azpadu's "Desert Ruins," creates a new thirst for an old, familiar past.

The highlight of Part Three, "La Famiglia in America," is Susan J. Leonardi's "Bernie Becomes a Nun," which is simultaneously a depiction of a saint's and sinner's struggle to belong to the world by separating herself from her family. Adria Bernardi, Phyllis Capello, and Giovanna (Janet) Capone, all present younger protagonists growing up in a world of Barbie Dolls, G.I. Joes, historical asassinations, unfaithful parents, divorce, and a stiff and stiffling Catholic Church.

The final section, "The End of a Generation," features an excerpt from Dorothy Bryant's novel, "The Test," which is a bittersweet a testimony to the immigrant generation: sweet is the fondness of a daughter for her father, bitter is the experience of having to deal with his aging. Anne Paolucci's "Buried Treasure," is a telling portrait of a man who is only truly understood by his daughter-in-law. And Lynn Vannucci's excerpt from "Driving" is the exclamation point that finishes the collection in a flourish!

The book's cover is a telling painting by Chicago artist Christine Perri. Entitled, "The Interruption," it serves as a warning label that this book contains works-in-progress that have been interrupted, that women at work are prone to interruption, but also that an eruption is occurring among Italian/American women and that the outpouring of literature has never been better.

*March 1994*

# Out from Garibaldi's Shadow

## Dorothy Bryant

*O*ne day, an Italian exile aboard a rebel ship peered through a telescope and discovered something that would change his life. "And I saw her, standing at the top of the Barra, a small sturdy figure, looking out over the lagoon, leaning slightly backward against the wind blowing from the ocean. Her feet were spread apart, one slightly in front of the other, bracing her against the wind. Her dark skirt whipped around her bare legs. Her shawl spread out over the air like wings. Her long, black hair blew around, above, and over her face like a thick veil. I was struck by the defiant posture of that little body, the way she threw back her head and shoulders to rest on the pressure of the wind."

The exile, was Giuseppe Garibaldi, the woman, Anita Ribiero de Duarte, a married woman who would become his lover, his wife and comrade in arms. While the beautiful language belongs to Dorothy Bryant, the story belongs to all of us. And in this novel Bryant has given new life to Giuseppe Garibaldi, that figure of Italian history who for so long has managed to remain in the dust of historical tracts.

While Garibaldi might be one of the most important names in the history of Italian unification, his impact on American popular culture has yet to move beyond the adoption of his name by a fast-food chain. In spite of the fact that Garibaldi was blond-haired and bearded, the restaurant chain uses the image of a tiny balding man with a dark handlebar mustache. This corruption of the image of Garibaldi masks a reality that should make him one of the most promising heroes of Italian/American culture.

Covering the years between 1835, when Garibaldi fled Italy for exile in South America, and 1849, when he returned to Italy, *Anita, Anita* brilliantly reconstructs the story of Garibaldi that only a handful of historians know. Using biographies, Garibaldi's memoirs, histories and visits to the places where they lived and fought, Bryant tells a remarkable story of the love of Garibaldi's life and the life of Garibaldi's great love.

The occasion of the novel's telling is the year 1851 when Garibaldi, during his second exile from Italy, traveled to Peru and visited Manuela Saenz, the lover and defender of Simon Bolivar. In alternating chapters, Bryant presents a first-person monologue using Garibaldi's voice together with a third person narrator from Anita's perspective. This combination of perspectives enables a variety of voices to be heard and provides a depth of coverage that has never before been attained by Garibaldi scholars.

While Garibaldi's incredible victories have become legendary, Bryant returns to the historical facts that underlie those legends to give us insight into how Garibaldi was able to win against overwhelming odds:

> This is my secret of winning battles against heavy odds. Give a desper-
> ate, despised man something to fight for, his own manhood, or, better
> still, something beyond himself — his country or a dream of universal
> freedom — and you will see the soul of the cowardly criminal set free
> to rise like a bird, transformed into a selfless, fearless warrior for truth,
> for freedom.

No doubt Garibaldi's eloquence relies more on Bryant's talent than historical fact, but what Bryant has done is give this historical figure a voice that both recaptures his legendary acts and redirects our attention to the important role his wife played in helping him achieve his heroic stature.

But more than dramatizing the heroism of the man who led the fight to unite his homeland, Bryant breathes life into the woman who was just as brave, just as heroic and just as important to Italian history. Anita, gave up her home, and eventually her life, to join Garibaldi as he led South American and Italian revolutionaries. Now, for the first time, we have a sense of the personality that belonged to this legendary woman who shared

> ten years of struggle, exile, lost causes. Ten years of love and hope.
> Fighting was our victory. Wandering was our home. She was my youth,
> my hope, my life. My Anita, Anita.

*Anita, Anita* is Bryant's tenth novel; she has also written three plays and a non-fiction book entitled *Writing a Novel*. She is also, along with her husband, founder and publisher of Ata Books, a press devoted to keeping Bryant's works in print. Dorothy Bryant's new novel deserves the attention of all Italian America for without a doubt, it is one of the most thrilling, rewarding historical recreations to ever come along. This one has Hollywood written all over it. It is filled with action, love, strong men and even stronger women.

*February 1994*

# Southern Lights

## Mary Bush

### 1

*M*ary Bush grew up in a house empty of books, but filled with stories. Born and raised in Canastota, New York, once a predominantly Italian town, she has been writing and telling stories for as long as she can remember. Her family spent much time sitting around the kitchen table talking and listening to stories. Fascinated by what she considered, as a child, to be the stupid way they talked, she tells of listening to them for hours: "Just to be a brat I would write down everything they would say. Many were the times when I loved what they said and the way they spoke and so I captured it all."

Her first major publication is a collection of stories entitled *A Place of Light*, published by William Morrow in 1990. Most of the stories are set in rural areas and deal with the conflict that results when different cultures come into contact. Whether it's white and black, male and female, small town and country, urban and suburban, Bush demonstrates a keen ear for dialect and a mastery of narrative development that makes her stories haunt you long after you've stopped reading. Mary's Italian background comes out very little in these stories, yet her ethnic experience has made her sensitive to life on the margins of society.

Most of her stories focus on women as both victims and victors. Mary experienced none of the discouragement or repression that is commonly recounted by Italian/American women who become writers. The oldest of four children, three girls and a boy, Mary tells of the many strong women role models in her family. "Our future plans were never constrained by anyone," she recounts. "The women were in charge of everything."

In her first novel, currently in search of a publisher, Mary turns to her Italian/American experience to tell a story of life on southern plantations during the early 1900s. Though they were called Italian colonies, to which Italians were shipped directly from Italy, many were little more than new versions of slavery. Her grandmother had gone to the south when she was seven years old.

Though this was a common experience, very little has been published about it. So, fueled by her grandmother's stories, Bush began to research the phenomenon for her novel. She found that Blacks and Italians lived next door to each other, in separate plantation shacks, and socialized with each other. Most of the Italians had not been farmers when they came over. "Quite often," says Bush, "the Blacks taught the Italians how to survive, how to work the farm, and how to speak English. There was almost no racial separation between the two. Eventually the adults did realize that the Blacks were treated differently and were frightened by that."

It wasn't until a few years after her grandmother's death that Bush tried to discover Sunnyside, the plantation that her grandmother's family had moved to in 1904. This plantation was one of many that were investigated in 1907 by the Federal government because of charges of peonage. "Italian agents had worked against their own people," says Bush. "They had them sign papers, the contents of which were never truthfully explained. Some people had their passage paid by the plantation owners, but they were instructed not to let anyone know this because it was illegal. They were told to say they were going to meet a cousin or a *paesano* who was paying their passage. In the end, no one was ever convicted of this peonage." Bush suggests that one explanation for this importation of Italian laborers is that white southerners, overwhelmed by the size of the Black population, wanted to diminish it by bringing in Italian workers. In no way, says Bush, were Italians considered to be equal to the whites.

Though Bush is obviously not an Italian surname, her parents were children of Italian immigrants (her father's side from Campobasso, Molise, her mother's side from Montegranaro and Senigallia near Ancona in the Marche). The family name Bucci was changed to Bush by school teachers, none of whom pronounced the name the same. "They called them 'Bookie,' 'Buckie,' or 'Butchie.' When they discovered they all belonged to one family they decided to call them 'Bush,' so they'd all be the same."

Mary graduated from the State University of New York at Buffalo in 1972 and then "bummed around" for six years working as a bus driver and onion picker. After a critical accident in which her back was broken — an experience that Bush says changed her life — she decided to try her hand at creative writing. One of her aunts, who had grown up as an onion farmer and who became a driving cultural force in their community, supported her education.

Bush earned her Master's and Doctorate in Arts from the graduate program in creative writing at Syracuse, where she worked with such luminaries as George P. Elliott and Raymond Carver. She taught at Syracuse University and Hamilton College, and in 1984, with novelist Rachel Guido DeVries, she founded the Community Writers Project in Syracuse. Just recently Mary accepted a tenure-track position in Memphis State University's English Department.

Of the dozen stories collected in Mary Bush's *A Place of Light* only a few deal with the representation of the Italian/American subject, yet they all speak from a knowledge that is sensitive to the lives of the people who, like many Americans of Italian descent, inhabit the margins of American society.

All of the stories take place in rural settings that Bush depicts in a style characteristic of some of America's best country writers. The spirits of Willa Cather, Kate Chopin, William Faulkner, and James Dickey are all resurrected by the tales that Bush spins, and yet Bush writes with a freshness that tells us she has come into her own as an American writer.

The texture of her writing, like the landscapes she creates, shifts from thick description to understated and bare suggestions of what is revealed to us. Bush presents the voices of the uneducated, the people we have come to call the "salt of the earth," in ways that depicts the humanity they share with the more sophisticated city-folk. In a time when artistic focus seems frozen on urban culture, Bush turns our senses to the culture of life far beyond the city limits.

## 2

*M*ary Bush is an exciting writer to read. Her stories vary from documentary realism to fabulistic folktales. Sensitive to the effects of cultural clashes that still occur in rural America, she depicts these confrontations with a literary flair that contains echoes of the folk wisdom of oral tradition, as evidenced by "Cure." In this story which opens the collection, Bush takes us, through the minds of Italian/American children, into an experience of the tension that results from the interaction of old and new world cultures. The children come to know that there is a stigma attached to those who, like Great-aunt Maria, keep the ancient beliefs. Maria comes "to make tea and say prayers and cook" for the family after the mother has fallen ill. Maria believes that all her niece needs is, "the Cure. Carp mole clay," something the father thinks is voodoo. "We believe in doctors in this house," he says. In spite of what their father believes, the children go off in search of the necessary ingredients that will effect Maria's Cure. Having found all but the carp, they begin fishing next to Old Man Otts. When Otts finds out they're fishing for carp, he tells them has one that he found on the ground. When they ask him for it he replies, "What you want with a carp . . . I can see you ain't no niggers . . . You must be wops if you planning to eat carp."

Much of Bush's work, like "Cure," centers on the family as it struggles to stick together or claws its way into disintegration. Whether recounting the loss of a young girl's innocence in a story like "Outlaws," in which an uncle's attention to his niece turns sexual, or depicting the realization of how the home world seems different after a stay in the hospital, Bush proves that even the mundane, ordinary acts of life can be turned into powerful fiction. Such is the case in "Glass," "Rude Awakening," "Muskrat," and "Difficult Passage."

Bush strengthens the tradition of American writing by deftly rendering worlds of women. This she does throughout all of her stories, but it comes through most successfully in the one from which the collection gets its title. In "A Place of Light," Bush in a manner reminiscent of Toni Morrison, depicts the interaction of two females strangers who meet. Their subsequent relationship poses a threat to white woman's racist boyfriend. Told from the daughter's point of view, the story becomes a tale of how shared gender eases the crossing of class and racial boundaries. When the white couple's car breaks down, the only assistance they can get is from an old black woman and her daughter. The car's trouble becomes a metaphor for the failing relationship. And when the car's repaired, it's the woman who takes control as a result of gaining strength and a sense of independence through her encounter.

Car troubles provide the entry into another story. In "Emergency" an old white woman leaves her son's broken down car and attempts to her way to a bus station in the heart of an off-highway ghetto. Predictably she cannot relate to a black woman whom she follows home in search of a phone. The old woman's disorientation becomes an odyssey magnified by her fear of blacks, demonstrating that a sense of sisterhood can't always escape the bounds of racial difference.

Two of the most daring stories in the collection are "Losing Willy Gleason" and "Hunters." Based on the rough characters from the hills, the type made infamous by James Dickey's *Deliverance*, both stories focus on the potential for brutality in rural life, reminding us that the pastoral life is not always peaceful. When Willy Gleason, an offspring of the town's most notorious family, "those idiot Gleasons," teams up with Sylvia Biddle, a young girl who is right out of the 1970s song "Ode to Billie Joe," they create a scene that becomes a town legend, the kind of event by which time is marked. And in "Hunters," what two errant hunters do to a young couple expecting their first child will have you rechecking the locks on your vacation cabin doors. In both stories, Bush treads well the tightrope over the dangerous trap of sensationalism, demonstrating a fine ability to create the dramatic tension that keeps you turning pages. The same feelings come through her "Underground Railroad," in which a brother and sister run away from home after their baby sister's crib death.

As is the case with many Italian/American writers, Bush's first collection has a tendency to keep her own ethnicity in the shadows. It's as if writers like Mary have to show the world that they are writer's first and Italian Americans second. But this in no way detracts from the success of the debut of her first major book. The stories here prove that another Italian/American writer has come of age in a time when work like hers is needed.

*May 1991*

# An Intelligence of the Heart

## Anne Calcagno

At first glance, there doesn't seem to be anything particularly Italian about the short stories in Anne Calcagno's first collection *Pray for Yourself.* While two of the nine are set in Italy, the rest are scattered about urban and rural America and are peopled with characters peculiar to America.

However, a closer look at these remarkably American short stories reveals an Italian foundation. Beneath the surface of the polished prose and carefully constructed sentences Calcagno has combined the the beauty of poetry with the complexity of prose fiction, capturing the lyrical rhythms and sounds of the Italian language through English. By weaving Italian sensibilities with unorthodox English syntax, she creates phrases that resonate in the mind long after the last page has been turned.

Calcagno is master of the sentence that says it all. In "The Story of My Weight," a woman meditates on her life now that she's middle-aged and thinks: "Age is an invisible train charging through the dark, wearing down the rails," and later in the same story the narrator remarks, "Age is a sort of overeating."

Many of the stories deal with the disintegration of the nuclear family and the interruption of normal life when change derails routine. Sometimes these disruptions are caused by forces outside the family, as in "Something Like a Risk," in which a father is fired from his job, or "Married You Are Not Alone," in which a husband loses his job to a corporate buyout of the company that has provided him with an identity. The loss of job, of a sense of who one is and where one belongs, sends Calcagno's ordinary characters off into extraordinary explorations of previously uncharted territories inside themselves.

While she creates stories that are more traditional than most of what passes for short fiction in these postmodern times, her plots are never quite resolved. At the end of nearly all her stories, there is a person, more often a woman, who is frozen in time. Having just gone through a life changing encounter, her characters are suspended as if someone hit the pause button on a VCR.

While there might be nothing autobiographical about these stories, they all reflect the experiences of a woman who has lived in two worlds. Born in San Diego, Calcagno was raised in Milan and Rome when her father's job transferred the family. At the age of seventeen, she returned to the United States to attend Williams College where the late John Gardner encouraged her writing by calling her "original."

At a recent meeting of the Italian Cultural Center, Calcagno talked about her writing and its connection to Italian culture. She spoke passionately of a struggle for her self-identity that began the moment she returned to America after thirteen years in Italy.

"Because I wasn't the exotic stereotype that most people expected of an Italian woman," she says, "it was hard for me to continue identifying with things Italian in America. And when I went to Italy, I was labeled as an American." This struggle repeated itself in her search for a language of self-expression. "I found myself trying to translate my Italian sounds and thoughts into American words. I wanted to get the emotional weight of the Italian language into English to create an intelligence of the heart."

After graduation she lived for a while in New York City, where she worked for *La Repubblica*. Later she earned an M.F.A. in poetry and fiction at the University of Montana and has published stories in literary magazines such as *The North American Review, Epoch, Denver Quarterly*, and *Tri-Quarterly*. In the past four years she has won a National Endowment for the Arts Creative Writing Fellowship, an Illinois Arts Council Artists Fellowship and, in 1993, the prestigious James D. Phelan Literary Award.

In spite of such success, publishers were not knocking down her door to produce a collection of her short stories. When *TriQuarterly* went into partnership with Northwestern University Press to create TriQuarterly Books, her collection was one of four projects chosen to launch the new publishing venture.

Calcagno, an assistant professor of English, teaches creative writing at DePaul University, and is working on *Struck by Dina*, a novel that deals with a family and Italian immigration during this century.

   *Pray for Yourself* is a strong step forward for a young writer who is at the beginning of what will surely be a great career. But don't take my word. Read for yourself.

*January 1993*

# Cross-Cultural Lines

## Alessandro Carrera

*A*lessandro Carrera's *The Perfect Bride/La sposa perfetta* is the witty and passionate bilingual record of a journey into postmodern American culture, a telling travelogue of a man and his mind encountering new lands and languages.

In his explorations of the territory of American culture, which we Americans too often take for granted, Carrera reorients our view of everyday life. He transforms the ordinary into the extraordinary, forcing us to think through the many common things that slip out of our consciousness. This collection tells us what it's like to be Ulysses again and in the process helps us to learn more about ourselves and our country.

The Italian and English versions of each poem, beyond mere translation, create a cultural dialogue which at times finds the poems debating, at times echoing, each other. Carrera presents difficult thoughts in simple language. Each line rings with music and echoes a variety of meaning. The force of making the foreign familiar is much of the power inside these new poems. Whether it comes through an airplane flight, as in his opening poem "Good Morning, I Am Your Pilot," or through self-ironic humor, as in "I Hear the Sounds But I Do not Understand the Words," Carrera is able to turn even the most American readers into strangers in a bus station.

The collection is composed of fifteen poems, divided into three sections. Section I, "Domestic Flights," presents eight poems which present the earliest impressions of America. Some of the poems set up a naivete which disappears by the end of the collection. The total effect make us observers of the narrator's growth, a growth that careful readers will also experience.

In the second section, "The Big World and Its Wonderful Music," the poet gives us six poems which reflect the realization of the American encounter. A most significant poem of this section is "The Red Caboose," a marvelous and haunting meditation of how the images of America can powerfully evoke Italian memories of a folksinger's travels and a father's tales.

In this section, the poet combines explorations of American and Italian history and myth in musical observations of contemporary culture. In Carrera's adept hand, lyric poems become mini-epics of how wandering down rivers and roads results in the creation of new myths. Using the classic figures of Tiresias and Ulysses in "Tiresias before the Sea," and "Ulysses Arrives in California," Carrera moves through the American landscape using the figures of the blind prophet and bold adventurer to echo the earlier dialogues of father and son through which wise advice is passed along to the reader:

> Roads and dust, roads and
> Mind the roots, my son,
> Roots are ravenous ... (62)

> The untransmittable wisdom of the old
> Is that the young, through memory,
> Will become more and more forgetful
> And, swelling with age, will sour
> Like wine turns into vinegar:
> The young, whose mere existence
> Confutes, by laughing, the whole line of descent. (64)

In the final section entitled "Farewell," Carrera leaves us with two poems which serve as retrospective reflections on the entire experience as well as commentaries on current events such as the fall of the Berlin wall and the Gulf War. His "My Father from His Grave Addresses the Berlin Wall" continues the theme of dialogue between the past and present through father and son. And in "A Song after the War" the poet, often with tongue in cheek, exposes and criticizes of some of America's most troubling faults.

The story of traveling to new lands, of immigrating to new worlds is an old story; in *The Perfect Bride*, Carrera while, never reaching perfection, should be applauded for making it new.

*November 1991*

# Sicilian Truth

## Gaetano Cipolla

### 1

*C*hances are, if there's anything happening with Sicilian culture in the United States, somewhere nearby, if not at its center, is Gaetano Cipolla. Since the early 1980s, this professor, translator and poet has been a driving force behind the revitalization of *Arba Sicula* (Sicilian Dawn). Cipolla has coached some of Al Pacino's Sicilian for *Godfather III*, and has edited books of Sicilian poetry and culture for Legas Publisher.

Born in Francavilla, Sicily, Cipolla immigrated to America with his parents in 1955. He earned a Bachelor of Science in Education, majoring in Italian, from New York University. After teaching junior high school for four years, he went on to Hunter College. In 1974 he earned his Ph.D. in Italian at New York University. Since then he has taught at NYU, Marymount College, Lehman College and, in 1978, he St. John's College where he's now a full professor.

Cipolla notes two distinct stages of his career. The first, as a critic and scholar, had nothing to do with Sicily. This stage was marked by his book: *Labyrinth: Studies of an Archetype*. Published in 1987 by Legas, this book, the first of the Legas series on literary criticism, presents a study of the labyrinth and its manifestations throughout the western world and elsewhere. His next two books, however marked a change not only in his career, but in himself. Cipolla translated Giovanni Meli's *Don Chisciotti and Sanciu Panza* and *Moral Fables*. These were the first translations of the great Sicilian poet Meli, to be published in this country. "While I was in graduate school, Luigi Ballerini had the idea of having each graduate student come up with a reading in their own dialects. I choose Meli. I did the recital and thought that was something that I should be doing. I got goose pimples. Poetry in one's own language can't be duplicated. It hit deeper than any other poetry I had studied and taught. I was finding part of my self in the works that I had covered up."

According to Cipolla, the Sicilian language had no standing in the realm of academia. "You don't parade your own ethnicity in academia," he says. "There was always a kind of awkwardness in using your own language which came from years of having one's Italian corrected. Years of schooling established the idea that speaking a dialect was inferior to speaking the standard."

Another obstacle Cipolla overcame was the stigma attached to translation. "Translations," Cipolla says, "were not always considered a scholarly endeavor. However translation is an act of criticism of the most elementary kind. If you don't understand the text, then you really can't translate it. I'm always fighting a battle to make people understand that there's more to translation than simply transposing words."

Soon he got involved in publishing others with Legas, a press founded in 1988 by Leonardo Sbrocchi, Professor of Italian at Ottawa University, which at that time was primarily publishing text books and book projects in other languages. Since Cipolla's collaboration, Legas has added a specialty of publishing Sicilian writing in two different series: Poets of *Arba Sicula*, which highlights works of single poets such as Vincenzo Ancona, with audio tapes. A forthcoming volume is devoted to the poetry of Nino Martoglio. "Martoglio is the most famous Sicilian language playwright of the 20th century. He spurred Pirandello to write for the theater," says Cipolla.

The second series is more scholarly and covers Sicilian history, sociology and economics. The first volume in this series is Giuseppe Quatraglio's *A Thousand Years in Sicily*. These series were designed to introduce Sicilian people and culture to America. Before Cipolla's participation in Legas, *Arba Sicula*: held annual live poetry recitals. However, in spite of the success of these events, there would be little impact other than on those who attended these readings. And so Cipolla decided these poets could reach more people, more frequently, if they were published. "Poetry is the window to the soul of the people," says Cipolla. "We have to have these things on record."

Current estimates figure that fifty percent of all Italian Americans are of Sicilian origin. This could mean that there are more than ten million Sicilian/Americans. Relationship between Sicily and Italy has always been complex. Sicily, after Garibaldi, united with Italy. Conquered Sicily and

Naples, and gave it to the king. "Sicilians always knew Italian, as much as other parts of Italy. When Italy was made in 1861 perhaps only three percent of the entire population knew Tuscan Italian, even the king himself didn't know. In the universities they taught Latin. Most of the people got along in their own dialect. In giving a common language they have stigmatized the dialect by putting them down, by having teachers correct students' dialects as inferior form of expression, creating a deleterious effect on the dialects. Sicilian is not a dialect; it is not a corruption of a language. Thirty years ago people used to say that dialects are going to die, but it hasn't happened. People have stopped using it in everyday conversation, but there is a greater use of it in written language, especially poetry. Among the intellectuals people use it more, because they no longer have to prove to anyone that they know Italian well. It used to be that if you spoke Sicilian, it was because you didn't know Italian. Now everybody speaks Italian pretty well so there's no need to prove anything. Sicilian is the first Italic language to be used for poetic purposes. The Scuola Siciliana was founded by Frederick II in the 13th century. In 1220 this school was the major school of poetry to use an Italic language, as its influence moved up north, imitated Sicilians. I've read different theories that have said that all of the different groups of people who have come to Italy have simply deposited their languages atop Sicilian, these can be identified through a type of archeological dig on the language."

## 2

*G*aetano Cipolla, the president of Arba Sicula and editor of the bilingual Sicilian-English journal of the same name, has completed an important and exciting new publishing project. *The Poetry of Nino Martoglio* (Legas 1993) is the first bilingual edition of selected poems by one of Sicily's most important poets. Cipolla prefaces his translations with an illuminating introduction that establishes the importance and outlines the achievements of one of the most famous Sicilians of the turn of the century (1870-1921). He also presents a sound formal analysis of two of Martoglio's longer poems that never gets bogged down in academic jargon. Like Martoglio, Cipolla writes for the people.

Considered by many critics to be the founder of the Sicilian theater, Martoglio is, without a doubt, one of the greatest contributors to Sicilian literature. He persuaded the great Luigi Pirandello to write for the theater. The two even collaborated on a few plays, and Pirandello called him, after Giovanni Meli, the most expressive poet of Sicily. Yet in spite of his fame during his lifetime, Martoglio, as Cipolla points out, has received scant critical attention.

Martoglio lived an exciting life. At the age of sixteen he founded his own newspaper, *D'Artagnan*, for which he contributed most of the articles under a number of pseudonyms. Because of his tough criticism he fought twenty-one duels with those who claimed offense. He served as artistic director of Morgana Films, and produced and directed a number of important films. But his greatest contribution to Sicilian culture is his poetry and *Centona* was his great collection.

As Cipolla notes, the theme throughout *Centona* is love — not love in the poetic ideal, but love in the real. Martoglio was a writer in the *verismo* or realist tradition, and like real life, he can move from undying love to life threatening hate in a single poem as he does in "Nica":

> How did I live my life until the time
> you came along and we together walked?
> I will not say to you I did not love
> because I do not wish to tell a lie.

And by the poem's end he confesses:

> Listen to me, I'll read your destiny
> I own a knife that's long and shiny bright
> with a strong point, and sharper than a razor,
> and I keep sharpening it day and night.

Any lover of opera will appreciate the wonderful dialogues that Martoglio was able to capture in sonnets and lyrics. There is a sense of humor here, that when restrained by the formal structure creates an interesting tension. The real beauty of this poetry lies in its original Sicilian, but the joy of knowing what that beauty means is given to the reader through Cipolla's fine job of translating the poems into English and Italian. There are times when, as he explains, he presents a literal translation, but more often than not he achieves an excellent sense of the poetic through his English renditions.

In the past Cipolla's verse translations have included Giovanni Meli's *The Origin of the World*, *Don Chisciotti e Sanciu Panza*, and *Moral Fables*, all were the first of Meli's works to be published in this country. This latest labor is a continuation of Cipolla's energetic devotion to promoting Sicilian literature through translation.

*July 1992 / May 1994*

# Father Knows Best

## George Cuomo

$\mathscr{I}$n an article in the *New York Times Book Review* (March 14, 1993), author Gay Talese posed the question, "Where are the Italian American Novelists?" George Cuomo, who has been writing novels for over three decades, while not mentioned in that article, is proof that the Italian/American novelist is alive and well and working hard in relative obscurity.

The latest novel by Cuomo is a fine example of how Italian/American characters can be utilized to tell a tale that speaks to everyone. *Trial by Water* is the story of the love of a father for a son caught up in a school rivalry gone deadly. Through the investigation of the drowning of two kids on prom night, we come to learn, as does the father, the competing influences that society and family have on a young man. We also learn that the ways of the past can be both useful and harmful when applied to the present.

Florian Rubio has successfully made his way out of the Bronx neighborhood where he was born, but fails in his relationship with his wife Elly, who takes off with a landscape designer for California, where she raises their three children. Rubio rebuilds his life and career in a small western Massachusetts town. His parents join him and, at age forty-seven, he's reliving his adolescence by riding around in a red Corvette and working on a new relationship with a married woman. His eye for the right piece of land which he buys at the right time gives him the freedom to work when he wants. But when his neurotic ex-wife sends their youngest son, Brian, back to live with Florian, because she can no longer control him, his whole life changes.

Brian forces his father to look back into his own past of which he remembered the two prime virtues expected of an Italian boy growing up.

On the one hand you were to show *furberia*, the quickness and cunning needed to get by on the streets of an unfriendly city full of strange customs. But at home you'd get cracked across the head if you didn't display *osservanza*, the proper obedience and respect and family loyalty.

But the question arises, is the backbone of proper behavior for one generation appropriate or useful for the next?

The answer lies in Rubio's ability to adapt the age-old wisdom of his parents and the new knowledge he gains about himself through his son. Cuomo uses the Italian/American family as a bridge between the families of old wealth and old poverty. Through them the towns of Trent and Medway come to know each other in ways they might never have.

In this time of fictional experimentation and minimalism, Cuomo's novel is a refreshing return to a more traditional way of writing in which a smooth style never detracts from the story being told. He creates three dimensional characters, even in the minor characters. His portraits of immigrant parents, the son, the grandson and even the townspeople, remind us that there are qualities of life that are inherited and those that we must invent as situations arise. Cuomo's gift as a storyteller comes through his ability to sustain a narrative and to color it with a variety of voices that reflect versions of reality that create competing truths. There's a real plot here, and while the pages slip through fingers like water, the images created are indelible.

*June 1993*

# *Border Crossings*

## Antonio D'Alfonso

### 1

Antonio D'Alfonso is an Italian/Canadian author of a number of books of poetry, prose, and fiction, written in French as well as English. With the publication of *The Other Shore*, a few years ago, he leads us into expanding our notions of what it means to be a product of different, and often competing, cultures.

In his own words, *The Other Shore* is a "notebook without a beginning, without an end, only a flowing towards being, a flowering; contradictions and explanations." But there is more integrity and coherence here than the author's modest attempt at explanation may lead us to believe. Divided into seven parts, the scattered reflections and recollections presented in prose and poetry (illustrated with the author's own black and white photos of Molise, his ancestor's homeland) combine to describe a voyage from self to other, a voyage in and through language from home to ancestral homeland. This book documents a process of self definition. It is as though the author has leapt into a sea fed by the rivers of many cultures. His writing is the act of coming up to the surface — up for air — and of swimming to the other shore. Much of what is presented in this book is the result of getting out and looking back over the area the swim has covered. This work documents the struggle for balance and understanding of all the varieties of culture that make up a single human life.

The first section entitled "L'uomo solo," or solitary man, is best represented by the entry entitled "Ghiaccio":

I am ice. I thaw with time. With heat. And become what I originally was . . . I taste the Atlantic and the Pacific. I taste the Tyrrhenian and the Adriatic. I drink polluted water and am cleansed by it. Water, never still, always changing, cannot be imprisoned by matter or metaphor. Water for mother, freedom, nomadism, the unconscious.

The sections here are very self-conscious, but D'Alfonso never lapses into nostalgic and sentimental melodrama. He keeps afloat in such dangerous waters by turning clichés inside out and by creating memorable phrases like:

Language is a voice that answers your questions, that questions your answers.

The second section, "Beyond My Limits," while focusing on descriptions of others, as in "The People Across the Street," tells us that the world is a mirror, and in others we can see something of ourselves.

An old couple walks on Lungomare called Via del Duca degli Abruzzi
— how can I escape from myself in Italy?

It is, D'Alfonso reminds us, impossible to get away from ourselves; no matter where we go and what we do, we are trapped inside ourselves. The only way out is through language of speech, of writing, of gesture.

In "Guglionesi," we follow the writer's return to his roots, and witness how the experience challenges and changes notions of self. "Romamor," a palindrome, plays with the idea of the enchantment of The Eternal City, and the writer's notions of sensual and platonic love. Here is a sensuality, a more mature and seasoned approach than in his earlier book of poetry, *Black Tongue* (Guernica, 1983). "To Criticize Oneself" contains the less polished prose and poetry of the collection. The language is obviously journalistic, yet it is sometimes only when we write down the obvious that we come to know it.

To write is to remember the voices of your people, the voices of those who came before you . . .

No writing without the critic. The critic solidifies the fluidity of language . . .

Those who are not frightened to criticize themselves know their way
to freedom. Have they come from the shadows?

The final two sections, "Six" and "Il nuovo barocco," complete the
voyage to a new land. In "Six," there is the juxtaposition of Italy and
Canada, friends and artists in both places. In the final section, we observe
the writer's struggle to create a new definition of both art and himself as an
artist.

*The Other Shore* is an important document of Italian/North American
culture; it is geography of one's soul designed in thoughts and mapped in
words; it tells the story of an emigration from the inside out, and the
outside in.

The work of poet, novelist, and publisher Antonio D'Alfonso is woven
from strands of the different cultures which have affected his life. Born in
Montreal, Canada, to parents who emigrated from the Molise region of
Italy, D'Alfonso defines himself as "French, culturally, English speaking, and
Italian as a human being." His earlier works have focused on his French and
English influences. With *The Other Shore*, he begins examining the Italian.

D'Alfonso first visited his parents' homeland in 1973, but says the
experience didn't affect him strongly. It was during a second visit that he
realized how close he was to them. "I found myself faced with the dilemma
of being two or three people in one. I needed to learn how to be happy
with that knowledge. I needed to achieve a certain type of emotional
security by being non assimilated, non integrated," he says.

D'Alfonso chronicles his experience in *The Other Shore*, a book of
prose, poetry, and journal writing that captures the process of creating a
self-identity. "We have to reeducate ourselves; you can't pretend you know
who you are; you really decide what it is you want to be; some people, and
rightly so, want to get away from that, but those who don't want to should
be allowed to do so."

D'Alfonso suggests that Italian culture is ultimately not one of language but of image. "I'm really in awe of the Italian/American filmmakers.
They're showing us that there is a culture that goes beyond language, one
that doesn't die even if it's five generations old; the language of presentation may change, but there's an essence there that carries over from one
country to another."

The forty-one-year-old author believes that the place for Italian North
Americans has always been in the margins society. "However, when we take
control of our culture by mastering the means of production, we can fix our

energies and efforts moving our own creations into the center of main-stream society; ultimately, the issue is that we own our own production, and we can produce the images that we create." In order to pursue these goals, D'Alfonso gave up a career of teaching and working in film. Over the years, his hard work had paid off in a strong network of publishing and distribution resources.

Guernica Editions Inc. was started in 1979 in order to create an alternative to the mainstream system of publishing. The primary interest of the press is Italian/North American culture. "Everything we do is filtered through the fact that it's Italian," he says. "Thanks to people like Anthony Tamburri, we're beginning to make inroads into the U.S. markets and we're getting manuscripts from Italian/American writers." For D'Alfonso starting his own press was ultimately a political gesture. "In Canada, small presses need grants to survive. I did get some small grants, but they weren't paying my bills," he says. "I've devised a format of small, good-looking publications, that distinguish Guernica as a publishing house. I'm creating my own vision."

D'Alfonso has big plans for Guernica. He's trying to get into the Southern American/Italian writing community and he'd like to have the works of North and South American writers of Italian descent translated into Italian. He organized a 1992 International conference in Canada which brought together writers, critics, and filmmakers of the Italian diaspora. Some titles include a work by Italian/American critic Anthony Tamburri and a book of poetry by Diane Raptosh.

## 2

*I*n 1986, D'Alfonso stopped writing in English because, as he says, "The reaction to the writing was negative."

During that period, D'Alfonso was hard at work on determining his relationship to his Italian heritage by birth, his French heritage through life in Montreal, and the English language through which he was educated. "That search for identity was being misunderstood," he says, "it was being taken for self-conceit."

When he returned to French, the language in which he produced some of his poetry and prose since 1973, the same work was received much better, but, as D'Alfonso says, a new problem arose. "Critics said: 'Ah, here's an Anglo who's turned to writing in French. He has become one of us.' People began taking my work as a cry for the very nationalism that was threatening minority identity in Canada."

*The Other Shore* captures the process of creating a self-identity. D'Alfonso chronicles the experience of searching for his identity. Published in 1986, the book was initially panned by English-language critics. "They hated it, in spite of the fact that it was written in English," says D'Alfonso. When translated into French, the response was quite different. It received much critical attention and was named as a finalist for one of the top poetry prizes in Quebec. D'Alfonso attributes this reception to the French/Canadian's obsession with the effects of bilingualism. This obsession with nationalism and the languages that represent it became a political issue in 1990 with the Meach Lake Accord, a legislative attempt by the Canadian provincial ministers to create a law stating that Canada is composed of founding people: the French and the British. Other cultures, such as the Italian Canadian, would be subordinate to those.

With *The Other Shore*, D'Alfonso feels that the quest for identity has been explored as content, and he is now free to move to other levels where he can explore how ethnicity affects literary form. "Once I came to terms with my identity," he says, "I needed a new direction for my writing. I needed to move beyond pasta and the nostalgia." D'Alfonso's latest writing begins the project of creating what he calls, "An Italian/American morality. I felt we needed to know what was behind all the signs and symbols that most of us equated with Italian/North American culture." The first step in exploring this new morality is *Panick Love*, D'Alfonso's English translation of his 1987 prose poem entitled *L'Amour panique*.

The foundation of *Panick Love* is the Odyssey, specially the encounter between Ulysses and Circe, a myth of intoxication and passion that D'Alfonso explored in *Circe's Cup*, his first short film. In *Panick Love*, he returns to it to chart the effects that mindless passion has on the soul of a voyager who refuses, unlike his men who are turned into pigs to succumb to Circe, and returns to his wife. *Panick Love* also serves as a commentary on the decadence that extreme nationalism leads to. To avoid the barbaric self-destruction, the traveler needs to go back to his roots.

*Panick Love* is the first of D'Alfonso's proposed trilogy on love. The second, entitled *A Letter*, explores marriage, and a third will be about beginning a family. D'Alfonso's decision to move from French into English stems from his curiosity with how, after so many years, *Panick Love* would affect the English reading and speaking culture. By choosing to write in

English, D'Alfonso is making a political as well as a personal statement. But, as he notes, "it's a totally different level of English that I'm using now. I'm using English much more consciously and more carefully."

D'Alfonso believes that the Italian/Canadian voice is very important and needs to be heard. "Until we re-master the Italian language," he says, "English will have to serve as the Italian language of North America, Australia England, and in many countries that have become homes to the Italian diaspora. Through English, we can speak to each other, expanding our audiences for and thus the impact of our literature."

To encourage this interaction, D'Alfonso, founder and publisher of Guernica Editions, has extended his publishing concerns into the United States, Australia, and South America. Publications planned for release this year include: Giose Rimanelli's *Benedetta in Guysterland;* Anthony Valerio's *Valentino and the Great Italians*; a collection of contemporary fiction by Italian/American women writers entitled *The Voices We Carry,* edited by Mary Jo Bona; Robert Viscusi's *Astoria*; and *Women as Lovers*, plays by Theresa Carilli.

# Paper Fishing

## Tina DeRosa

*I*'ve known Tina DeRosa's writing a lot longer than I have known her. A few years ago I heard her read at a conference on Italian/American Writing organized by Professor Dominic Candeloro as part of the Italians In Chicago project. At that time I was beginning work on my own novel. As a young, inexperienced writer I was hoping to extract a few words of wisdom. She told me what I had to do was unplug the phone and stop going to family affairs. I took her advice and six years later I completed my own novel.

I read her first novel, *Paper Fish* soon after as it was published. I did a review of it for the American Italian Historical Association's newsletter. I have included an excerpt of that review as a context for better understanding this interview.

> *Paper Fish* is an important work of art because it preserves what Italian Americans must never forget. It is the story of memory and the recall of indelible images that recreates the Italian/American experience in the city. Tina's skillful use of words brings back the old neighborhood (Taylor and Halsted) in a way that has never been done . . . The beauty of the book is in the ability of the author to bring the reader right into the characters' minds . . . She preserves the Bellacasa family in a photo album of poetry . . . It is a book that I didn't want to end, and when it did I wanted more.

When Tina was a child she realized she couldn't become an altar boy or a priest, so she decided to be a writer. It was the third best choice. "Creation is close to priesthood. It's taking the ordinary and turning it into the extraordinary," she said.

Tina began writing when she was seven or eight. She remembers reading children's books and the *World Book of Knowledge*. "I memorized the 'Gettysburgh Address' and decided I wanted to write something that strong and that beautiful. My father gave me a diary, a real book with blank pages and I began writing stories that were all generally religious: a little girl grows up in a convent and sees God."

Tina was educated in Catholic schools through college, attending Holy Guardian Angel Grammar School, St. Mary's High School and Mundelein College. "I was completely lost in college until my junior year. I was one of maybe three people from my neighborhood who went to college. I began to major in English, then I changed disciplines several times and finally began work in sociology when I was a junior. I also worked on the college paper."

During her freshman year her family moved away from the Taylor Street area. The neighborhood as she had grown up in was gone. It was an abrupt departure for her. During her senior year a nun she had grown close to asked: "Tina, what are you going to do with all this?" (referring to her Liberal Arts education). She replied, "I don't know. After graduation I first did social work. After six months I realized I couldn't do it. I was a case worker in the Audy homes. Then I decided I wanted to work for a newspaper, so I photocopied all the articles I had written for my college newspaper and went to the *Chicago Tribune*."

Tina was hired as secretary to John Fink (then editor of the *Chicago Tribune*'s Sunday Magazine) with the understanding that she wanted to be a writer. Within three months she was writing for the magazine. "While working for the magazine, I began writing children's stories. A writer on the magazine read them and encouraged me to write fiction, by telling me: 'Someday you're going to be doing this for real.'"

Tina began taking her writing seriously and applied for fellowships. She thought she was writing a book, which she has since discarded. She calls it "a hopeless work." During this time she held a number of professional jobs, such as editor for *Encyclopedia Brittanica*'s Film Division and staff writer for *Sphere* magazine. She has always worked as a writer. "I don't think my family really understood what I was up to. Sometimes I confused them. But when they saw stories in the *Tribune* magazine with my bylines they strongly supported me. The very first story I ever had published was about growing up on Taylor and Halsted."

As she started to write more fiction, she began to feel very lonely and wanted to be with other writers, so she enrolled in the writer's program at the University of Illinois at Chicago, intending to get a Master's degree in

English. "At the University of Illinois I met Michael Anania who became my mentor. He offered a lot of direction." Generally, reactions to her writing (mostly poetry and short stories) were favorable. She was beginning to write *Paper Fish*. The first fifty pages of the novel were part of her Master's thesis. She was teaching composition classes at the same time.

"At some point in the program I realized there was at least one book in me; Michael said the same thing. He read the first draft of *Paper Fish* (I thought I had finished it.) Michael said a lot of nice things to encourage me and after the praise he said (and I don't know if he'll remember this): 'Tina take the first two hundred and fifty pages and throw them out. I think in the last fifty pages you have the beginning of a book.' " She didn't look at the manuscript for a year after that.

In 1977 she was asked to give a reading from the book. Jim Ramholz, publisher of The Wine Press and a friend of hers, came up after the reading and said that he wanted to publish her novel. She didn't take him seriously. The following year the book took hold. Tina continued working on the book. In August of 1978 Jim called her and said he had received a grant and wanted to publish her novel. "I was working two jobs and coming home to my basement apartment to work each night. I was saving my money to move. The pressure of a publishing deadline grew. In the fall I applied to the Ragdale Foundation and was given residency from October to December of 1978. Ragdale was a place where I could go to finish the book in peace. I finished it there. If it weren't for Ragdale I don't think I could have completed the work in the amount of time I had."

I asked her why the title *Paper Fish*. She said that the people in the book were as beautiful and as fragile as a Japanese kite, so the title. *Paper Fish* is the only novel featuring Italians in Chicago and the Old Taylor-Halsted Little Italy. About the book she had this to say. "The neighborhood was becoming a myth in my own mind. It was gone; I was not in touch with anyone else who had lived there; I was living in an entirely alien world; I was constantly telling stories about where I had grown up and people found the stories interesting. Michael Anania encouraged me to write them down. I wanted the neighborhood to live again, to recreate it and so many of the people I was close to, especially my grandmother and father who had both died. I think I was haunted by it all. I wanted to make those people and that neighborhood alive again. I wanted the readers of the book to care about it, to realize that something beautiful had existed and that it was gone.

"Taylor Street had become a myth of terrible beauty and terrible ugliness. It was a world complete unto itself. The further I got away from it the more I could see it as a small, beautiful, peculiar world. I had so many conflicting feelings about growing up there, especially because of the reactions I'd receive from people when I told them where I had grown up. Everyone knew about it. Everyone had some crack to make about Taylor Street. They didn't realize the beauty that was there. I never realized all the beauty that was there until I started to write about it. In fact I never realize my own truth until I start putting it down on paper."

Tina did no research for this novel. For her, Italy was always an imaginary country. "I still haven't been there. I could always imagine Italy because I heard so many stories about it from my grandmother and from the people in the old neighborhood. There is a section in the novel that deals with my great-grandparents, about whom I know nothing. I imagined my great-grandparents and Italy. I have had people who have read the book ask me if I have been there.

"Because I grew up with such a rich heritage I can see now how myth and reality in your imagination become so confused. Growing up in a neighborhood like that is not merely being confined to streets that other people are afraid to walk down. You're growing up with an entire mythology. Your grandparents carry that mythology with them and try to pass it on so that it becomes a part of you.

"When I sat down to write *Paper Fish* I was not only haunted by my memories of the family members who had died and the neighborhood that was gone, but also by the stories that were told to me. It was an immensely rich, complex world that no longer existed except in my imagination."

*Paper Fish* is out of print, though Tina does have a number of copies. An excerpt has been included in *The Dream Book*.

*May 1985*

# Wiseguys Aren't Smart

## Albert DiBartolomeo

### 1

*B*orn in Tasker Homes, a South Philadelphia housing project, novelist Albert DiBartolomeo knows what it's like to have a family broken to pieces. "My father was diabetic and didn't work; he died when he was thirty-four; I was eleven. We were six kids, and my mother sent three of her four boys to Milton Hershey School for Boys, a private school, free for orphans and semi-orphans, that was set up by the guy who invented modern chocolate production."

DiBartolomeo, educated at Hershey's from sixth to twelfth grade, was cut off from his native neighborhood, an experience that provided him with an outsider's perspective to south Philadelphia. "I was always an inward looking individual. I used to write letters home to my older brother who always thought I was more intelligent than him, and I knew that he was stronger than I was. So there was always this unspoken rivalry between us. I wrote him a letter once in which I confessed my feelings and evaluated our relationship. I think he was knocked down by it and told me I ought to be a writer. After that I started to write seriously. Nothing happened for a long time."

DiBartolomeo attended Temple University as undergraduate where he studied business. During his junior year he took a literature class which captured his imagination and his future. After graduating from Temple he taught for five years in the Philadelphia school system. From there he started a woodworking business. After surviving a car accident he sold his business and enrolled in Temple University's creative writing program where he studied with novelist David Bradley. He graduated with a novel that was almost completed. "I sent it to Candida Donadio, she was John Cheever and Mario Puzo's agent. After three months she decided that it was too heavy, and that she didn't want it. So I cut out 200 pages right away. Another brother in New York, passed it on to a friend, who in turn passed it to another friend and it found its way to Walker and Company."

The novel became a family affair. His brother, owner of Circa 86, a graphic design company, designed the book's cover, and his wife, Susan Banka, took the back cover photo.

DiBartolomeo didn't set out to write a thriller. "I was very much preoccupied with the family and its splitting up. Vincent continues to live in the old family home because he's tied to the idea of the family that it once housed. And although he can leave it all behind, as did his brothers and sister, he doesn't. The Hershey episode of my life was traumatic, as I now know. My family was ruptured by my father's death. I see now that what has preoccupied my writing is the family, not just the Italian, but the American family as a unit, a support system, the net; and it's been destroyed by modern life. I found it very tragic, and what Vincent is holding on to in the house is the time when they were all a family. Naming the character Vinnie was a tough call," says DiBartolomeo.

"I know it conjures up the stereotypic TV Italian, but he's marked with that. It's part of the web in which all these characters are trapped. Even though Vinnie is more of an American than an Italian, he's still connected to the web."

DiBartolomeo takes life in South Philadelphia as seriously as Faulkner did his small towns in the South. "The same things are going on in South Philly," he says. "For example, the corruption in Faulkner's work comes from the sin of slavery, for South Philly, it's source is the mob. I found myself wondering about it all, thinking this isn't right. And so I wrote about it."

DiBartolomeo didn't grow up with books in the home; and although he is told that his father was an intelligent man, and that he read, Albert doesn't remember it. "In school I read the American classics by Steinbeck and Salinger. But it wasn't until college that I read Faulkner for the first time, along with Hemingway, and the English writers Dickens, Huxley, and Joseph Conrad. I also remember reading *The Carpetbaggers* and *The Adventurers*."

A close reading of DiBartolomeo's work will identify influences from the classics and popular fiction. He speaks of what he calls "the pleasure of recognition" that happened when he came across books like *The Godfather*,

*Christ in Concrete,* and those by John Fante. "It is something that you don't get in precisely the same way when reading other American writers." Though he acknowledges his Italian/American heritage, DiBartolomeo says he didn't want to just be looked at as an Italian/American writer. "Don DeLillo has a Jewish character in his novel *Endzone* who's preoccupied with wanting to de-Jew himself. I remember reading that in my early twenties and I thought that it was a worthy thing to do. I really did have problems with being seen as Italian. In Hershey, in the 1960s, I was called a wop. This would never have happened in Philly, but in rural Hershey, the wops were seen as not being far from the blacks.

"The situation is interesting: here I am, I look Italian but I don't speak Italian; I happen to live in an Italian area, but I see myself as an American, yet they call me Italian. And I've come to realize that I was born into it and brought up in it, and that for better or worse it's going to inform anything I do. On the one hand it rubs me wrong; on the other hand it would be stupid to ignore it. My book would not be the same if I was not Italian."

His mother's side immigrated from Abruzzi. "I don't even know where my father's side is from," says DiBartolomeo. "And this not knowing is an indication of how little I was concerned with being Italian. My father would take us to his mother's house or to the place where he gambled. There was a culture clash. We were poor in the project and they seemed so rich; they had their own home, and though it was just a row house, the meals were full of luscious food, and this all gave me a sense of Italian ethnicity.

"But I really wasn't aware of being Italian until I was in Hershey, where it was thrown it my face. When I returned to Philadelphia I really wanted nothing to do with anything Italian. I hated it all — the loyalty, tradition, everything. But eventually I came to realize that it was a marvelous thing to have this support system."

*The Vespers Tapes* is his first publication. Albert has written other things with non-Italian characters, but he says there was a comfort he felt when writing about life in South Philadelphia that he didn't feel when writing those other works. DiBartolomeo is currently a part-time instructor at Drexel University teaching literature and composition; his wife is a technical writer at Temple University. His next publication will be a segment that was edited out of the novel which will appear in the next issue of *Italian Americana*. He is also at work on a second novel. DiBartolomeo is hoping for a chance to turn his novel into a film. Recently the film rights were purchased by Larry Bresner, the producer of *Dead Poet's Society* and agent to Robin Williams and Billy Crystal.

## 2

*A* Review of the Film *Godfather VII*

> Italian gangsters,
> all my life, Italian gangsters:
> there's the one with the scar;
> there's the good-looking one with the curls
> who is a coward;
> there's the little murderer who loves his mother;
> there's the ratty one in the white car
> blowing on his nails;
> there's the dignified old Don who turns good,
> and dies;
> there's the big, oily one being gunned down
> in the restaurant — his head sinks
> into his bowl of spaghetti;
> the man with the machine-gun is Italian too,
> and grinning.
> all my life Italian gangsters;
> you too, Leonardo, and Galileo,
> and you too Pop.

Felix Stefanile

It's unfortunate that nearly every book or film that deals with organized crime gets compared to Mario Puzo's *The Godfather*. Puzo's romanticist portrayal of Italians in crime, paired with Nicholas Pileggi's realistic portrayal in *Wiseguy* (and the Martin Scorsese film *GoodFellas*, based on it) seem to be the two accepted ways of portraying criminal elements of the Italian/American community. It looks like the Italian/American gangster has become a permanent stock figure in Americana, as permanent as the cowboy, the Indian, the mad German Scientist, the hot-blooded street gang Latino, the lusty African/American slave. These stereotypes have become a type of visual shorthand for the television and filmmakers whose livelihoods depend on repackaging proven blockbuster formulas.

This year, with these names back in the Hollywood headlines — via the publicity and the Oscar nominations for the films based on their fiction — we seem to be inundated with the larger than life gangsterism that overshadows the Italian/American presence in American media. This is a phenomenon that perhaps will never go away.

So what are we to do when a young Italian/American novelist tries his hand on the Italian gangster material? The two blurbs on the back of the book, by respected figures in American literature — David Bradley and Jerre Mangione — refer to Albert DiBartolomeo's *The Vespers Tapes* in terms of *The Godfather*; Bradley calls it *"The Godfather* with real people,* " and Mangione says that it is "written in the tradition established by Puzo's *The Godfather* . . . refreshingly free of stereotypes."

To the contrary, there is a great deal of difference between DiBartolomeo's work and all the gangster books that precede it. DiBartolomeo can think, he can write, and although he cannot escape the lure of the gangster material, he has the talent to turn out a thrilling tale that is plotted at a nonstop pace, which all makes for an interesting read. While we can understand the sales potential inherent in the Puzo reference, the connection does a disservice to DiBartolomeo's refreshing style and point of view. It keeps us from getting to the real story in this novel, the story beneath the gangster surface.

DiBartolomeo's story revolves around school-teacher Vincent Vespers, younger brother of Frank, a local hood loyal to Don Tucci. Tucci, a dying gangleader, is reaching the end of his life, a life that while scarred by crime is nevertheless one he would like to set straight through an autobiography — an element that reminds us a bit of Gay Talese's *Honor Thy Father*. Tucci, can't write, so he turns for help to the college educated Vincent. Through his sessions with Vinnie, we learn that Tucci has the secrets to more than just some of the Philadelphia Police's missing persons' cases. Tucci can explain family mysteries to any number of Vinnie's contemporaries who have no clue how their family's history is part of Tucci's life story. The interconnection of all these lives becomes the fuel that thrusts this novel beyond the limits of the typical gangster tale. This is a story we can all relate to, the breakup of a strong family caused by the material corruption of contemporary American life.

The excitement begins when Vinnie becomes the center of attention to Tucci's family, his soldiers, and Government agents. Everyone's future depends on the information on those tapes. The knowledge gained from the Don's oral history has the power to change the past as well. *The Vespers Tapes* is an exciting thriller. And while it is not destined to make the reading list in an American literature course, it is certainly a worthwhile read. Don't be surprised if you see this book turned into a film; it has all the right ingredients for that blockbuster formula; the difference is that it is a new voice telling that story. The distance gained by a being a generation removed makes for a new way of viewing a staple element of Americana.

## 3

*I*f Martin Scorsese were writing novels instead of making films, he might produce something like Albert DiBartolomeo's second novel. In *Fool's Gold* DiBartolomeo returns to the streets of Philadelphia where he set *The Vespers Tapes*, his fine debut in 1991.

On the surface, *Fool's* covers some of the same turf as *Vespers* in a much more formulaic way. It's got all the right ingredients for a popular crime story. Its quick pace and intricate plot keeps the pages moving even faster than his earlier work. But behind this popular facade lies the real story that DiBartolomeo is after: how people strive to reproduce family structures out of the materials at hand. Take a man whose child was murdered, whose wife abandons him, whose new lover is kidnapped and saved by a homeless street kid and you have the makings of the strange, postmodern family created in this novel.

Like Scorsese, DiBartolomeo pulls no punches and leaves the cameras rolling long after others, less talented, would have turned them off. What separates DiBartolomeo from those who romanticize crime figures is his ability to get into the minds of the flashy, street thugs and to give us the psychology that drives such psychopathic behavior. DiBartolomeo is as comfortable with street talk as he is with narrative threads and his ability to infuse it all with a great sense of humor makes *Fool's* more than just another crime story.

The most interesting aspect to this latest effort is the juxtaposition of Benny Bean, a street punk, with Paul Fante, a well-meaning, hardworking craftsman who gets mixed up with the wrong crowd in an effort to make a better life for his family. Benny and Paul are two sides of the same street and remind us that good can't exist without evil and that whenever they meet there's a good fight to be seen. There's gold in this here novel; and while it's deep down, it's worth the digging.

*April 1991 / May 1993*

# Immigrant Workers and Saints

## Pietro di Donato

## 1

"*The* wop is in the wheelbarrow" — words spoken to a young Pietro di Donato by a New York cop when asked if he had any news as to his father's whereabouts following a construction accident, became di Donato's call to write a short story that changed the direction of his life.

Born in Hoboken, New York, in 1912, of Abruzzese parents, di Donato became a bricklayer, like his father, after his father's tragic death on Good Friday, 1923. Fourteen years later, di Donato wrote *Christ in Concrete*, a short story of his father's work site death, and sold it to *Esquire* magazine.

Within two years, the story grew into a novel which became the main selection of the Book of the Month Club, chosen over John Steinbeck's *Grapes of Wrath*. Di Donato never intended to be a writer, but the novel's success placed him in a national spotlight. As an essayist, di Donato's words have been published in some of America's most prestigious magazines and journals.

Now, just fifty years after its momentous publication, *Christ in Concrete*, like its writer, lives on the margins of mainstream American culture. There was no golden anniversary edition or celebration; in fact, until recently, all of di Donato's books *Christ in Concrete, This Woman, Immigrant Saint, Three Circles of Light,* and *The Penitent* were out of print. *Immigrant Saint: The Life of Mother Cabrini,* reissued this year in St. Martin Press's Religious Miracle Series, could be a sign of renewed interest in di Donato's writing. Di Donato says that the biography of America's first saint began as a film project. "Sophia Loren wanted to play Mother Cabrini in a film. The heads of 20th Century Fox called me to write the material. I went into it for the money, but soon fell in love with the material. By the time I finished Loren was talked out of the project by her husband."

Di Donato then took the material to his agent who got him a book contract that enabled him to travel to Italy where there was a great deal of material by and about Cabrini written in Italian that was kept sacred among the nuns. Within one year the book was completed. di Donato handed it over to Kitty Messner, the woman who had edited and published *Peyton Place*. "When the news got out that she would be publishing the Cabrini book," di Donato says, "the Catholic Church got up in arms, prevailing upon me not to be published by the people who had published that book. Messner called up McGraw Hill and they took it.

"This is a book that speaks to today's reader as well as it did to the reader of thirty years past. It is not a fairy tale; this Italian immigrant was a modern woman. She drank beer, had a keen sense of humor, and in spite of poor health accomplished much. Everybody loved her. Until her arrival in America the Scalabrini missionaries had been impotent in their attempts to assist the Italian immigrants. She could accomplish whatever she set out to do: education, hospitals, orphanages."

The leather bound copy reserved for Cardinal Spellman, the representative who gave the book the Church's official *imprimatur*, was instead sent by di Donato to Jackie Kennedy. "I don't know if he ever got his copy, but I was more interested in getting her impression than his," says di Donato. "Three weeks later she responded personally. There is an evolution in all work, a progression from life to death to an afterlife, and I believe the Cabrini book gives testament to this process. Ours in an age of benign fascist democracy; now, more than ever do we need to be reinspired by self-less saints like Mother Cabrini."

At nearly eighty, di Donato continues his cultural criticism in a daring new project called *The Gospels*. A segment of his latest novel will appear in the fall issue of *Voices in Italian Americana*. A writer whose education came more from the streets than from schools, di Donato predicts a brighter future for today's Italian/American writers. "Our time is now. I see it, because our writers are no longer *figli dei muratori*. They go to school and are children with brains. The true artist is a truth seeker, a person with a mind of his own, and you must remember that real education is truth."

*Italianità* is vitally important to nearly everything Pietro di Donato has written. Through much of his work we gain insight into the mysteries of

Italian immigrant life and especially into Italian Catholicism. Whether he is describing a work site or a bedroom, his imagery vibrates with the earthy sensuality that early Italian immigrants brought to their American lives. This vitality is what makes his biography of Francesca Maria Cabrini, the immigrant who became America's first saint, more than just a record of her life achievements.

The story of Mother Cabrini, in the hands of di Donato becomes a model story of Italian immigration to America. In *Immigrant Saint*, he presents the founder of the Missionary Sisters of the Sacred Heart in the social and political contexts of her time. Cabrini's life roughly spans the early days of Italian democracy. Through her life we review the Italian *risorgimento*, turn-of-the-century mass immigration, and the arduous adaptation of Italian life to American lands.

Born in 1850, in a small Lombardian village, Francesca Maria Cabrini was a frail woman whose incredible faith in God enabled her to battle poverty, homelessness, and prejudice against immigrants. Armed only with her faith, she thwarted the attempts of corrupt politicians, revolutionaries and apathetic clerics and successfully established a network of orphanages, schools and hospitals throughout Western Europe and North and South America. *Immigrant Saint* tells the story of a self-less woman's drive to carry out her Savior's work among the poor. Denied admission to a religious order, she went on to found her own, the Missionary Sisters of Sacred Heart. By the time of her death it had grown into sixty-five houses with over 1,500 sisters. For her life's works she was beatified in 1938 and canonized December 22, 1946.

The prose is heavily punctuated with letters, prayers, and newspaper accounts. But more than placing research on the page, di Donato dramatizes her life. Through his strong, research fueled imagination he is able to recreate her life. Through his empathetic recreation of her encounters with Popes, politicians, and her people, he successfully brings us into the mind of a thoroughly modern woman. From her Cinderella beginnings inside an Italian orphanage to her experience with Tammany hall politicians, di Donato paints an inspirational portrait of how one woman confronted problems which still plague us today: poverty, homelessness, and poor education. Cabrini combats apathy and corruption to build hospitals, orphanages, and schools. Her work in America brought Italian immigrants together, helping them to realize that life in America would only be better than life in Italy if they took control of their lives.

Of particular interest to Chicago area readers are the accounts of her meetings with Bishop Scalabrini and the building of Columbus Hospital. Mother Cabrini died in Chicago December 22, 1917, of malaria. Through di Donato, the story of Mother Cabrini's life becomes both a lesson in history and an act of cultural criticism. The author's own politics, though always mediated by Mother Cabrini's ever optimistic point of view, remind us that the problems of the past never disappear entirely. In this sense, di Donato was perhaps the perfect biographer. They both share the same lust for life and justice. This is the key which enables this book to speak as strongly to contemporary life as it did thirty years ago. Both the author and his subject share the belief that only through faith and hard work can the impossible be realized.

## 2

This year *Christ in Concrete*, reprinted as a Signet Classic, has returned to inspire us during what Studs Terkel, in his Preface to the new edition, calls "a new Depression, euphemistically called a recession." According to Terkel, *Christ in Concrete* "is a powerful contemporary novel. And while for too long novels of working class life have been out of fashion, the hard reality of our day makes them as pertinent and timely as ever." Di Donato, who died last year at the age of eighty, was born in West Hoboken, New Jersey on April 3, 1911, to Abruzzese emigrants. He took up writing during a period in which he was an out-of-work bricklayer. His first story, "Christ in Concrete," dramatized the early death of his father in a construction accident. Published in Esquire magazine in 1937, it was included in Edward O'Brien's *Best American Short Stories*. Within two years, the story grew into a novel of the same name and became the main selection of the Book of the Month Club, chosen over John Steinbeck's *Grapes of Wrath*. *Christ in Concrete* sold nearly 200,000 copies during its first few months — an incredible accomplishment for a first-time novelist, especially one who had never intended to be a writer. The novel's success placed him in a national spotlight and he took advantage of his new found fame. He took care of his brothers and sisters, traveled around the country, visited with the likes of Ernest Hemingway in Cuba, and spent money wildly. He saved just enough to start-up his own construction company.

At the start of World War II, di Donato registered as a Conscientious Objector and worked in a government camp in Cooperstown, New York. In 1942, he was married to Helen Dean in a civil ceremony presided over by New York Mayor Fiorello H. La Guardia. They had two children. In 1949, *Christ in Concrete* was made into a film directed by the blacklisted Edward Dmytryk and adapted for the screen by Ben Barzman. The film, titled then as *Give Us this Day,* won an award at the 1949 Venice Film Festival. However, without Hollywood's support, the "outlaw" film never had the exposure it deserved.

*Christ in Concrete* has become a literary classic because it presents di Donato's own true story as a founding myth of Italian/American culture. As a myth it presents an heroic figure, Paul, who searches for God, in the form of Christ, whom he believes can save his family from the terrible injustices brought upon them through a heartless society. The novel is divided into five parts: "Geremio," "Job," "Tenement," "Fiesta," and "Annunziata," each focusing on the key figures in the myth. In "Geremio" and "Job," di Donato presents Job as the antagonist which controls the Italian workers lead by his father Geremio, through the human forces of Mr. Murdin, the heartless foreman, the State Bureaucracy that sides with the construction company during a hearing into Geremio's death, and the Catholic Church through an Irish priest who refuses to do more than offer the family a few table scraps from his rich dinner.

In "Tenement" young Paul comes to learn about the forces of good and evil in the world and that good comes only from the workers' community, which is portrayed in "Fiesta." Paul's mother, Annunziata, in the chapter devoted to her widowhood, attempts to raise her children according to the Christian myth. However, in the process her son Paul loses the faith she hopes to pass on to him through recollections of her husband's show of faith.

For di Donato the immigrant laborer may become a hero through martyrdom, but his life is not a model to emulate. By directing his characters' rage at the employers who exploit immigrant laborers, Pietro di Donato argues for solidarity among American workers and requires that they look to each other to solve their problems. Just as it is the Italian community through the extended family that keeps Geremio's family together, it is the extended family of the workers that must help each other.

When di Donato died last year, Italian America lost one of its most colorful and critical voices. With this new edition, Pietro di Donato's continuous struggle for truth is rekindled. Finally, *Christ in Concrete* can take its long deserved place among America's classic novels.

*September 1991 / September 1993*

# DiStasi's Big on
# Italian/American Culture

## Lawrence DiStasi

## 1

*T*hrough his writing, Lawrence DiStasi works to extend the limited view that most people have of Italian America. His first book, *Mal Occhio: The Underside of Vision* (North Point Press, 1981) is a study of the phenomenon of the "evil eye." This work, which began as an attempt to understand aspects of his ancestral culture, led him on a path away from his Italian/American family and into the family of the world. "For a lot of American kids in the 1960s," says DiStasi, "the search for pre-industrial age knowledge led them to American Indian thought; for me it led back to Italy."

As a result of this journey, DiStasi has added to our understanding of the role that both vision and its representation plays in Western culture. DiStasi has always been interested in the commonalities shared by the ethnic and minority experiences. "My mistake early in my life was thinking I could connect with the larger culture without first coming to terms with my own background; there was a lot I had left undigested."

This awareness has led DiStasi to serve on the board of directors for the Before Columbus Foundation, a group which promotes the multicultural dimensions of American life and arts and awards the annual American Book Award, one which DiStasi received for *Mal Occhio*. DiStasi has always been interested in fitting what he knows into a larger context. "What I've been discovering in my own work is that there's a tendency to place the folk wisdom that I grew up with in a dignified or scholarly context. The subterranean force in much of writing has been the non-scholarly, almost the non-verbal. There's a book, *The Cheese and the Worm* by Carlo Ginsburg, that traced the cosmological thinking of a non-lettered miller in 16th century northern Italy to a deep strand of pre-European thought. That thinking dovetailed with what I had done in *Mal Occhio*. Ginsburg's book put the Italian immigrant into a perspective that I had never seen before."

This tension, between the personal and the public, between the scholarly and the folk, is what gives DiStasi's work its rich depth. *Mal Occhio* has that strand, and the same feel comes across in his most recent publication, *The Big Book of Italian American Culture* (Harper Collins, 1990), a book which resulted from his intense investigation of Italian/American culture. "With this book I wanted a mature presentation of the culture, without any apologizing or complaining; I wanted to say, 'Look we have all this to claim; we don't have to go back to Michelangelo and Dante to find an identity.' *The Big Book* is filled with examples of that utopian strand found in people like Joseph Cardinal Bernadin, Mariana Bertola, Ralph Fasanella, and Vince Lombardi; it's an aspect of our culture that doesn't get any attention due to the predominant stereotypes that prevail."

The response to *The Big Book* has been overwhelmingly positive, though it hasn't been widely reviewed. Perhaps, as DiStasi suggests, "because its 'coffee table' look makes it seem like a book that's easy to underestimate and dismiss. The one response that DiStasi treasures most comes from his twenty-five-year-old niece. "She didn't know anything about these people and she feels that this validates so much of what she is. And that validation is more necessary now than every before. I know this guy who told me he used to act like a character out of *The Godfather* because that was an expected public way for Italians to be. He's an example of this general perception that Italians have made it, and that Italian things are good; yet there's this corrosive, underlying image that everybody's carrying and not knowing how to deal with. What's left of Italian America as far as the general public is concerned is crime; people love that stuff. We're at this curious phase where we haven't acknowledged our literature yet. That's going to take some consciousness raising; the Italian/American community, particularly the younger segment is going to have to learn that it's important to know about themselves. The 'I Love Italy' attitude via the Gucci appeal is diverting a lot of attention from what we really need to know."

DiStasi, born in Connecticut in 1937, says he did not grow up wanting to be a writer. After his father died he went off to college to become a doctor. "Like most Italians I know, there were few books in my home. We didn't have a bookshelf, but I always liked to read. I used it as an escape; I used to stay up reading long into the night. In a certain sense the lack of a writing context in my early life has made my growth as a writer more difficult; I have had to learn it all as an adult."

The first book he set out to write was to be a non-fiction study of food phobias and taboos. "There had been a kid in this college where I had taught who had done a lot of fasting. I was fascinated by his story and started writing regularly. After thirty pages I decided to try fictionalizing it and the result was a first novel entitled *Eat*, which got a good response from one publishing company. Everyone who read it encouraged me to continue. I discovered I had the discipline and really liked writing."

In his second novel, excerpts of which have appeared in *The Big Book* and the first issue of *Voices in Italian Americana*, DiStasi plunged into Italian material, and the result was *A Family Matter* which DiStasi says is essentially a book about his father, who was born in Telese, Italy, a small town between Naples and Benevento. His father followed his father to America at the age of twelve and worked as a barber and then as a hairdresser; he also had a penchant for science, which he learned on his own. "What I always thought was a disadvantage, that is growing up Italian, actually turned out to be a gold mine. So I mined that ore for *Family Matter*. It looks back at my father from the point of view of a narrator being in Italy. That first trip back to Italy had a strong effect on me. There were things that happened there that I really wanted to keep, and writing helped me to do just that." Currently he's at work on a novel based on his mother's story which she wrote, without any literary pretensions, towards the end of her life. Working on her story, says DiStasi, has made him more conscious of his mixed Eastern and Western heritage. His mother was a Hungarian Jew, who, disowned by her Jewish family, "thought, cooked, and virtually became Italian." Di Stasi, who resides in Berkeley, California where he works as a freelance writer and lecturer at the University of California, says he does whatever he has to keep writing. "My father was a gambler, and my writing is the way I've inherited his gambling. Writing is a gamble, far more than playing the ponies. It's what I do, what I have to do, and I'm very content with that."

## 2

*F*rom Columbus to Coppola, from La Madonna del Carmine to the Madonna of pop rock; from *lo zappatore* to Frank Zappa, Lawrence DiStasi's *Dream Streets* covers the culture of Italian America as no other book has. *Dream Streets* is by far one of the best of the "big books" of Italian/American culture; it is certainly far too big to fit into this review.

Sure the line-up contains the usual hit parade of Italian/American biggies from Columbus to Cuomo, Capra to Coppola, and Capone to Costello, but what makes DiStasi's contribution unique is the way the articles are written, grouped and the style with which they are presented. DiStasi has pulled together contributions by some of the finest American writers of Italian descent. Diane DiPrima, Lawrence Ferlinghetti, Sandra Gilbert, Angelo Pellegrini, Gay Talese, and Anthony Valerio — you've got to read his "Mario Lanza's Nose;" it's worth the price of admission alone — are among the many fine writers in this volume whose work has had a significant impact on American culture. DiStasi's own well-crafted contributions round out what is perhaps the best executed collection of Italian Americana in print.

*Dream Streets* uses brilliantly designed visual collages to compliment the written profiles and memoirs gathered under headings such as: Workers and Anarchists (Labor); An Empire of Food; Saints (Religion); Sinners (Crime); the Electronic Puppet Show (Entertainment); da Vinci's Children (Invention); Artists of the Possible (Politics); The House of Valentino (Film); and Revisionaries (a miscellany). Each section contains well produced photographs and original illustrations that compliment the writing making this a book for readers as well as lookers, a scrap book as well as a photo album. This book is a symphonic synthesis of dream and reality, a bridge connecting the skies to the streets, as the author explains, "Urban dreamers, then. These are the people who people this book. Heroes who dream the millennial dream, but one tempered by several millennia of city dwelling." It is a book that belongs to all of America; it just so happens that this time, the key players are Italian Americans.

There is an hilarious scene in *The Godfather Part III* in which Michael Corleone is presented with the Meucci Award as that society's Man of the Year; holding the plaque, he looks up and asks: "Who's he?" The presenter (played by Joe Mantenga) responds, "Why he's the one who invented the telephone a year [actually it was four years] before Bell!" This parody of an

Italian American's ignorance of the contributions of his own people to American culture need never surface in your life if you pick up and read Lawrence DiStasi's *The Big Book of Italian American Culture*. First issued in hardcover as *Dream Streets* (1989), this paperback reprint should make this collection more accessible and easier to add to your home library. It's part encyclopedia, part storybook, and all worth its $14.95 price. DiStasi guides us through a perspective that reveals much in our American history that we need to take note of and have pride in. *The Big Book* reminds us that we do not have to extend our reach into the Renaissance to find something to identify with.

*March 1991 / July 1989*

# *Evviva John Fante!*

## John Fante

### 1

$\mathcal{N}$ineteen-eighty-five was a good year for readers of John Fante. Black Sparrow Press went on a publishing binge and brought back much of his collected works in beautifully designed and printed editions: *The Wine of Youth*, a collection of short stories; *On the Road to Los Angeles*, a first novel that was discovered by his wife after his death; and now *1933 Was a Bad Year*.

That you don't know much about Fante is not surprising. If it wasn't for regional fame, John Fante would have died practically unknown. But as so often happens to the truly talented, Fante's stories will be reaching more readers after his death, than ever while he was alive. All three of these early works are united by a common voice, that of a narrator looking back on his days when he was on the brink of adulthood; a common struggle, that of finding a place to fit into a world outside his family and ethnic culture; and a common style, that captures strong images and emotion in well focused sentences. All this is evident on every page, as this excerpt from *1933* demonstrates:

> I knew her troubled soul, and I pitied her. She was lonely, her roots dangling in an alien land. She had not wanted to come to America, but my grandfather had given her no other choice. There had been poverty in Abruzzi too, but it was a sweeter poverty that everyone shared like bread passed around. Death was shared too, and grief, and good times, and the village of Torricella Peligna was like a single human being. My grandmother was a finger torn from the rest of the body and nothing in the new life could assuage her desolation. She was

like all those others who had come from her part of Italy. Some were
better off, and some were wealthy, but the joy was gone from their
lives, and the new country was a lonely place where "O Sole Mio" and
"Come Back to Sorrento" were heartbreak songs. (18)

So often the Italian/American audience has had to observe its history
and culture through the eyes of those non-Italians who, though sometimes
with utmost sincerity, never reach more than a superficial portrayal of the
Italian/American experience. The market calls for gangsters, spaghetti din-
ners, and the trials of the displaced immigrant. Fante chose to ignore the
market and tell the universal story of class, of family, of individual, of Italian
life in America. And in having made this choice, his fame has been delayed.

*1933* is the story of a young Dominic Molise's struggle with the reality
of foreign born parents living in poverty and the dream of becoming an
American sports hero. This novel is at once the story of class and the
individual's struggle during hard times in America. What makes this novel
appealing to readers of all ethnic backgrounds is that once shared belief that
if greatness can be achieved then there is no better place for a misfit to have
a chance than in America.

Edison was deaf. Steinmetz was a hunchback. Babe Ruth was an
orphan, Ty Cobb a poor Georgia boy. Giannini started with nothing.
People thought Henry Ford was crazy. Carnegie was a runt like myself.
Tony Canzoneri came out of the slums. Poor young men, touched with
magic, lucky in America. Thank God my father had the good sense to
leave Torricella Peligna! Times were bad, to be sure, with the
depression going full strength, but what a glorious future lay ahead for
those touched with fame. (52)

Fante's strength as a novelist is in his ability to pen irony without
melodrama, to use humor without absurdity, to allow a story to flow
without editorial interruption. You are at once caught up in the plight of
Dominic Molise and a social commentary about America. This novel, as the
rest of the body of literature this man has left us, is truly a testament to the
ability of an Italian American to tell his story in the tradition of great
writers.

## 2

*T*hough John Fante has been dead for more than three years, he lives on in the fiction that Black Sparrow Press keeps finding and publishing. *West of Rome* is two novellas — "My Dog Stupid" and "Orgy" — that both deal with dreams and how they affect our lives. The former deals with growing old in the 1960s and the latter, with growing up in the 1920s.

"My Dog Stupid" is the story of a disgruntled screenwriter whose real dream, to write great novels, is disrupted by his need to finance his family's needs and wants. He lives with the fantasy of escaping it all and moving to Rome. The story takes place during Vietnam War to which both his sons are vulnerable. The action revolves around the finding of a dog. The narrator adopts the dog, which he names Stupid; this adoption creates chaos in the family. Eventually his children leave home and the dog runs off. Finally the narrator is free to head for Rome. He liquidates all his resources only to later use his life savings to ransom the dog. The characteristically lean prose of Fante is sharpened in this work. His concern with family is again the main theme of the work and he tells us that as the family disintegrates so does the individual.

In "Orgy" we have yet another parable, yet this one is truely Italian American and relates the second generation's insistence that hard work is the only way. "Orgy" is the story of the friendship between the narrator's bricklaying father and his atheist friend, a left-handed bricklayer named Frank Gagliano. The narrator's mother abhors this man who ". . . hates God" and chases him away from the house by spraying him with holy water. Frank responds by saying "I don't hate God; I just don't believe in him," as he is chased off the property. The father is given the deed to a gold mine by a black hod carrier whose investments in penny stocks one day pay off royally. This gift becomes the an excuse for father and friend to disappear on weekends. They are supposed to be digging for gold, but when the mother insists that the narrator accompany the men, we find out that all they're really doing is digging into a floozy. The young narrator in this story reminds us of Arturo Bandini from Fante's *Wait Until Spring, Bandini!* The characteristic ironic voice and naivete make this a story that matches the best of John Fante. However, "Orgy" seems unfinished; perhaps this is because we want more from one of the best Italo American writers ever. And we hope Black Sparrow continues to find more Fante. We need him.

*January 1986 / June 1986*

# One of America's True Bards

## Lawrence Ferlinghetti

## 1

$\mathscr{H}_e$ is a well known poet, editor, playwright, artist, novelist, truth seeker, and truth sayer and, at seventy, Lawrence Ferlinghetti's poetic vision and voice are stronger than ever. What he contributes to the American conscience is a depth, a concentration and a simplicity that few of today's writers can match. He has published and defended controversial literature in courts, has traveled to "enemy" countries, and has shared those experiences through his writing.

Lawrence Ferlinghetti grew up as Lawrence Ferling, a decision made by his older brothers. "They shortened the name because Italian at that time was like the dago gardener who was the lowest thing on the scale, smelling of garlic and pepperoni," he says. "My brothers tried to get away from that as soon as possible, especially in the rich suburbs of New York. They shortened the name and never told me. Years later I was applying to get into the Navy and wrote for my birth certificate. It came back with 'Ferlinghetti.' That was the first I knew of it. It took me a few years to get around to restoring it. It seemed the thing to do. Ferling sounded Scandinavian or something. During the 1950s and 1960s we were all getting back to our roots."

Born in 1919, Ferlinghetti was the youngest of five boys. His parents met in a Coney Island boarding house. His father had a real estate office on 42nd Street. The family was completely broke when he died. At that time they were living in Ossining, where Sing Sing is located. "My brothers were in their early teens when my father died. None of them got any education. One lied about his age and got a job at the prison. He became an assistant warden. I wrote to him after I restored the name to Ferlinghetti. He was furious and told me: 'I'm too old to start explaining this to my secretary.' For all those years he had passed as an Anglo-Saxon.

"My father came from Brescia in 1900, probably on the same boat with the Godfather. He came through Ellis Island and settled in Little Italy. He was an auctioneer. That's about all I know about him. He died before I was born, so I missed the Italian influence."

Ferlinghetti's mother was born in New York. She was Spanish and Portuguese Sephardic. Her family migrated from Portugal during the Spanish Inquisition to Nice, France. Some of them moved on to the Virgin Islands on a Danish Crown colony expedition. From there they came to the United States. Ferlinghetti was taken to France shortly after his father's death and lived there until the age of seven. His first language was French. He received his M.A. in Literature from Columbia University and later returned to France after serving in the United States Navy during World War II. He earned his doctorate from the Sorbonne. He has two children who have made their own lives outside the field of letters, Julie, twenty-six, and Lorenzo, twenty-five.

"I find the hereditary bloodline has a lot to do with people's natural capabilities," Ferlinghetti says. "Lorenzo was always a poor student. He doesn't read or write much in English. But he went to Mexico a few summers ago and met a girl who didn't speak any English. And ever since, he's been corresponding with her and taking Spanish. And he took to it. It's something in his blood. His teacher says he even sounds Spanish, and he's never been to Spain."

Ferlinghetti says the same for his experience with Italian. "I go back to Italy, and in a couple of weeks, if I'm traveling with Italians, I can speak quite fluently and read the papers. But when I come back here it disappears. After about a month I can't even speak to my landlord in North Beach. My older brothers could still speak Italian if they wanted to, but they don't."

Ferlinghetti has spent much of his life in San Francisco. He lives in North Beach, where his City Lights Press and Bookstore are located. The area was once the city's Italian district, but the Little Italy is now disappearing. "Now it's being bought up by the Chinese," he says. "I think there are less than 500 families left. Most of the Italians have moved to the suburbs. They've lost their sense of community. They're sitting out there in the suburbs and wish they had it back. But it's too late. Now they're trying to regroup. There used to be an Italian daily paper called *L'Italia* but it's gone."

His poem, "Old Italians Dying," is a testament to the dying immigrant culture and was first published on the op-ed page of the *Los Angeles Times*. "I couldn't write that poem today," he says. "They're all gone; they're not sitting in the square anymore."

Ferlinghetti is an accessible poet whose works often appear on the op-ed pages of major U.S. newspapers. He calls this accessibility "public surface." "Not much poetry today has visual excitement. People are writing poems about walking down the street but they are not seeing what's there. 'Old Italians Dying' is an objective description of sitting in the square — a sticking to what's going down right in front of me. But you can never make it completely objective. I see the coffin as a black boat without sails. The person in the coffin is like a fisherman on his last trip to the sea."

Much of Ferlinghetti's poetry deals with political subjects. His voice can be heard wailing against injustice and for peace. A *Booklist* reviewer once referred to him as ". . . one of our ageless radicals and true bards."

## 2

*L*awrence Ferlinghetti is a rare poet whose work appears quite often in the op-ed pages of our nation's largest newspapers. His work has, what he calls, "public surface," an accessibility that has often hampered critical appreciation of his poetry, novels and prose because it just seems to be too easily understood. Since he began writing in the late 1940s, Ferlinghetti has never avoided head-to-head confrontation with political subjects and his style and diction never leave us in doubt as to what his political convictions are. He is a street-smart intellectual whose voice has been heard for over five decades wailing against injustice and for peace.

His life story is certainly, in many ways, characteristic of the America of his time, in *Ferlinghetti: The Artist in His Time* (Warner Books), Chicago poet, editor, and writer Barry Silesky tells both stories well. Of the three biographies of Ferlinghetti, Silesky's is by far the best. If you have never read Ferlinghetti's poetry, prose, and drama, this book will make you want to; even if you have read every word of every work by this dynamic and inspiring artist, Silesky's book will make you want to go back and reread Ferlinghetti all over again.

Silesky uses many approaches in trying to represent Ferlinghetti's life in words. His narrative is a verbal composite of interviews with Ferlinghetti and friends such as Allen Ginsberg, Gary Snyder, and Nancy Peters, critical readings of Ferlinghetti's major works, excerpts of Ferlinghetti's personal journal and an incredible synthesis of what must have been many, many months of research. Silesky's writing is not without its flaws. Awkward phrasing at times slows down the reading, but it is only because the rest of the book is so well crafted that the flaws can be jolting.

As with any major artist, the life story of Ferlinghetti is also a tale of the times surrounding his life. Silesky wonderfully recreates the eras of American history that Ferlinghetti's life has encountered. Born in 1919, Ferlinghetti was the youngest of five boys. His parents met in a Coney Island boarding house and later his father, an Italian immigrant from Brescia, had a real estate office on 42nd Street. The family was completely broke when he died. Because his father died before he was born, Ferlinghetti has missed the early childhood the Italian influence. Ferlinghetti's mother was born in New York. She was Spanish and Portuguese Sephardic. Her family had emigrated from Portugal during the Spanish Inquisition to Nice, France. From there they came to the United States. Shortly after his father's death Ferlinghetti was taken to France and lived there until the age of seven. He was adopted by a wealthy New England family after spending a few years in an orphanage. With their help, Ferlinghetti received a privileged education.

World War Two had started and after earning a B.A. in Literature from the University of North Carolina at Chapel Hill Ferlinghetti had enlisted in the U.S. Navy as an ensign; later he was promoted to lieutenant. After the war, he completed a M.A. in literature at Columbia University (where he had met such to-be-infamous writers as Allen Ginsberg and Jack Kerouac) and a Ph. D. at the Sorbonne in France, both on the G.I. Bill. He returned to the United States and took up residence in San Francisco and opened City Lights, the nation's first all-paperback book store.

Book sales soon led to book publishing as Ferlinghetti began City Lights Books. One of the company's earliest publications was Allen Ginsberg's *Howl and Other Poems*, now a classic, then the subject of an obscenity trial that launched Ferlinghetti's career as a public spokesperson for truth and a defender of our freedom of speech. This is during the post-war era that we have come to know as the days of The Beats. And in spite of the tremendous amount of writing that has been done about the beats, Silesky's insights and his style of presentation make us see it anew.

Since the 1950s Ferlinghetti has traveled all over the world and been part of the international poetry and peace scene. The key to Ferlinghetti's success has been his ability to connect words to actions, to put his body where his words ask us to go; he has continually denounced government support of the arts and has never taken a penny from such sources as the NEA. He has been involved in anti-war protests and community organization. Most recently he spearheaded a movement to rename a number of San Francisco streets after the city's writers.

Most interesting in Silesky's book is his presentation of what Ferlinghetti's been up to in the 1980s and 1990s. His poetry no longer sells in the hundreds of thousands as it once did (that doesn't keep it from going out-of-print), but that is not the reason Ferlinghetti has stopped writing; he's focused his greater efforts these days on his painting, an art that Silesky reminds us has always been a part of Ferlinghetti's life. Over the past few years, with the City Lights business doing well, and with his two children out on their own, Ferlinghetti has been able to produce enough work for a number of one-person shows, both in the U.S.A. and Europe. He continues writing, but it's his painting he wants to promote. Perhaps the best compliment we can give Silesky is to admire his ability to evoke Ferlinghetti's "public surface" through his own.

*May 1986 / November 1990*

# A Woman for All Seasons

## Maria Mazziotti Gillan

### 1

*I* don't know much about Paterson, New Jersey, except that it has been the home of some of our country's great poets. The weather there must be ideal for creative writing for it has certainly been inspiring for William Carlos Williams and Allen Ginsberg, two of the city's famous sons. But what of its daughters?

Maria Mazziotti Gillan is one of Paterson's daughters whom I first met in *The Dream Book*. One stanza of hers particularly haunted me for months afterward.

> Remember me ladies
> the silent one?
> I have found my voice
> and my rage will blow
> your houses down.

This, the finale to "Public School No. 18: Paterson, New Jersey," did much to make me realize that the literary silence of Italian/American women writers was over. In such simple words, Gillan had evoked a presence that was permanent and powerful.

Gillan is a highly honored poet. Her work has won her the prestigious Walt Whitman Prize and Sri Chinmoy Prize for poetry as well as a number of New Jersey State Council on the Arts awards. Her poetry was selected for the 1985 Editor's Choice Award and was nominated for the Pushcart Prize. She is the director of the Poetry Center at Passaic County Community College and is a candidate for a Ph.D. at Drew University. Gillan's *Winter*

*Light*, published in 1985, was translated into Italian (*Luce d'inverno*) by Nat and Nina Scammacca and was awarded the 1987 American Literary Translator's Award.

Now Gillan comes to us with *The Weather of Old Seasons*, a chapbook in the Women Writer's Series of Cross-Cultural Communications. A few of the poems are translated into Italian by the Scammacca team and by Enzo Bonventre. This beautiful publication (truly a lesson in what chapbooks should be in terms of style and production) is illustrated by Bebe Barkan, an illustrator noted for her work with the Sicilian *Antigruppo*.

*The Weather of Old Seasons* contains over two dozen poems, many of which have appeared elsewhere — together now for the first time. Most deal with the themes of family and individual memory. Just as one season blends into the next, creating a cycle only observable in retrospect, Gillan's memories of childhood and adult life blend into each other, forming threads of images and ideas that she weaves into beautiful poetic tapestries. It would take pages to introduce you to all her poems, and in choosing one I risk mistaking the whole for the part; but the beauty of Gillan's work is that each poem echoes the whole collection. Gillan's direct language masks the complexity of thought that is behind it. For this poet, language is a veil through which a tantalizing thought waits for uncovering. I have chosen one poem, but really it could have been any one, to represent the whole collection. Poems such as "Distances" (dedicated to her son) point to the continuity of life and the difficulty of separating our past from our present and future. It also reminds us of the continuity that a sense of family life carries on from generation to generation.

> 1
> Going and coming through days
> noisy with telephones,
> the thought of you
> moves through my mind,
> persistent
> as an underground river;
> yet when I speak to you
> there is distance,
> distance in your voice,
> your eyes.
> My mother poured her life into me
> as though I were a beaker
> that could never be filled.

I thought I would be different,
but I have poured and poured.
Now, when your eyes tell me
you no longer need me,
I don't know how to stop.

2

After the stalled traffic hunching
toward the Lincoln Tunnel,
after the day in the conference room
at the Sheraton Hotel,
after the blinding light
of the crystal prisms,
after the heat of the room,
after the voices I tried not to hear—
I fall back into the yellow house.
The soft lights of Oak Place
glow into winter evening.
You call. Your voice searches
for some word to give you courage.
You have years to go on the path
you are building brick by brick.
I see it stretching into distances,
feel the thread that binds us break;
suddenly I know,
in the future hidden behind the rim
of mountains, you will wake one morning,
and, in your mirror, you will see my face.

Once again Gillan has left us with a haunting finale, powerful and permanent. We can see our parents in our reflection, no matter how we try to be our own person, we are also the people who raised us. This is the power of Gillan; to take the personal and give it to all people.

## 2

*Taking Back My Name* is a great way to meet one of the Italian America's best poets. This small chapbook, published by malafemmina press, contains ten of Maria Mazziotti Gillan's poems that explore her experience as an Italian American. Gillan's previous work has won such prestigious poetry prizes as the Walt Whitman Prize, the Sri Chinmoy Prize and the Editor's Choice Award. Her first book length collection of poetry, *Flowers from the Tree of Night*, appeared in 1981. Four years later, her second book, *Winter Light* was published. The Italian translation, *Luce d'inverno*, by Nat and Nina Scammacca, was awarded the 1987 American Literary Translator's Award. Both books have gone into second printings. Two years later Gillan published *The Weather of Old Seasons* and won a commendation in the Chester H. Jones National Poetry Competition. A driving force behind the Passaic County Cultural and Heritage Council, Gillan also directs the Poetry Center at Passaic County Community College, which showcases America's best poets; she also edits the *Paterson Literary Review*.

The title of her most recent publication reflects a dual perspective by which she views her life as an Italian American. In one sense, Gillan says, she voluntarily gave up her name. "While I was growing up, having this long Italian name was a negative thing; when I married I got this nice short name without any z's in it. For a long time I was accepting society's definition of me, buying into the negative images that were out there, erasing my past as I went along." In another sense, Gillan feels her name was taken from her. "I grew up never hearing anything positive about Italians. Nobody was ever held up as a successful role model. The image I was getting was that those Italian Americans who made it did so only in terms of money. They were the ones who put plastic seat covers on their couches, had ornate lamps with dangling things on them, and were crass boors. In that sense, my name and the culture that created it were being robbed." And so Gillan felt she had to redeem her identity.

While most of these poems have been published elsewhere, their appearance here represents a powerful display of the forces that drive this poet's talent. "Growing Up Italian" tells the story of how and why she returned Mazziotti to her full name. "In Memory We Are Walking," "Public School No. 18: Paterson, New Jersey," "In the Still Photograph, circa 1950," and "Talismans" are all image rich depictions of her Italian past. "Betrayals" is the ironic portrayal of how her attitude toward her parents' differences is inherited by her child when she becomes a parent. "Arturo" is a tribute to her father, while "My Grandmother's Hands" is a meditation on the responsibility of transmitting heritage from one generation to the next. "Connections" deals with the fragility of a mother's presence. "The Crow" is the embodiment of the voice of the outsider that encourages self-doubt to echo throughout one's life. Gillan credits Rose Romano, malafemmina founder and editor for the success of "Taking Back My Name."

"Rose has a great instinctive feeling for how to arrange a series of poems. She has shown great skill in *la bella figura*, the journal she founded, and she's now applying it to these collections of poems by individual authors." Gillan sees Romano's work as indicative of the renaissance that's occurring in Italian/American culture.

"Just in the past five years, things have taken an incredible leap forward for Italian/American writers. Books like *The Dream Book* and *From the Margin*, along with the journals, *Voices in Italian Americana, Italian Americana*, and *la bella figura* have really pushed us forward."

In spite of these gains, Gillan feels Italian Americans still have a long way to go. "We need a strong, well backed press that will publish the many books were are creating. Until that happens we'll always be struggling to have an impact in the libraries, the schools, and the universities — all the places where stereotypical media images can be challenged." Gillan feels that publishing is the only way to perpetuate the Italian/American writer who, "will pick up this thread that we've found and reinterpret this experience for the generations to come. At this point we are more an international community, so our connections need to be made to Italians living in Canada, South America and other parts of the world. I'd like to see an international conference of all these writers and artists. Maybe if we got to know each other, we'd find ways to strengthen our presence."

One of the obstacles that we have got to overcome, according to Gillan "is this sense of sole ownership of any territory, this belief that person A is the one and only poet, or fiction writer or essayist who can represent Italian Americans. Perhaps happens because there's so little space in the mainstream for Italian/American writers. But if we are ever going anywhere we have to start saying, if I push an Italian/American writer, then I'm pushing all Italian/American writers. This has got to happen in reviews, in conferences, in publications in all the ways that we gather and network and disseminate our work."

*October 1989 / February 1992*

# Critic Turns Novelist

## Josephine Gattuso Hendin

*J*osephine Gattuso Hendin has wanted to be a writer since she was eleven years old. The daughter of a Sicilian immigrant father and a Neapolitan mother, Hendin was born in a Manhattan Little Italy. She became attracted to writing by reading. "The library was between where we lived and the Astoria Park and pool, which was my vacation home away from home every summer. I started to read, largely as a means of entertainment. We didn't have the money for a television set, so we'd take a walk and watch Sid Caesar through the store windows." Hendin grew up in what she calls a typical Italian/American family. "It was the sort of family in which whatever you did was fantastic if you didn't do something drastically illegal or stray from the path."

There is no doubt that Hendin has chosen the right path. Her first novel, *The Right Thing to Do*, follows two books of literary criticism and marks the beginning of a new direction in her life. Hendin had no idea where she was heading when she left home at sixteen and enrolled in City College. Her mother had encouraged her to become an elementary school teacher, but the family made no strong efforts to map out her future. "My father was mainly concerned about my brother, who was more interested in cars at the time," she says. "He eventually became a pharmacist and owns a drug store in Astoria."

When she looks back on her youth, Hendin says she is reminded of A. Bartlett Giammatti's introduction to the book, *The Italian Americans*, which laments the loss of the contributions of many Italian/American women because of the pressures against them. "I must have had the feeling on some inarticulate, subconscious level that it was impossible to achieve anything within the context of that family, which is why I left. I wanted to get out. I was unhappy there. It was more a feeling that I wanted to be on my own and partly a sense of wanting more identification with the people in the literature I was saturated with."

When she took a term off during her last year of college and landed a job as a social worker in the Bureau of Child Welfare in the South Bronx, her father, a former pharmacist turned Depression era social-worker, said she was "finally doing something useful." The next year Hendin returned to school and graduated magna cum laude, winning a Woodrow Wilson Fellowship to Columbia University. Afraid of losing her fellowship (colleges weren't generous with women during that period), she completed her Ph.D. in four years. "At commencement my mother looked at me and said: 'Well I'm glad you got an education, but who will marry you now?'"

The following year she was married and teaching at Yale. In 1970, she published her first book, a critical study entitled, *The World of Flannery O'Connor*. Her husband's job brought them back to New York City, where she taught at the New School for Social Research and wrote literary and cultural articles for *Harpers, The New York Times Book Review,* and *Psychology Today*. She returned to full time teaching at New York University, where she is now a tenured professor of American Literature. In 1978, *Vulnerable People*, a critical examination of American fiction since 1945, was published by Oxford University Press. She also contributed a chapter on experimental literature to *The Harvard Guide of Contemporary Literature*. Hendin did not identify strongly with her Italian heritage early in her college career. And she says she discovered one of the strengths of being Italian American only recently.

"I don't see a very high value placed on self examination and introspection. I think Italians can be very thoughtful, but they are not always thinking about their own feelings. Our cultural focus is very much oriented towards behavior, from whence comes the title of the novel. There is an emphasis on doing the right thing, the right behavior, perhaps more so than on certain kinds of emotional configurations such as knowing the self in the sense of psychoanalytic explanations or psychological understanding. I think that is really an enabling factor. I see other friends of mine who tend to get lost in figuring out every nuance of how they feel at a given moment. I've never particularly been that interested."

*The Right Thing to Do* received favorable reviews in *Booklist, Kirkus,* and *The Worcester Sunday Telegram*. Though the novel has an autobiographical feel to it, Hendin says it comes more from the emotions than the actual events she's experienced. "The parents in the novel," she says, "are really a composite of many other people, of many other parents." Her father's background mirrors to some extent the father in the novel. "He had wanted to be a doctor," she says. "A well-to-do uncle was going to subsidize him through college and medical school, but it took my father five years to work his way through high school. By the time he was applying to colleges, his uncle died and his aunt would not deliver on the promise. So he went to Columbia Pharmacy School and became a pharmacist. During the Depression he left the drugstore and became a social worker.

"Willa Cather said the most important things that happen to a writer happen to them before they're eight. After being away from my background for a great many years I discovered how connected I was to it and how much I had derived from it. In many ways the book is kind of a love letter to that; I have the feeling that the people I grew up with were in many ways more real and more alive than many of the much more sophisticated people that I have had to deal with in my later life."

Though the first draft of the novel was written over a period of nine weeks during the summer of 1985, it took Hendin over a year to revise it. The novel vividly presents generational conflicts that are universal. In terms of style and structure it represents a real coming of age of the Italian/American experience in American literature. It is an important novel in that it presents a rare look at the old world-new world crisis in light of a father and daughter relationship. "The father has a rigid notion of what is beneficial or helpful to his child," says Hendin. "Ultimately he comes to realize that he's going to lose that fight and that perhaps there are other areas in which the connection is going to last."

Hendin's novel brings to the current literary scene the willingness to make moral discriminations and judgments and to see life in terms of the assumption of responsibility for oneself, something that she doesn't see in much contemporary writing. "Sometimes it's an anti-theme," she says, "as in the work of Robert Stone. I think my Italian Americanness implies a willingness to be responsible to my characters, and to create characters who operate from a feeling of the necessity to protect people they see in danger, even if their efforts are misguided."

*August 1988*

# *Beyond Bensonhurst*

## Salvatore La Puma

### 1

*W*ith the Flannery O'Connor Award for Short Fiction in hand for his first collection of stories, *The Boys of Behsonhurst*, Salvatore La Puma has established a strong new voice in American literature. Since winning the prestigious award, La Puma has published his stories in some of the top literary reviews in the country. "Guys Under Their Fedoras" was published in the *Antioch Review*, and "The Gangster's Ghost" was published in the *Kenyon Review*. And most recently the editors of *New Brooklyn Fiction* selected "The Mouthpiece" for inclusion in the anthology.

La Puma was writing stories while he earned his living as a Madison Avenue copywriter. When he moved to Santa Barbara, California, where he now lives, he got into a whole other business to take care of the family. But after the kids grew up he started writing again. "My wife wanted to know about my origins and my early days and I started to tell her these stories," says La Puma. "She suggested that I put them together in a collection. She's the one who found this contest and encouraged me to enter my stories. It really was a total shot in the dark. It's a miracle that they were published and I have to thank Charles East, the editor who took the book. The University of Georgia Press took the collection even before the *Boston Review* published my first short story "Gravesend Bay."

Charles East, editor of the Flannery O'Connor Award series, recalls his reaction when coming upon La Puma's manuscript: "I think I must have read 150 manuscripts by then and I wasn't sure that I would know a good story if I saw one. Then I picked up *The Boys of Bensonhurst* and there was no doubt about it — here was a writer! Salvatore La Puma had brought a world alive for me."

## A Bensonhurst Boy

Born on a kitchen table in Bensonhurst, La Puma feels there was little difference in his neighborhood and the Sicily of his parents. "I guess my birth was just as I might have been born on the island if my parents had remained in Sicily. They came over as babies. My father's family comes from Palermo and my father is one of those blue eyed Sicilians that keep showing up in my stories. My mother's side came from Sciacca."

La Puma's stories recreate pre World War II life in the Brooklyn neighborhood of his boyhood. "Generally, I don't think that anybody in the neighborhood really believed they were in the new world in the sense that they just connected to each other in the same old ways they might have back in the old country. And everything pretty much remained the same, the food, the ideas, the church. My mother pushed her kids toward the American way while my father held back a little because the old ways seemed better to him.

"The children got an inkling of what the American experience was through the school and by meeting other ethnic groups. There were a lot of Jewish kids there and I'm sure they had a similar introspection as we did and they huddled to themselves. We felt very compatible with each other. I don't know if it broadened our views any. It was a lovely place to grow up though at times it was pretty crazy."

## A Writer's Beginnings

La Puma started out as an advertising copywriter. "When I first started looking for work in the business I said my name was Salvatore and I thought I saw somebody wink. So I backed off from it in order to find a job and began using my middle name 'John,' which was Giovanni.

"Apparently my parents had told the person who recorded the births that my name was Salvatore John, but the clerk was from the old country and she put down 'Giovanni.' For nearly a dozen years I used John and it created a split personality because my family thought of me as a Giovanni.

"Then I decided that it really wasn't a nice thing for me to do so I took my name back. You can do these things out of insecurity when you're young, but sooner or later you find out later on that it really wasn't worth it."

Writing was something that La Puma started to do when he was young. "It started out in junior high school. An Irish teacher insisted that I read everything I wrote out loud to the class. And that made me think: 'What does that mean? Maybe I should keep doing it for my own amusement if not for anyone else's.' "

Sal says his father was a storyteller. He came from a family that puts on the La Puma Opera Workshop in New York. "When I was thirteen they made me and my brother try out for the opera. I had a bad time and flunked, but they wanted my brother. He didn't like the whole idea. Anyway, my father had a tradition of entertaining people with his stories. He was a pastry man, as was his father who had his own shop.

"The business of having a pastry shop required working around the clock, seven days a week. When I was about eleven or twelve my father used to take me with him into the shop. We'd go at night. He would bake it and take it out of the oven and I would have to pile up all the biscuits into pyramids. I had a lot of little opportunities like that which were educational now that I look back on it. And they provided me with plenty of good material."

La Puma's bakery experience comes alive again in the story "Guys Under Their Fedora's." La Puma graduated from St. Francis of Assisi College in Brooklyn in 1950 with a degree in English Literature. After an Army stint in Korea, he returned home and went to work as a copywriter for BBDO, an advertising firm on Madison avenue. "When I was in college I wrote for the college publications and won some prizes. So I had a handful of samples and I knew that that's where my future was. I was planning to continue my work in fiction with Eugene O'Neil Jr. who was teaching at Fordham. I signed up to take an M.F.A. with him. I had been very excited about working with him on a novel. After his tragic death I was pretty shook up and I dropped that idea to work in advertising because there was some money to be made in that business."

## A Family First

La Puma has always been torn between doing his writing and having a family. "I liked the idea of having a family. And I concentrated on that for a while; now I have six children. It was tough; it was hard, but I loved every minute of it. We started out thinking we would have a dozen children. But my wife got pretty sick with asthma so we moved out to California where her illness cleared up. But then we split up. By then the kids were mostly grown, but they've all done pretty well. My baby is now twenty-three."

La Puma's work has been praised by reviewers around the country. The *Library Journal* called it:

> A delightful picture of the lives of a group of teenage boys in Bensonhurst, Brooklyn, 1939-1943. Their encounters with girls and their relationships with parents and friends are dictated by Sicilian tradition and bravado, behind which lie the omnipresence of the Church and the mob . . . Authentic and recommended.

And *Kirkus Review* said:

> La Puma, with a fine ear for dialogue and dialect as well as an equally satisfying prose style, paints lots of nice cameos . . . La Puma is obviously a talent, and much here is as touchingly sharp as an aging Kodak print.

La Puma is now working on a novel and writing more stories. His newest stories are about guys who had their origins in Bensonhurst. *The Southern Review* will be publishing another story this summer "about a guy who grew up in Bensonhurst who's still a *paesano* and a hustler. It's called 'In Delphine's Bed.' I'm working on what these guys are doing in contemporary times and what happens when they drag their baggage with them. I write much more now. I have a bad a feeling when I don't write a sentence. It's like dope. Now I'm a freelance salesman and can work my own hours. I've cut back substantially on that. I'm trying to get by on what little I've got in order to stick to the writing. I've got to put it down now."

## 2

*O*ne of the traditional wedding photos certain to be preserved in family albums is that of the bride and groom cutting the cake. In many ways this novel reflects many of those more traditional "Kodak" moments of life after marriage. However, what the bride does with the knife after the cake-cutting is anything but traditional in this passionate, exciting, first novel by Salvatore La Puma, winner of an American Book Award and a 1987 Flannery O'Connor Award for his collection of short fiction, *The Boys of Bensonhurst*.

*A Time for Wedding Cake* recounts the story of two Bensonhurst brothers who return to the old neighborhood after serving in World War II. Mario, a war hero turned bricklayer and Gene, a medic turned school teacher, are the Leone brothers whose Bensonhurst travails form the center of this story that moves across the pages like a literary tornado.

La Puma is adept at rendering traditional Italian family interaction of the post World War II era, and while his characters move dangerously close to the stereotypical hot-blooded Sicilians, they never fall into the pit of predictability. La Puma's players are the three-dimensional humans that only good fiction depicts. These are people, all full of life and driven by unchecked passions in love and even in death. When words fail, there is always the knife; and in a darkly humorous way, the knife, like the inherited passion, becomes a family heirloom of sorts.

La Puma reminds us that the same passion that unites the family can also destroy it, and that in life we live in the heavens and hells that we create. While it is easy to see why this novel got picked up by a major film studio — it's full of wild characters, exciting action and disarmingly simple dialogue — we are always reminded that there is more to La Puma's work than lights and action. There's a self-mocking irony present in this first person narrative that reminds us of the best of John Fante, another Italian/American fiction writer turned Hollywood scriptwriter.

La Puma never over-writes, and his use of understatement echoes the style of Ernest Hemingway. La Puma deftly balances the narration and dialogue in this work, and this is an important balance to maintain. The story easily could have fallen apart in the hands of a less poised writer. It is quite obvious that La Puma has been working hard at his craft. Since his prize winning collection of stories, *The Boys of Bensonhurst*, La Puma has grown in his ability to integrate narrative with dialogue. He has also moved away from the more autobiographical material which suffered a tendency toward sentimentalism, and in *Wedding Cake* he has turned his talent towards more imaginative writing. And while his earlier work focused more on the male-side of life, La Puma, in this novel, has developed strong female characters who not only stand up to these wild men, but also assert their own identities that take them in independent directions.

If one wished to find some fault in La Puma's novel, perhaps it lies in its brevity. At just under three hundred pages, a typical size for novels these days, it seems to be over before we've started. We want to know what happens to all these characters after they've made it through courtship, adultery, murder, artificial insemination, and sanctuary in a hospital psych-ward. Perhaps, it will come to us in a sequel; perhaps we'll never meet these wild *paesani* again. But to leave readers wanting more is a present that only the good writers can give. And we thank La Puma for sharing his remarkable storytelling gifts with us.

## 3

Salvatore La Puma's *Teaching Angels to Fly* is a literary flight out of the more traditional and folktale-like world of his earlier work. With this latest collection of fourteen stories La Puma successfully steers his talents into the larger and more complex world of contemporary literature. While *The Boys of Bensonhurst,* a 1987 Flannery O'Connor award winning collection of short stories, and *A Time for Wedding Cake*, his first novel, established La Puma as a major voice of Italian America, *Teaching Angels to Fly*, is evidence that La Puma's talent is not limited to spinning yarns about the old neighborhood.

There were hints of La Puma's eccentricity in *A Time for Wedding Cake,* but the proof is in this collection of stories which range in style from simple neo-realism to sophisticated magical surrealism. In the opening story, "Lightning," those familiar with La Puma's writing will probably feel they're reading someone else. The story revolves around the flirtatious encounter between Wally, a middle-aged pharmacist and a twenty-three year old angel named Uriel who lands on his rooftop with a wing in need of repair. "Lightning" introduces a more playful, surreal aspect to La Puma's writing that is carried off well in many of his new stories.

La Puma continues his trademark play with history and memory, but with this collection he shows off his ability to play with imagination. He approaches the world of adulterers and divorcees from strange angles. In the next three stories, "The Four of Us," "Photograph," and "Murderous Myrtle," he dramatizes those how ex-lovers, for better or worse, never really leave each other. In "Sailing" he uses the play of children to remind us of how innocent adultery can seem and how dangerous it can be.

With incredible insight La Puma finds love in the strangest places. His account of the contemporary world of the homeless in "Inside the Fire" reads like the best of William Kennedy. "Number Ten for Potatoes" presents the unique world of two mentally retarded people who are brought together by well-meaning parents who realize they've made a terrible mistake when the couple, against their warnings, have a child. In "First Cousins," he explores the life-long fantasy of two cousins whose mutual dream of sleeping together is realized too late.

The familiar characters from Bensonhurst still inhabit La Puma's stories. There's Giovanni, an assistant in Carlo's Pastry shop in "Cakes." First published in the anthology *From the Margin*, this story uses La Puma's own experience as a baker. In "Your Country Wants You," Tommaso Scarlatti, a local mafioso who is close to retirement, is paid a call from a U.S. government agent who offers to stop indictment proceedings if Scarlatti will assassinate a foreign leader. "In Delphine's Bed" recounts a fantasy turned reality when a local bookie pulls a fast one on the mob in order to gain the girl of his dreams.

In "The Hangman," La Puma draws on his experiences in the Korean War to set up this story of a rebellious soldier and his strange friendship with the company's top sergeant. "Loose Change" recounts the story of a Puerto Rican kid struggling to get over on his mother's sweat shop boss. La Puma returns to the surreal in "A Marvelous Feat in a Common Place." In this, the collection's strange finale, we meet a professor "lifelong ambition has been to write a definitive history of the bedbug over the millenniums." When the professor's only friend, a cat, dies, he has it stuffed and mounted. La Puma loosens all ties to realism when the cat returns to life and the reader is treated to a trip into the world of magical realism.

All in all, this collection should fulfill La Puma's wish not to be pigeonholed as an ethnic writer. Although many of these stories transcend the boundaries of reality, they never stray from human possibilities. There's a deeper understanding of human psychology at work in these stories that enables LaPuma to render characters and worlds his earlier work rarely touched. *Teaching Angels* reveals a greater sense of a mind concentrating on more than mere nostalgic recollection. It's as if his earlier work was a warm-up for the more vigorous mental workout these stories evidence. In this collection, La Puma has not only shown us he can *Teach Angels to Fly*, but that he can teach us to read the world in new ways, and that is a lesson that only the best of our writers can offer.

*September 1987 / February 1991 / January 1993*

# *La Sorte's* La Merica

## Michael La Sorte

*M*ichael La Sorte is a Professor of Sociology at the State University of New York, Brockport. He received his Ph.D. in sociology at Indiana University. La Sorte started out in theoretical and family sociology. Then in the early seventies he became interested in historical demography, particularly in 19th century America. In the late seventies he got involved in migration and fertility studies in Italy in regard to regional, class and historical differences. He was also working with some of the census materials in both Italy and America and became interested in the migratory movements both within and from Italy.

In 1979 he had an opportunity to study Italian dialects at Stanford University. It was there that he started to dig into material regarding the private lives of immigrants. That was the beginning of what became *La Merica*. He continued to work in that area and produced some papers. He obtained diary materials and brought together a bibliography of works about immigrants. Realizing that at that point he had more than an article or a series of articles, be began thinking in terms of a book. "When I returned from Stanford, in 1980, I began the extensive work on the book in 1981 and completed a first draft in 1983.

"Then I added material I had obtained from the Immigration History Research Center in Minnesota. By the spring of 1984 Temple University Press had indicated interest. They sent it out to a reviewer, who said many good things about it and that hooked them. I was also fortunate with my editor, Janet Francendese. She's of Italian background. She was interested in bringing something out in the Italian area."

*La Merica*, though it was published by an academic press, does not read academically. In both the content and style of the writing, La Sorte has taken his years of research and made the immigrant experience accessible to the every day reader. *La Merica* is a book that speaks clearly and vividly, as though the subjects of the book were speaking directly to us. La Sorte first allows the immigrants to speak as individuals and then provides the reader with insight into the larger context of the immigrant experience.

Says La Sorte: "I started to conceptualize it in a way that would somehow be different. I wanted to present the material more from the point of view of the immigrants, seeing the experience through his eyes. Little by little the manuscript took shape."

## Academic Origins

"I was very much an academic at the beginning. My audience was small. I was having difficulty getting the material published. There are a lot of journals out there. The kind of analysis I was using did not appeal to those journals. I asked myself where is this all getting me. In response I started to tone down my style and to play with the material in a much more casual fashion, without bringing in theory or methodology. I always considered my self somewhat of a maverick. I drifted away from statistical sociology and became more interested in social history. This took me away from sociology and the kinds of papers that sociology journals are looking for. At one point I couldn't even get my papers accepted for the American Sociological Association meeting. They were not statistical enough."

La Sorte accomplished the full professorship level and received tenure in 1974. Having accomplished this he became more and more alienated from sociology. It had changed dramatically since he had entered it back in 1958. He found himself a total stranger at the Association meetings. So he quit the Association completely. Because Brockport is a small institution La Sorte has been able to move around. He's taught Italian, Freshman English, and now along with his courses in sociology is teaching a Modern European History course. "There are a lot of Italians in Rochester and a substantial number of them come to Brockport. There's a potential pool out there but there isn't that much interest. The class I have is small."

# A Book for Us

*La Merica* sold well over a thousand copies in the first nine months. La Sorte hopes that the Italian/American population would read it. He wrote it with us in mind. La Sorte argues against the notion that Italian Americans do not read books. "I think we've been taken in by the kinds of generalizations you find on the front pages of newspapers and in popular magazines. Magazines of every type appealing to all audiences are being published today more than ever before. The bookstores are full of them. You find them in every drugstore. There are certain kinds of books that individuals who do not normally read will pick up. The Iacocca book is an excellent example.

"I know all kinds of Italians and I know they don't read as we [professors] read. After all we are professional readers. That is what we do for a living. So it's not fair to compare our reading habits to theirs. Now here are these people that you couldn't get to read a book. But they all read that book and they loved it. Because it really appealed to them."

That is what La Sorte has done with *La Merica* created a book that would appeal to Italian Americans as well as to the larger audience interested in learning more about the Italian immigrant experience.

# Italian/American Identity

La Sorte believes that the time has come for Italian Americans to base ethnic pride on a strong foundation of understanding our heritage. He has been to Italy four times and has made contact with relatives in Bari and Genoa. "I think that we're finally coming out of the closet regarding our ethnicity. I agree with Vecoli's argument: that our feeling of our Italianess has always been there, though we kept it submerged, mainly because when it did come out we were criticized.

"Italian Americans have a bad image. Part of it, perhaps, is our doing, but much of it has to do with the American public's fascination with the more unusual activities that have been associated with the Italians. That is, either we're funny people or we're criminal people. One thing that always irritated me and I guess it motivated me to do the kind of book I did, was that there are such a variety of Italian/American experiences in America. And only a few of the more sensational stories are getting all the attention. We're a diverse people. We occupy a number of positions in American society. Today we're solidly middle class. And as we become more middle class I think we will start to look back at our heritage and our background and be more willing to talk about it in a straightforward manner."

La Sorte feels he was typical as a young man in that he kept his Italianess to himself. "It didn't do any good to bring it out. The negative feelings were there and you got tired of that." He grew up in Endicott, a small factory town in New York. A large Italian population shared the area with a mixture of immigrants who came to work in the town. It was founded in the early 1900s. "That kind of ethnic mix meant that you were always being confronted with your ethnicity and the best thing to do was to play it down, to fit in as much as possible. In fact, that was my father's philosophy. If any one said anything thing negative, you never said anything in response. Generally the reaction was to look somewhat embarrassed and hope it would all go away. This is quite different from the Jewish reaction, which more often than not is to verbally attack negative remarks."

La Sorte says he still gets this reaction from his Italian/American students. "If I have occasion to bring up material about ethnicity, there's a very profound silence in the class. Ethnicity embarrasses them. But if I bring it up in a particular kind of way, that is not just talking about these people as objects, but talking about them in a positive way as you would anybody else, sometimes they perk up. It's a long process."

It took La Sorte a long time to come out of his shell. And now he feels he's out of it completely. He's proud of his heritage up front and doesn't care how people respond to him. It's that kind of confidence he sees coming out more and more, particularly in the middle class Italian. "I see a much more intellectualized pride in our heritage which involves learning about ourselves, learning about our relatives and learning about Italy, making that connection across the Atlantic.

"When I became a professional, I thought I finally got away from all that prejudice. Then I was called a wop three times by three of my colleagues; all with Ph.D.s in sociology. When I became Chairman about fifteen years ago it was obvious that they weren't going to take me seriously. One day I finally figured it out. I said to myself: 'Look Mike, you might just as well face it. They consider you to be a dumb wop and a dumb wop you'll always be. So I said, OK, I'll be a dumb wop.' And I've been a dumb wop ever since and I've been much happier. I mean it. I understand the redneck.

I have some of the redneck in me. But I fully realized it when a former President of Brockport college told an anti-Italian joke at a meeting and thought it was funny. The vice president who was Italian laughed, and that was a bit too much for me."

## Man at Work

Currently La Sorte is working on other material he came across when he on sabbatical leave in Italy last year. It also has to do with the private lives of immigrants. What he's doing is to try to look as deeply as possible into the marital relationships of the immigrants. "This is an area that has pretty much been neglected. I've looked at the family studies of Italian Americans and I was surprised to find that I came up with relatively few of them and most of them have to do with the structure of the family — much of what I take to be cliché. The question of the extent to which Italian customs and norms have changed in being transplanted in America and that sort of thing. Nothing much has been done in looking at the internal dynamics of the Italian/American family system."

He's focusing on the marital relationships. He asked: "What do we really know about these people." La Sorte's been looking at the way the novelist handles the immigrant couple's relationship. "The stereotype that I'm finding in the literature is that it's a closed system. We grow up in a family where the secrets are not only kept in the family, but they are kept in the relationships in the family. In other words, you really don't know much about mommy and daddy who were born in Italy. We grow up and some of us become writers who use material from family experiences, like Jerre Mangione. His material is fascinating, but he's really outside his mother and father's relationship. He can't get inside it. The only way he can get inside it is for them to let him come inside it. And this doesn't happen that much.

"I'm arguing that even though it is a closed system, it is accessible in some ways. Through novels for example. So I'm looking for novels that might show this access. I'm looking for the immigrant's story."

# *Italglish*

The excerpt from his chapter on Italian/American English that appears in this issue comes from a well researched look at the way the immigrants fashioned new words from both English and Italian. Though such speech is hard to find these days, it does represent a linguistic phenomena that bears a place in the history of American English. Many people feel that it is degrading to use the Italian/American dialect in print and La Sorte says he can understand how Italian Americans can feel offended by use of the Italian/American dialect. "It's legitimate point of view. But they can grow out of that. If it's possible to go beyond that sensitivity, then they will find some confidence in their pride. The fact that my mother didn't speak a very good English embarrassed me tremendously as a kid. I understand the process."

La Sorte says that the Italian American has always wanted to fit in. We came over here with an inferiority complex and it grew as we tried to assimilate. We felt that by fitting in we would finally be accepted. Of course he realized that even though he fit in, he still wasn't accepted. "I tried to be an English gentleman. Every time I see this happening to others, I feel like saying: 'Be yourself.' There's something more here to ethnicity than cultural conditioning. What you try to repress keeps bubbling up to the surface. Finally one day I grabbed it and I played with it. And now I've made it an integral part of my personality now. I'm being what I really wanted to be."

*March 1986*

# Confessions of a Critic

## Frank Lentricchia

$\mathscr{A}$fter nearly twenty-five years of writing award winning literary criticism that has earned him a reputation as one of America's best cultural critics, Frank Lentricchia has shaped a controversial book out of various pieces of his own life.

Not a traditional autobiography, *The Edge of Night: A Confession* is as imaginary as it is autobiographical. Throughout the work, we witness a constant recreation of a man's self so that there is no single identity that can be pinned down and explained. By doing this, Lentricchia more accurately reflects the realities of a postmodern world. At the same time he maintains a silence about just who he might really be. In this way, he fashions an ironic example of bella figura through its brutta counterpart. The result is not what you'd expect from a nice boy with a "proper" education.

One critic called the book "an Italian hoodlum act." One publisher refused the book saying she would not want to meet its author in a dark alley. And while the book invites such misreadings, *The Edge of Night* is more about writing and reading than about a man's life. Lentricchia admits that his interest lies more in the process of writing than in the resulting product. "I never existed except in this doing," he writes.

In each of the book's four sections, a different *I* emerges. In the first section, we get a sense that this famous literary critic is about to reveal the darker side of his life. In the next section "Part One: To the Monastery (May 1991-September 1991)," a middle aged academic seems to be looking for a Catholic past by going to Mepkin Abbey where he gains a new sense of religion.

In the next chapter, a different Frank Lentricchia takes off for Ireland the homeland of his literary self and of one of his cultural grandfathers —

William Butler Yeats. On this trip he transports a new self that he has begun creating in writing; he is paranoid about losing that self — an extremely fragile self that is newly created on paper. These two selves — the newly literary and the critical Franks — come together in a fanciful encounter between Don DeLillo and Yeats at Dominick's Restaurant in the Bronx. He returns to this trip toward the end of the book to learn that the name Frank does not exist in Irish. Can it be that our literary critic has realized that he can no longer depend on literary subjects for his identity?

In the third chapter we witness a transition in which the literary critic becomes the self critic. Previously published in *Harper's* as "My Kinsman, T.S. Eliot," this section explores the social consequences of achieving literacy through an intellectual version of Nathaniel Hawthorne's short story, "My Kinsman, Major Molineaux." The moral of this section is that our heroes never last.

Throughout the rest of the work Lentricchia delves deep into both his historical past and his imagination; he begins not only to fantasize, but also to criticize his past, as in this example in which the narrator imagines his daughter saying:

> You know, when it suits you, you come on like a wop right off the boat. You're proud of this, to put it mildly. It's like a weapon, like a knife, your ethnicity. Why did you take relish in teaching us those words when we were young? Wop, greaseball, dago, guinea, spaghetti bender. You like those words, but they just bore us. We don't care.

Lentricchia knows that the price of social mobility is the creation of alternative selves that adapt to the new situations one encounters on the journey away from the family and into society. He writes:

> The more I went to school the more I became the stranger in the house. Which, of course, was the point. Which is what we all wanted, a gulf, the gulf made by their love, though we would never have thought to say it that way. My son the college teacher . . .

When Lentricchia returns to his Italian/American past to examine that gulf, he carries with him every Italian American who has ever left home.

Unlike others, his is a triumphant return; in the writing he maintains control over the ghosts that have haunted him and creates a way to haunt them back. With *The Edge of Night*, Lentricchia has proven that he can create literature as well as he can criticize it.

*April 1994*

# A Journey: From Film to Book

## Susan Caperna Lloyd

𝒮or years a major theme of Italian/American storytellers has been Italy as the old country of immigrant parents and grandparents, with a focus on the lives of earlier generations. But now there is emerging a new phenomenon, Italy as the "new" country of discovery by the children of those American immigrants. One of the best portrayals of this experience comes to us in Susan Caperna Lloyd's *No Pictures in My Grave*. In the book, Lloyd tells the story of her trips to Trapani, Sicily which began out of curiosity and ended with her finding a lost part of herself and a new home inside Sicilian culture.

More than a record of one woman's quest for identity in a postmodern world, *No Pictures* speaks for all women, especially for those with old country roots. In the tradition of *The Odyssey*, Lloyd encounters ancient goddesses on the cave walls of Levanzo, at the shrine of the Black Madonna, and in the faces of modern day Sicilian women. The tale is told as a mystery in which she escapes the clutches of evil men, and is transformed into a modern day goddess. The search is over when she becomes the object of her quest.

Lloyd has crafted a dramatic tale of a spiritual journey that reads like a novella. The plot presents the question: can a panic-attack prone, rootless, contemporary American feminist (and mother of two) find her roots and their origins in pre-Christian, pre-patriarchal culture. And if she does, what will she do with them? This autobiographical travel story is woven with myth and history, all told in a deceptively simple style that informs as it entertains, enchants as it depicts contemporary Sicilian small town life and its relationship to its pagan past. The writing is beautifully illustrated with Lloyd's own striking black and white photography.

## A Journey: From Film to Book

*No Pictures in My Grave* comes two years after Lloyd's award winning documentary film, *Processione: A Sicilian Easter*, which recorded the Santa Maria Addolorata procession, a Trapani Holy Week tradition dating back 400 years. The film garnered the Blue Ribbon at the 1990 American Film Festival, the Bronze Apple at the 1990 National Educational Film and Video Festival, and a top honor at the 1991 UCLA Film Festival of Folklore and Popular Culture. Lloyd's connection to Italy comes from her father's side of the family who immigrated from Terracina in the early 1920s.

During World War II, her father came out to California to serve in Merchant Marine, where he met his wife and where Lloyd was born. She grew up in Oregon, where her Italian identity was shaped by grandmother's stories and food.

Lloyd earned a Bachelor's degree in Art and a Masters in photography for which she prepared a thesis on the *Santos* in Latin American churches. "What attracted me to them was their difference from the Catholic churches I had been familiar with," she says. "I explored the relationship between Our Lady of Guadalupe and the Aztec goddess."

Lloyd explored the pagan references in these statues, knowing there was some connection between the two cultures. This experience, which also included trips to Peru and Equador, prepared her to study the same relationship in Sicilian culture. Lloyd says the Sicilian search, culminating in the film and book, all started with her first pregnancy, during which she left college teaching and began exploring mother/son relationships in both her studies and her art. "I began looking into my relationship with my father and his relationship with his mother. I didn't want some of the same things to happen between me and my son."

Lloyd started a series of portraits of herself and her son. "I also wrote these long texts about how my world view was changing now that I had a child. I believed that by giving birth to my son, I had experienced a death, of my old self, and the birth of a new me."

With a grant from the Oregon Arts Commission, Lloyd started looking at old family photographs and remembering her own childhood. "I was trying to understand the smothering love going on in my own family which kept my father from being a man. I decided to go to Italy and research the photos of the family in Italy to get a better sense of the values that had shaped my grandmother's life and her relationship to my father." Lloyd returned to Sicily with her husband Tom and her son Sky, to film a documentary on the Easter Procession. After the film was completed, she returned alone in 1990, and that is the experience captured in her book. "I don't want pictures of my sons in my grave," she says, explaining the books title. "I don't want to play the role of the Madonna for life and thereby make my sons weak. I don't want them to have to need my protection, even in death. I want them to be able to take care of themselves."

*April 1992*

# Italian/American Folklore

## Frances Malpezzi
## and William M. Clements

*S*ince the 1938 publication of *South Italian Folkways in Europe and America* by social worker Phyllis Williams, a book designed to help social workers understand their clients, there's only been a handful of book-length studies of Italian/American folk culture. Most of these have focused on individual storytellers and their tales, as in *Italian American Folktales* by Elizabeth Mathias and Richard Raspa, which features the life and stories of Clementina Todesco, an immigrant from northern Italy.

Finally, with *Italian-American Folklore,* by Frances Malpezzi and William M. Clements, we have an effort to map out the largely unknown territory of Italian/American folk culture. Malpezzi and Clements, a husband and wife team, are quite thorough in their research as they present the elements that make up Italian/American folk culture. More importantly they analyze those elements and present their observations in a style that makes for easy reading.

As they admit in their introduction, their aim is to represent the breadth and depth of the field and not to be all inclusive. While this approach limits the number of examples that can be included, a survey of this rich field is precisely what's needed. Clements and Malpezzi, both professors at Arkansas State University in Jonesboro, have been at work on this subject since the early 1980s and plan future publications that will be more narrow in focus. The use of secondary sources such as earlier articles, studies, and fictional accounts, is enlivened by combining informant interviews with Malpezzi's personal reminiscences. Malpezzi, a native of the ethnically diverse Masontown in southwestern Pennsylvania, adds recollections of family members which helps personalize the approach.

The book is divided into ten chapters and opens with "Setting the Scene," a discussion of the vital roles that regionalism and *la famiglia* play in the creation and transmission of Italian and Italian/American folk culture. Malpezzi and Clements remind us that folklore is a means of communication, and their chapter entitled "Conversation" deals with language and the dialect that was created when Italian and regional dialects met. In this chapter they chart the development and use of folk speech and proverbs. Special attention is given to southern Italian culture and especially Sicilian culture from which come their examples of proverbs. In "The Life Cycle," we follow Italian/American life from birth through death. If you've ever wondered what those Jordan almonds were doing at your wedding table or how you got some strange birthmarks, explanations are offered. What's left out here is the importance of grave visits and the custom of picnicking at grave sites. In "The Traditional Calendar," Malpezzi and Clements take us on a tour of events and rituals which occur on liturgical and secular holidays. They offer an excellent explanation of the importance of the traditional Sunday dinner. The emphasis of this section is on the Christian holidays, like Christmas and Easter. While this section lacks commentary on or reference to the pre-christian roots of this culture, this connection is somewhat explored in the next chapter, "Folk Supernaturalism," in which the differences between Italian, Marianist Catholicism, and American Irish Catholicism are explained. The authors also illuminate the phenomena of *malocchio,* monsters, and luck. Their chapter on "Folk Medicine" explores the role of magic and medicine and the use of herbs and minerals in the healing process. In "Recreation and Games" we are reminded that the games we play, *bocce, morra,* card games, and drinking games such as *passatella,* are important ways of identifying with our ancestral culture.

"Stories and Storytelling" provides examples and an explanation of how we process and transmit experiences from one generation to the next through the oral tradition. In "Drama, Music and Dance" Malpezzi and Clements explore the relationship between traditional performance and the rise of Italian/American presence in American popular culture. The final chapter, "Foodways," explains how today's Italian Americans, especially those of the third, fourth and fifth generation, retain the strongest connection to their culture through the rituals of preparing and eating those large family meals.

Their narrative is followed by a fine bibliography which alone is quite an achievement; never before have such resources been gathered in one place. This is a remarkable effort which paves the way for future studies.

*Italian-American Folklore* is a book for all of us and we owe Frances Malpezzi and William Clements *tante grazie* for their fine work.

*November 1992*

# Spring's Eternal Hope

## Rose Tavino Manes

*I*n August of 1986, her mother five years dead, Rose Tavino Manes was sound asleep when she heard a voice call out: *"Rose, è stritt', è scritt'."* The voice was so real that she jumped out of bed with a vision of her mother carrying a jug of water on her head. Thinking of the hardships that her mother often spoke of brought a stream of visions that drove Rose to the typewriter. That night she wrote fifty pages of what would become, after three years of research and writing, *Prima Vera,* her second novel.

*Prima Vera* spans eight decades and recounts the continuity and perpetual renewal of an Italian family and its American extensions through immigration. By breaking the Italian word for "spring" into two, Manes suggests the idea of "first truth" and "first wedding ring," *vera* being colloquial Italian for wedding ring. And it is the marriage between Enrico and Lucia that is the heart of this novel.

The novel is based on the lives of her parents and grandparents. Beginning with the birth of Lucia, the novel, in journalistic fashion, follows the life of Lucia and her *contadino* family in Benevento, Italy through to its third-generation as they celebrate America's bicentennial. *Prima Vera* is told from a distant, hovering point-of-view, as though the author is narrating a series of family photos in a written documentary which covers the earthquakes, political wars, and economic hardships through which the family not only survives, but thrives.

While lives come and go, sometimes in sentences, Manes presents aspects of family life that often get ignored in similar immigrant sagas. Reminiscent of Jane Austen, Manes details regional customs and domestic rituals, depicting the culture that these people lived in and their connections to the earth. Manes reminds us that our ancestors were very much aware of their relationship to nature and worked hard to maintain ecological rules that we have very much forgotten in this country. She mixes story and history to make *Prima Vera* an interesting ethnographic study of Italian life in America.

Manes' writing experience began early as she took on the task of family scribe, writing the letters back to Italy. In 1967, Manes returned to Italy and spent six weeks in the home where her mother had grown up. Relatives there were able to fill her in on aspects of her family's history she did not get from her parents' stories. "We didn't have television," says Manes, "and so on long winter evenings my parents would talk about their childhood experiences and we would ask questions. It was a tremendous learning experience."

Manes attributes her success to her parents. "They supervised our very being to make sure that only the very best would come out of us." Rose graduated valedictorian from her class, as did her sister the following year. "We were competing as first generation Americans in classes that emphasized Anglo-Saxon culture," she says. "This had never happened before nor has it since. Our younger brothers became well respected builders and architects."

Without money for college, Rose was sent to business school in New York City. She earned secretarial certification and was employed in publishing. In 1945 she married and was widowed at age thirty-two with one child. She took a job in the health field to get her daughter through college. When, at age forty-nine, Manes was told that her hard work intimidated her co-workers, she quit and went to college. She completed her Bachelor's of Science degree *cum laude* in two years at Hunter college where she majored in health sciences and studied Italian history, geography, and language with Mario Fratti.

Rose put her studies to work in writing *Prima Vera*, which sets the families in the context of Italian history. She also relied on a sense of oral tradition. "While writing the book I asked myself, 'Now what do I want to tell my grandchildren?' I have two beautiful grandchildren, and in today's busy world I don't get to see them as often as I'd like. Writing became a way of passing on some of their history."

In spite of contributing two books and a number of essays, Manes doesn't feel she's had much impact on Italian/American posterity. "Perhaps," she says, "the best we can do is set a good example and hope that it takes root at some point."

*March 1992*

# Where Writing Leads Us

## Renee Manfredi

*In* 1993 Renee Manfredi became the first Italian American to win the prestigious Iowa Short Fiction Award. That same year she earned a National Endowment for the Arts fellowship and a Pushcart Prize. These are major accomplishments, especially considering that Manfredi, like many Italian/American writers, grew up in a house without books and was seen as eccentric by a family that did not read much beyond the newspaper.

A native of Pittsburgh, Manfredi characterizes her family as a cohesive group with traditions and customs dating back to Catanzaro, Calabria, on her father's side, and Sicily on her mother's. The first of her generation to attend college, she began as a pre-law major at the University of Pittsburgh, but fell into creative writing one summer when the other classes she wanted were closed. "Once I started this class, I became serious and focused for the first time in my life," she says. A year later she published her first story in the *Carolina Quarterly*. Encouraged by instructor Montgomery Culver, she began writing every day. And while she was thinking of graduate school, her family was expecting marriage. "There was an underlying ambivalence about my going to college," she says. "To them family is the most important thing; beyond that, ambitions are modest."

From Pittsburgh she went on to study at Indiana University where she met Tony Ardizzone. "I feel very lucky to have studied with him," she says. "Tony is like a lot of the Italian men in my family; he's very engaged and passionate in the classroom; you always know what he's thinking and where he stands. If he didn't like one of my stories he would tell me. He's been very supportive of me and my work."

Ardizzone directed her thesis which became the foundation for her story collection.

Most of the stories in *Where Love Leaves Us* are set in Pittsburgh's Italian/American neighborhoods. They all revolve around relationships among fathers, mothers and their daughters, and explore the connection between memories and voices. In "The Projectionist," a sleepwalking father's depression is formed out of past that haunts him and a present that he can't face. Afraid of losing his daughter to American men, he begs her: "'Promise me that if you lose your heart, you'll let your memory follow it. Otherwise, no one will know where to find you.'"

In "Bocci," a young girl, "whose imagination sometimes intersects inconveniently with truth," is lured and lulled into molestation and worse by a friend of the family at an Italian/American club banquet. After the horrifying encounter she finds her father and tells him she wants ". . . cymbals in case I get lost. I could just stand still and crash them and you will always be able to find me." Her father assures her that all she has to do is call for him and he'll find her. Her haunting reply is: "But what if I have lost my voice, too?"

"Truants" is the story of a father and daughter who "take a sabbatical from life," leading double lives. "Keeping the Beat" explores the relationships of three generations of women: grandmother, mother, and daughter and the new men in their lives. The young daughter, a gifted music student, has developed "musical autism" and returns home to live with her grandmother. At a picnic, her grandmother leads her back to the natural rhythms of life that first inspired her.

In "Ice Music," a deaf widower learns to love his daughter only after she defies him and leaves him alone. Out of the new solitude he manages to shape a language of sincerity which he speaks on her wedding day. "A Kind of April" uses the Jewish Holocaust to frame a story dealing with the relationship of personal history and public humor. "The Mathematics of Pendulums" portrays the difficulties of two young children in dealing with their father's death and their widowed mother's new romance. "Tall Pittsburgh" is a humorous exploration of a widower's attempt to raise his daughter. He hires a consultant to shape his daughter into a woman and to prepare her for the "Miss Tall Pittsburgh Beauty Pageant." The final story, "Where Love Leaves Us," features a daughter who is called home from school by her widowed mother who needs her to learn how to deal with men again. "Ice Lady," as the daughter calls her mother thaws only after the daughter spills curling lotion on her mother's face — accident or twisted revenge?

# DAGOES READ

While Manfredi drew little from her actual experiences for these stories, she is reluctant to have her family read them. "My family has never read much of what I've published," she said. "Months after the book's publication I still hadn't sent them a copy. When I showed my mother the first story I ever wrote she told me, 'The characters are nice.' I asked, 'Oh yeah, which ones?' She replied, 'The "Ws" and the "Ms."' She was talking about the typeface! My family is very literal like that. Maybe that's why it's taken so long for me to develop a sense of irony and to realize sarcasm. They just don't relate easily to the intellectual or the ironic. Now that they are finally seeing me as a writer, I'm both relieved and anxious."

*May 1994*

# The Passion of Sicilians

## Jerre Mangione

### 1

*F*irst published in 1968, then in 1972, *A Passion for Sicilians* has once again returned for one more encore. As most of Jerre Mangione's work, this book seems to have a never ending life. (Recently *Mount Allegro* was reprinted by Columbia University Press, with a new final chapter by the author).

All of Mangione's books are as apropos now as the day when they first appeared. Perhaps this is because his style of narrative at once distances the reader — enabling us to observe and analyze the action presented, and involves the reader — forcing us to participate; his eye for the lasting image and ear for the dialogue worth eavesdropping upon combine to create movement and metaphor one rarely finds in a book labeled "Sociology — Social History."

*A Passion for Sicilians* is the story/report of Mangione's study of the methods and actions of Italian social activist, Danilo Dolci. Supported by a Fullbright Fellowship, Mangione and his wife Patricia traveled to Sicily in 1965 to observe Dolci's work. He joined Dolci's staff and came in contact with supporters as well as enemies of Dolci's radical methods of empowering the people. Dolci is a northern Italian, who since 1952 has been leading Sicilians in non-violent crusade against such staunch forces as the nature of Sicilian land and climate, the years of government neglect, and the infamous mafia. He has been called, *diavolo* and *santo,* and is often referred to as the "Ghandi of Sicily," because of his practice of hunger strikes, "strikes-in-reverse," and other uses of non-violence to draw attention to the problems that not only have been ignored by governments, but endured by citizens for many generations.

Where once the answer was either to bite the bullet and live with the problems or to emigrate, in less than a lifetime the work of Dolci has offered the Sicilians a much preferred alternative — to live and prosper in the land where they were born.

Mangione is at once journalist and cantastorie, weaving history, observation and dramatic elements in such a fashion as to make reading a near act of physical participation in the events portrayed. Through Mangione we meet organizers — both Dolci loyalists and betrayers; Church leaders who distort Dolci's intentions; mafiosi who despise Dolci's work, but fear his fame; government officials who at once loathe and envy Dolci's ability to lead; and the local inhabitants who wonder why a guy like Dolci would bother with problems they've expected to pass on to their children. Dolci's efforts build dams that change the course of nature and bonds among people that change doubt and suspicion into belief and trust. This success is not without failure and it is Mangione's writing that depicts the tension, the sorrow, the release, the joy of the world around Dolci.

Not to leave this new addition bound to the past, Mangione has included a final chapter which updates Dolci's work and the lives and deaths of the many important participants. As Dolci says: "If people explore their own shadows and lights, the explore the daylight of others." In *A Passion for Sicilians,* it is through Mangione's lucid prose that we are treated to a light show on one of the darkest stages ever — the mysterious, miserable, miraculous, and magnificent island of Sicily. *Bravissimo.*

## 2

*J*erre Mangione and Ben Morreale have spent most of their lives writing about Italian/American culture. Mangione's memoirs, most notably *Mount Allegro,* his social histories, and his novels, have always pushed beyond personal testimony to document the history of America since the 1920s. Morreale, primarily a novelist and playwright, has established himself as a fine cultural critic. Now, these two writers have teamed up to produce a major contribution to American history.

*La Storia: Five Centuries of the Italian American Experience,* begun by Mangione more than ten years ago, is the result of more than a collected century of the authors' gathering, digesting, and disseminating information on Italian/American culture. Together they have created a powerful historical narrative, a story of the many stories that make up the Italian/American experience. Their efforts harken back to the *Cantastorie* or history singers' tradition of southern Italian culture.

*La Storia* is the best of the most recent attempts at documenting the Italian/American experience in books. It goes beyond the name dropping of Philip di Franco's 1988 *The ItalianAmerican Experience*. And while it is a more traditional approach to history than Larry DiStasi's innovative *Dream Streets*, it far surpasses any of the earlier attempts to record the trials and tribulations of the hundreds of thousands Italians who left a home in Italy with the hopes of making a better one in America.

While written for all readers, *La Storia* is tremendously useful to the most advanced scholars of the subject. This narrative is written cleanly and clearly and is punctuated with historical photos, oral histories, and extensive research that is not weighed down by cumbersome notes. However, there are scholars out there who would have benefitted greatly had such information appeared at least in an appendix. The chapters move chronologically. In "Italians Among the Colonizers," we read of Venetian artisans who came in 1621 to make glass beads that would be used in trading with the Indians, the Garibaldi Guard's contribution to the Civil War and a short-lived movement to beatify Columbus in 1866.

The sections entitled "The Land They Left" and "Emigration Fever" tell the story of Italy's struggle for unification and its impact on southern emigration which is well explained in a section entitled "The Politics of Miseria." If your parents or grandparents never told you why they left Italy, it's all explained here. "The Land They Came To" tells how Little Italys were formed, what life was like inside them, and why they took so long to dissolve. "New Roots Across the Nation" surveys Italian presence in major American cities like Baltimore, Boston, Chicago, and New York, and contains seeds for future books.

As with any good realistic portrait, Mangione and Morreale do not ignore the warts that too often have been inflated to deface Italian Americans. In "Crime and Prejudice," the authors quite thoroughly debunk the myth that Capone created organized crime in Chicago by reminding us that people like Michael Cassius McDonald were major criminal forces long before Capone's arrival. In this section, the authors present one of the finest contexts for understanding both the criminal elements of Italian/American culture and the impact they have had on distorting the public's perception of America's Italians. One innovation is the introduction of the idea of cultural anger, the result of the bigotry of Americans who use organized crime to discriminate against Italian Americans. This is an idea that Morreale has depicted in his most recent play, one that might be the key to understanding the bitterness found in many Italian/American novels.

"Work, Politics and Divertimenti," "Assimilation," and "Old Wine in New Bottles," covers the cultural contributions to modern and contemporary American culture, providing us with an excellent history of the working class and the movement into the middle- and upper-class America. There is one unforgivable shortfall in this book and that is found in its discussion of literature. There's not a word about Mangione's or Morreale's important contributions to American literature. Modesty should have been overcome here, for their work is as important as any they discuss. They also could have used some help in research and proofreading. Key names are misspelled, much important information has been overlooked or perhaps cut out due to publishing constraints. In any case, *La Storia* should not be considered the final word in Italian/American history, better it be used as an introduction to the wider range of work that has and is being produced.

Beyond the range of the experts in Italian/American history, *La Storia* has already received great praise by American critics. *Publisher's Weekly*, designating *La Storia* as a book of unusual interest and merit, called it, "A magnificent saga that illuminates a century of accomplishment and struggle." The task ahead for this book is to enter the homes and minds of the people who have made the stories that it recounts. This combined effort of Mangione and Morreale should do more than re-awaken a sleeping history; it should return us to our own stories, to those we make, and to those which have made us.

*August 1986 / October 1992*

# A Reluctant Radical's Truth

## Carl Marzani

### 1

$\mathscr{C}$arl Marzani has spent his life fighting against injustice through his writing. At the age of ten, he published parodies of Fascist songs. In the past seventy years, he has written six books, dozens of pamphlets, and film documentaries. In each case, his goal has been to make America a better place to live.

Now at the age of eighty, the writer, whom Italo Calvino called "The only man truthfully and completely in love with the United States," has shifted his focus to recount the story of his life. And what a story it is! *Roman Childhood* is the first in a series of five or six small books through which Marzani will recall the eight decades of his education as a reluctant radical. The second installment, *Growing Up American,* is due out this October, and he is currently at work on the third volume entitled *Spain, Munich and Dying Empires.*

*Roman Childhood* covers Marzani's life from his 1912 birth through his immigration to America in 1924. Marzani is proud of his Roman heritage which he can trace back through twenty-seven generations. This rich background, he claims, has always made him confident even as an immigrant. "No ten-generation Yankee family like the Adams, could ever make me feel inferior," he says. "I always said I'd rather be a pre-Columbian Roman than a post-Columbian Yankee." *Roman Childhood* is a joyous book that documents the author's movement from self- to other-consciousness. While recovering the rich, Fellini-like images of his childhood, Marzani interweaves references to his future. The result is a dynamic tension that traditional intellectual autobiographies rarely achieve. Marzani explains: "If I laid this all out in an essay it wouldn't correspond to reality as you see it. So using the memoir form, I can present it as I see it, and people might say, 'maybe he's right.' "

Marzani had used some of this material in *The Survivor,* his only novel, published in 1958. That was seven years after he was convicted of "defrauding" the government by concealing a reluctant, one-year membership in the Communist Party. In the novel, Marc Ferranti, a Marzani-like character, is acquitted — a verdict achieved through the help of a senator who reads Ferranti's unpublished autobiography. This was not the case in Marzani's real life. In spite of his "exemplary" service in the O.S.S. during World War II, in spite of his Williams College and Oxford graduate school education, and in spite of the First Amendment, Marzani's "un-American," or what he calls "non-conformist," activities landed him in a federal penitentiary for three years.

While all of this is alluded to in *Roman Childhood,* this first book concentrates on the scenario against which an incredibly rich future will play. The book opens with an "Appreciation" of Marzani by Italo Calvino who met Marzani during a 1960 visit to the U.S.A. What follows is a depiction of his childhood; Marzani contrasts his life with that of his best friend who later on became a staunch fascist and then a corporate businessman. Both joined the Youth Catholic Explorers, a Boy Scout-like group and often found themselves battling the Balillas, a Fascist youth organization.

*Roman Childhood* is an immigrant story unlike any other written by an Italian. Marzani's personal style always avoids the temptation to be obviously literary. He includes family photos, proverbs, song lyrics, and the combination creates a document that is charming, historically important, politically vital and never dull.

Marzani's first-hand experience of Fascism enabled him to recognize it approaching the U.S. "The key to an understanding of fascism," he writes, "is its destruction of 'existing' democratic institutions." Marzani saw the 1947 loyalty oaths for public servants, ordered by Harry Truman and the American Cold War policies, as the first steps towards Fascism in America. Remembering his father's lament that the Italians should have fought Fascism in Italy, Marzani dedicated his life to combating it in America. As he told a prison psychologist, "I felt duty-bound to defend Roosevelt's policies, which Truman was perverting. I did it reluctantly; I had no choice."

He never dreamed of a life of political activism. A budding theater director, Marzani was planning for a career as a dramatist when, in 1939, he left Oxford University for Spain. There, he joined the Partisans in their battle against Fascism. "I knew then that if Spain fell the world would be drawn into another war," he says. Marzani has dedicated his life to preserving American democracy and to him, that means economic change. A staunch Marxist, Marzani is not dismayed by the fall of Communism in Eastern Europe and Russia. "It wasn't a failure of Communism, but a failure of Stalinism," he says. "People don't understand that our problems today are not political, they're economic. Our congresspeople are not the ones to blame; they're just errandboys for the corporations; throw them all out and the problems will still be the same. I give capitalism another fifty years. This is no recession we're in; it's a lingering illness that government as it is now will never be able to cure."

Marzani's future volumes will document the experiences that led him to his position as a radical patriot of American democracy.

## 2

*Growing Up American*, the second installment of Carl Marzani's memoirs, *The Education of a Reluctant Radical*, is now available. Marzani continues the story of his life which he began with *Roman Childhood*. From immigration to America through graduation from Williams College, this volume captures the transformation of Marzani from Italian/American greenhorn to Oxford scholar. Through a steady stream of beautifully crafted vignettes, Marzani recreates all the emotion of his life without drowning in the nostalgic melodrama often associated with such accounts.

As in *Roman Childhood,* Marzani recounts the major events of his life and comments on contemporary American life. This combination of historical recollection and cultural criticism separates Marzani's memoirs from most immigrant autobiographies. Beginning with his adolescence in Peckville, Pennsylvania, where he was a thirteen-year-old first grader, Marzani brilliantly recalls his education and social indoctrination into American life. Within six years he went from grammar school through high school and earned a scholarship to the prestigious Williams College. This volume features the teachers who both supported and thwarted his attempts to succeed in America. At Williams, Marzani revived the school's literary publication and was elected "Most Brilliant" and "Biggest Drag with the Faculty," nosing out Richard Helms who would become Director of the

CIA. There he met the anti-fascist historian, Gaetano Salvemini, whose *Under the Axe of Fascism* he helped edit.

Besides formal schooling, Marzani supplemented his education with a cross country hitchhiking trip during the height of the Depression. "The trip," he writes, "made me a citizen inside what I had achieved was more than a rite of passage — a testament to personal stamina and ingenuity . . . This was now my land, my patrimony, bestowed by previous generations of immigrants, freely and generously, on one Carl Aldo Marzani — newly minted American."

His exploits as a young adult experimenting with the new freedoms afforded by American democracy feature sexual and travel adventures that never give way to braggadocio. Marzani, the elder dean of true blue American radicalism, reminds us that you don't have to be a Republican to be a patriot or a "self reliant" WASP to be an American. In typical Italian/American fashion he does not separate his accomplishments from his family. "The family had been my fortress." He writes:

> . . . from its keep and redoubt I had sallied forth unafraid, because I knew I could always scuttle back to security. My heart was full of love for them and their pride in my success — it was a vindication of Father's choice of America as a place of exile.

*Growing Up American* ends with Marzani on his way to England to study on an Oxford scholarship awarded to him by the President of Williams College who overruled a faculty committee's objection to Marzani's candidacy. His next installment, *Spain, Munich and Dying Empires* is due out early next year.

## 3

# Marzani Marches On

With all the attention World War II is getting these days, it's refreshing to get a sense of what was going on behind the scenes before the war even started. That's just what Carl Marzani provides us with in the third volume of his memoirs, *The Education of a Reluctant Radical*.

## A Reluctant Radical's Truth

In *Spain, Munich and Dying Empires,* Marzani recalls his student days in 1936 at Oxford University. Out of curiosity and a strong anti-fascist beliefs, the young scholar visits Spain and finds himself fighting fascism alongside the anarchists in the Spanish Civil War. And while his stay was brief, his insights into the battle are those of a seasoned veteran. The experience became one in which his "life was altered forever."

When he returns to Oxford, he meets up with actress Edith Eisner — a member of the American Communist Party, and the woman he would marry.

Because of her he reluctantly joined the Communist Party, an action which he had not given much thought to at the time. "[I]t never crossed my mind that joining the party might embarrass or harm me by jeopardizing my future or making me an outlaw in American society. Given Spain and the CIO, most Communists and Communist sympathizers were accepted and even respected."

And while those actions would later become the foundation for Marzani's persecution, the bulk of this installment is devoted to an incredible honeymoon-hitch-hiking tour of Nazi controlled Germany, Eastern Europe, Syria, India, Laos, China, and Japan in which Marzani and his bride meet Ghandi, Nehru, Chinese generals and Japanese secret police. The trip begins in Oxford in August of 1938 and ends with the couple's arrival in San Francisco in April of 1939. Marzani's penchant for keeping track of even the tiniest detail enables him to figure out that the trip cost a little over a penny per mile or 67 cents per day.

Once again, Marzani interrupts the narration of events to analyze the events he and his bride experience from both the perspective of his past and the present during which he is writing. The result is part political science, part history and all interesting.

*June 1992 / September 1993 / August 1994*

# A Postmodern Virtuoso

## Carole Maso

*I*n 1986, Carole Maso made a most impressive debut as a novelist. *Ghost Dance* told the story of a third-generation ethnic who, unlike earlier generations, has the option of picking and choosing from the many traditions that make up American culture. What Italian characteristics the protagonist, Vanessa Turin, does not inherit directly through experiences with her grandparents, she imagines and re-invents to fulfill her needs.

Few novels capture so well the effects of the fragmentation that occurs when solid cultural traditions are fractured. In *Ghost Dance,* Maso re-invented an *italianità* through her recovery of the myths that have made up her ancestral past. Her father's mother immigrated from Sicily, and her father's father from Genoa. Her mother is of German, English, and Armenian ancestry. Out of these diverse cultural roots, Maso has fashioned a unique perspective on life and art.

"My father was a jazz musician," she says, "who was interested in all the arts; he would listen to opera, make spaghetti and weep. My mother was very practical; she kept things going and gave me my sense of discipline." The oldest of five children, Maso thought she would become a painter. "I was not a voracious reader wanting to replicate life through writing; I had lots of music and ballet lessons, and it wasn't until I was a senior at Vassar College, majoring in English, that I turned to writing as a form to express this passionate desire that had been nurtured through the arts."

After graduating from college, she followed the advice of her writing mentor and stayed away from graduate school and any work that required writing. She supported the creation of her first novel by working as a waitress, an artist model, a fencing instructor, and a paralegal. When *Ghost*

*Dance* was published, her parents, who had been skeptical about her choice of a career, were relieved and proud. Able to spend the next four years just writing, thanks to a Vassar prize, a NEA fellowship and a fellowship to a fine arts center, Maso completed her second novel, *The Art Lover,* which was published in 1990. When her publisher, North Point Press, closed shop in 1991, she took a position at Illinois State University as an artist-in-residence. Last year she was writer-in-residence at George Washington University in D.C., and next year she'll be teaching writing in Columbia University's MFA program.

Maso says she's always been aware of what being Italian was. Her father's parents would visit her family every Sunday and projected their Italianness in interesting ways. "My grandfather wanted to be American, but in reacting against being Italian, it became quite clear to me what Italian was; he never gave up any of his Italianness. My Grandmother, who missed Italy very much, would sing Italian songs and make us Italian meals."

Maso believes that contemporary writers, especially those who are grandchildren of immigrants have the freedom to be more inventive. "Though some of the past is revealed through stories we are told and the investigations we do, so much remains concealed that we have to use our imagination; we have to understand that not having access to that experience won't alienate us from the culture. Today you can write about people on the periphery, and Italian/American literature will reflect a great diversity; that's why I have become more and more comfortable with the phrase Italian/American writer."

Maso's latest writing reflects an interaction with contemporary Italy that comes from her two-year residence in southern France. "What struck me about Italy is the idea that there they thought they could do anything. I felt this imaginative territory that other people had said: 'Oh, not possible, you can't do that.' I see that in Fellini and Giacometti. Over the years it has become more and more obvious to me how Italian I really am."

In her latest novel, *Ava,* the experience of Italy greatly affects the protagonist, Ava Klein, a Jewish/American professor who tells her story on the bridge between life and death. *Ava* represents a daring step into new forms of narrating a novel that marks Maso as a major American writer. The novel, composed of fragments of recollection, lacks traditional narrative threads that usually weave a coherent plot and requires the reader to construct a story out of the silences that constantly interrupt the voice. The result is that the novel, no matter how many times it is read, is able to generate new connections that create new meanings. Her next novel, *The*

*American Woman in the Chinese Hat* will be published by Dalkey Archive Press in 1994. She is currently at work on another novel entitled *Day of Angels.*

*July 1993*

# From Storyteller to Autobiographer

## Elizabeth Mathias and Richard Raspa

*Italian American Folktales* is an important book, one that every Italian American should own. It is the story of the tales as well as the teller. This book is most important because it preserves a memory, chronicles the process and entertains. Here we have many books in one. First there is the academic presentation of the methods employed in collecting these tales. It reads much like a dissertation. But take the time to move through the language and you will be rewarded with a better understanding of the importance of the story teller and the stories told in the context of Italian and American culture. Then there is the history book that documents the place and culture from which these stories come. Again this reads a bit too academically, but is worth the wade.

Then we come to the biography, the story of the tale teller. And this is where the book comes alive. It breathes, because Clementina Todesco remembered. And her daughter Bruna along with the authors, wouldn't allow her to forget. Clementina immigrated to America in the early 1930s from a village in northern Italy. She carried with a strong oral culture that she was born into. Her story is one of the thousands that have been told, but one of few written. Her daughter, Bruna carried on her mother's tradition by writing these stories down. However, Bruna died before she could complete her work. Fortunately these authors carried on.

It is almost enough to have Clementina's stories of her life, but there is more. There are the folktales. These twenty-four stories are written versions of what had been passed on by word of mouth for generations. There is something that happens to the storyteller's voice when someone else writes it. It loses the simplicity and nuances of the story teller's style. You need only compare the written tales to the Clementina's personal narratives to hear what I mean. However, the stories are there and preserved. We should be thankful for that. This section of the book could have been published on its own, for it is the gold of this collection. These are truly tales of folk, not the watered down Disney versions that most of us are more familiar with. There is joy and sadness, wine and blood, evil step-mothers, good witches and kings and so much more. We are told that Clementina's children would often cringe and cry at the telling of some of these stories. She tells us that she told her children only the ones that she thought they should listen to. She tells us more. So here you have many books, all for the price of one. Worth its weight on your bookshelf. Clementina is an artist, a *cantastoria*, a history singer. The authors of this book are quite the producers.

*February 1986*

# The World at Noon

## Eugene Mirabelli

*A*t fifty-three, Nicolo Pellegrino finds his life is out of control. He has a loving wife who's not afraid to go after what she wants, a mother in the hospital, a dead father who keeps showing up in the strangest places, three children who zip in and out of his life, few real friends and a girlfriend old enough to be his daughter. By juggling the pieces of his past and present, Nicolo keeps from having to face his future.

There's a bit of Nicolo in every man who finds himself caught between old age and youth, a time very much like noon. This sense of being trapped between morning and night, between memory and fantasy, is what novelist Eugene Mirabelli captures in *The World at Noon*.

Mirabelli, a native of Arlington, Massachusetts, is the child of American-born parents of Calabrese and Sicilian descent. He earned degrees at Harvard and Johns Hopkins, and is Professor of English at SUNY-Albany. With *The World at Noon*, Mirabelli has broken a nearly twenty year silence since his last novel, *No Resting Place*, by producing a work quite different from his earlier novels, *The Burning Air* (1959), and *The Way In* (1968), which were well received by critics.

This novel is a tumble of scenes disconnected from any traditional plot. Nicolo, a college professor, is married to Maeve, a talented editor and publisher; they're not as wealthy as they had hoped to be, but they live comfortably with their three children. They met in the 1960s, and while they have settled into a traditional life in New England, neither is quite certain that an old-fashioned marriage is really what they want. The family, while falling apart finds, ways to pull itself back together.

Part myth, part memoir, and part love story, *The World at Noon* shifts from among a number of styles and points of view in an attempt to capture the story of three generations. What works best in this novel is the sense we get of how a person is shaped and haunted by his past and how uncertain he is about what his future may hold.

Mirabelli is good at mirroring the psychological state of his characters through language. Long, lyrical sentences often lure us into chapters, as in the prelude to Nicolo's realization that he is falling in love with his daughter's friend:

> I suppose the snow that fell that winter was no different from the snow that fell in winters before, whether it sifted down as if from a gently tapped flour sieve or came like crushed diamond driven at a slant, or what I liked most, floated here slowly in blossoms and loose petals, I don't know why I liked it again after so many years of not liking it, welcomed it . . .

The combination of the endless sentence, when Nicolo's is a state of reverie, and the shorter, staccato-like sentences when he's agitated, help vary the narrative pace.

Mirabelli's at his best when he spins a folk tale, as the one that is told to Nicolo by his Aunt Gina about his grandfather:

> The first time Ava saw Angelo naked was on their wedding night (11 May 1860) when he strode into their bedroom, accidentally revealing to her startled eyes that from the waist down he had the hindquarters of a horse.

Mirabelli's hot Mediterranean legends mix well with the icy cold realism of life in New England.

While Mirabelli's style is smooth, he runs into trouble when he tries to set his pictures in motion. He's more successful at describing characters than he is at making connections between them. The problem could be that he tries to pack too much into one novel.

The affair between Nicolo and Roxane, his daughter's friend, could have been the material for a novel. Roxane, a student photographer could have taught Nicolo to revise his life. But instead, she reminds him how foolish it is to be chasing after his youth. The story of his grandparents and parents could also have filled another novel, as could the story of Nicolo being seduced by his widowed Aunt Gina during his youth. However, when they are all combined into one novel, they detract from each other. In the end, *The World at Noon* becomes the sketch book of a talented artist. One of the finest sketches is when Mirabelli lets us see things through Maeve's eyes, but since he only does this in one chapter, he leaves us both wanting more and somewhat confused about where she stands later in the work. What keeps us interested in the novel ultimately is the man, Niccolo — not what happens to him, but how he experiences it and articulates his reactions.

*October 1994*

# Prisoner of Love

## Anna Monardo

*The Courtyard of Dreams*, a first novel by Anna Monardo, is a young woman's coming-of-age story set in the U.S.A. and Italy. As the opening dream sequence suggests, the courtyard is a place where young women can be educated and protected from the outside world by old women until their dream men come to take them out into the world. But the gate to the courtyard is ever guarded by the father.

Not since Josephine Gattuso Hendin's *The Right Thing to Do* (Godine, 1988) has a novel by an Italian/American woman provided such insight into the complexities of a father/daughter relationship. Monardo uses this interaction to highlight the contrasts between Italian and American cultures.

"The Italian part of me has been at war with the American me for as long as I can remember," says Giulia DiCuore, the novel's narrator. "When I was young, the Italian me was the voice of my father, Nicola, who was always trying to send me to Italy for a vacation. He wanted me to see how many relatives I had over there."

Giulia's mother, born on a ship between Italy and America, provides her American identity, while her father's stories "pulled me too far away — they slapped me down a challenge that would eventually have to be met." When her mother dies, Giulia feels that America is slipping away from her and that the women who take her mother's place are there "to protect my father and me — protect us from the Russians, from hunger, from American food, from America itself."

After the funeral, Nicola rents an old convent, the cellar of which becomes a cantina where Italy is a combination of smells leaking out of stored foods and images from tomato cans. He begins protecting her from America — from the Beatles on television and from neighborhood gradu-

ation parties. When Giulia makes it through high school, it's no surprise
that her father wants her to attend a local college, where he can keep track
of her; he also decides she's going to Italy for the summer.

Giulia expects Italy to be filled with oppressive men (like her father)
and subservient women (like her aunts). But from her Italian relatives she
learns that "to be Italian in Italy was very different from anything I'd been
taught at home." She also learns how women can maneuver within the
constraints of the patriarchal courtyard.

In spite of the smothering attention from her Italian family, Giulia
finds a way to fall in love with Luca, her cousin's friend who takes her for
long rides on his scooter. While the love story between Luca and Giulia is
rather predictable, the writing that brings it to us is clean and clear. Monardo is at her best when Giulia is on her own, experiencing the difference
between Italian and American life and learning that her Italy is not her
father's Italy.

Monardo punctuates her love story with accounts of what life was like
in Italy for her father and his brothers whose father ignored the warning
not to make his sons better than himself. Nonno Carlo, "a man who had
been to America and back" had a dream of making his sons doctors. He
lives in poverty to make his dream come true. Nicola, the brightest of the
brothers, falls in love with an Italian/American woman visiting Italy with
her parents and they move to America where Giulia is born. Nicola, in spite
of his education becomes like his father:

> Once you have known the love of such a powerful father, you can
> never be rid of the need for him. And if he is gone from you forever,
> and you can't find him anywhere, you have no choice but to become
> that man yourself.

Later in the summer, when Nicola arrives — returning for the first
time since he emigrated — he becomes furious with his family for not
keeping Giulia away from young men. His reaction ignites a family feud as
once again Nicola grabs the reins of his daughter's life. Giulia is free only
when they can't take the same plane back to America. That's when she
makes a daring move; she decides to remain in Italy with Luca.

This act of defiance, easily done as they are separated by an ocean,
eventually takes it toll on her. A budding photographer, Giulia delays her
own college plans to try living in Rome with her handsome Italian student
lover. Eventually she realizes that life with Luca is not much different than

was life with her father. She returns, in a way, resigned to the stronger need for her father's love.

While Giulia has made the "old country" new, by learning to speak like a native, Monardo leaves us wondering if Giulia has learned what it takes to gain control of her own life back in America and escape from her father's courtyard.

*September 1994*

# Morreale Uncovers His Sicilian Roots

## Ben Morreale

*B*en Morreale, novelist, story teller and professor, was born in Manhattan in what is now known as the Roosevelt Park area on New York's lower east side. His parents came from Racalmuto, a small town near Agrigento in Sicily. His mother's people were poor farmers and his father's side of the family were impoverished sulfur mine owners. Bad accidents and a steep drop of sulfur prices forced the whole family to emigrate. They came to the United States in 1910 during that great immigration era when more people left one area than ever before in history. His parents met on the lower east side. His father worked in factories and during the twenties went into real estate. Some of his uncles made films and operated a spaghetti factory.

The Depression changed their lives quickly. His father became a tailor and worked in a factory the rest of his life. With the help of the GI bill, Morreale was the first of his family to be educated. "Back then your parents wanted you to work. Before the war my father demanded that I go *zappare* like everyone else. It was a struggle. Sometimes we had terrible arguments about my going to college, but I insisted upon going to school. I had spent four years in the Army Air Force in the Pacific during World War II. I guess he eased up on me figuring that if I had been a soldier I must be capable of handling my life."

Morreale's father proved to be a secret fan of his son's work. "One of the touching things was that after my father's death, I found that he had kept all my books and the reviews in a secret place." Morreale's father was literate, but not comfortable in either language. He wrote a lot of poetry, some of which Morreale uses as song lyrics in *Monday, Tuesday, Never Come Sunday*.

"On the whole I often thought that if my father had had a more formal education he might have done a little better for himself and maybe have done something creatively."

## Sicilian Roots

The Morreale family returned to Sicily twice. The first time when he was four they stayed for a year. When they came back to America Ben says he didn't know a word of English. The second trip occurred when he was ten years old. "We were going back to stay. It was a great adventure for me. There's a nostalgia for me in both Sicily and that age. Jerre Mangione shared that same experience. You find it in all Sicilian writers such as Pirandello and Vittorini. It gives you that controlled poetic quality that most other writers don't have."

After serving in the Air Force, Morreale studied history at Brooklyn College and completed his degree at Columbia University. He majored in history, because, as he says, "I often think I didn't major in literature because I liked it too much." After Columbia he went to France where he lived for seven years. He received his Doctorate from the University of Paris at Sorbonne and says he never thought of writing fiction until he got to Paris. "By accident I became friends with Max Steele, one of the editors of the *Paris Review*. I made frequent trips to Sicily and I would tell him stories. He said why don't you put them down on paper. That's how I began to write. He helped me tremendously. I sort of took creative writing courses from him. We'd sit in cafes until two in the morning and he'd tell me where to put this and that. Finally he took one of the four stories I had submitted. It was one called, 'Hate' and was about Sicily. From that story that I received letters from editors all over the country asking if I was writing a novel. Of course I said yes."

In 1958, the result was Morreale's *The Seventh Saracen*, which unfortunately is now out of print. The novel is the story of a Sicilian American's return to the birthplace of his parents. "I wrote about things I knew about and felt strongly about, the things that moved and touched me. In looking at it now it's really a young man's book; it's too romantic for me."

## *Early Influences*

Morreale read a lot as a kid. He was brought up on Russian writers, such as Tolstoi and Dostoevsky. He didn't get to the Italian writers until he went to college. "I read a lot of Sicilian history and discovered Vittorini and Pirandello, who was a great dramatist and story teller. I first wrote *The Seventh Saracen* as an imitation of Vittorini's *Conversations in Sicily.* The editors at Coward McCann talked me out of it. I think they were right." Morreale says his books come to him when he sees the ending. Once he has an ending then he can start the book. *Monday, Tuesday, Never Come Sunday* (published in 1977 by a Montreal publisher, Tundra Books) came when he saw himself as a young boy running down the street with milk during the depression. It's about growing up Sicilian in Brooklyn.

All of Morreale's books have received critical acclaim, however, they've never achieved the financial success that they deserve. "There are a lot of other writers that don't give the editors, whose bottom line is money, what they want. Right now mafia is so popular. If you write anything that's not along those lines. You're going to have difficulty publishing.

"Many of the Italian writers are hindered by the fact that Italians haven't been known as a group of readers. I don't think many of the people I grew up with were really readers.

"One of the great difficulties we have as Italian writers is that at the very crucial time when you're beginning as a writer, you don't have that audience that's going to give you that confidence, that push to keep you writing.

"The Jewish writers have had that and I think one of the reasons that they've had so many writers is that Jews read and that the Jewish writer always has that steady audience." An unpublished novel of his was bought by some people in Hollywood. He's been working on a film script for two years. "The things I'm learning help me understand what happened to Puzo. They dangle success in front of you saying: 'You're going to be a rich man; you're going to have a Mercedes.' Then you say: 'O.K., what changes do you want?' It's a strong pull."

# Mafia Mystique

A *Few Virtuous Men*, his second novel, published in 1973 and translated into Italian, is a literary thriller about Sicily and what it is like to live on the other side of the Mafia. It's main character is a priest who recounts his life among *mafiosi*. Morreale says that although Italians are shadowed by the Mafia you can't ignore it. "Historians don't like to write about Mafia" they leave it to sociologists, newspaper people and guys who want to make a quick buck, like Puzo. To be fair to Puzo, he had written some really nice books, like *The Fortunate Pilgrim*. Then I guess he got tired of making six or seven hundred dollars and went the way of *The Godfather*. He certainly has left an imprint on all Italians which is horrendous. When the book *[The Godfather]* and the film achieved success, Italian kids in high schools were beginning to organize Mafia groups." Of Puzo's latest effort, *The Sicilian*, Morreale who had his reviews of it published said: "It was a lazy, slap dash book. He's getting tired." In the research that he did, Morreale found that Italians come into criminal activity almost in a progression of ethnic groups. The Mafia existed in America before Italians immigrated. Lincoln Steffens dealt with it in his *Shame of the City*. Italians and Sicilians learned it here. Morreale says that in the future other ethnic groups will take up the process. He has developed a course called Mafia in America from Alexander Hamilton to Richard Nixon.

# The Writer in Academia

In 1972, Morreale published *Down and Out in Academia* (Pitman Publishing Company). The book is his non-fiction account of university life. "For a long time I was very angry with academia because things like committee work and fighting for raises took me away from my writing. That book got me in a lot of hot water. For example, I'm still the lowest paid full professor in the state university system. But overall I think it was worth it. I simply don't go to meetings any more. I just teach my courses, which I enjoy very much.

"The academic world is not a good place to be in right now. The people coming in will do anything for a job and that's not going to make for a good atmosphere. You're getting very timid, unstimulating people."

Morreale teaches European History at the State University of New York in Plattsburgh. His Ph.D. work was in the French Revolution. He gives courses on European Civilization, France in 1789 and has gone into other areas such as Film in History and Mafia in America. "Now I'm giving a course on American and European Ethnic Heritage. I'm doing it for the first time this semester and it's working out very well. Besides reading a lot on immigration history I'm having the students develop a history of their own families and set it into the immigration history scene."

## Man at Work

Morreale is currently working on a play entitled, Ava Gardner's Brother-in-law. It takes place in Sicily and is a confrontation between an American of Sicilian origin and a Sicilian who's known as Ava Gardner's brother-in-law. "In rehearsing the play, I'm getting more ideas. The difficulty is that if it doesn't get produced no one can experience it. Unlike writing a book, a play requires collaboration, and I enjoy working with people I like." Though most of Ben Morreale's work is out of print, you can still find copies of his *A Few Virtuous Men* and *Monday, Tuesday, Never Come Sunday*.

*April 1986*

# A Sicilian not by Birth

## Joseph Napoli

*A Dying Cadence: Memories of a Sicilian Childhood* is a *piccola gemma* (a small gem). Not brought out by a large press, I'm afraid its fate is predictable. Without advertising campaigns, talk shows, and major reviews, it will remain in the shadows of lesser works. However, it is written, it is published and it is available. And for that an Italian/American audience should be thankful and supportive.

Jerre Mangione, author of a number of widely praised books about Sicily and Sicilians calls it, ". . . one of the most engrossing memoirs of the American ethnic experience that I have ever read. Joseph Napoli is an accomplished writer with a style that is a delight: lucid, sophisticated, and eminently readable. His book deserves a wide audience and a long life."

*A Dying Cadence* is the reminiscence of an orphan who was adopted by Sicilian parents. The story travels from his childhood, through his parent's lives and ends with his experiences during and after World War II. There is a most powerful scene in which the writer confronts his father upon his return home after serving three years in Italy where he has been part of the fighting, experienced the black market and served in the American transitional government:

> I saw him from the distance, sitting on the back steps near the pump, unwashed and bent over in weariness. He looked up in surprise when he heard my steps and a small unfamiliar smile replaced the customary impassivity. As I approached to embrace him he offered his hand to be kissed and moved slowly toward the pump to wash his massive torso.

Through Napoli's words we gain insight into the often mysterious life of the Sicilian family and the history of Sicily.

His images are tender and often must surface through tough and sometimes tangled prose, but they make it. There is no sloppy sentimentalism here to mask the reality of his experience. The book is not organized into memorial niches. In one paragraph he could be recalling his mother's habits and in the next he'll be presenting a slice of Sicilian history. And perhaps it is this method of organization that keeps the book moving at a slow pace. On the other hand, the book moves as the mind moves in recalling past events: a moment on an image, a dwelling upon a fact, a fantasy; it is filled with good times and bad, with understanding and confusion. It is reportage of the war experience filled with anecdotes and the many attempts of one man to know himself through his people. *Bravissimo* to Joseph Napoli, for telling his stories and for never letting us forget that at the same time it is also our story.

*June 1986*

# A Novelist Turns to Poetry

## Joseph Papaleo

### 1

*Picasso at Ninety-One* is the latest publication by Joseph Papaleo, author of the novels *Out of Place* and *All the Comforts* and director of the writing program at Sarah Lawrence. This is his first collection of poetry. While not always written in the grandest style, Papaleo's poetry speaks truth in simplicity and finds wonderful words for even the most absurd of subjects. Especially worth reading and re-reading are his poems concerning the Italo-American experience. "American Dream: First Report" is an excellent example of a recurring theme in Papaleo's work: now that we've made it, what happens to our ethnicity:

> First nobody liked us, they said we smelled
> and looked too short and dark.
> Then the TV proposed marriage, and we said yes.
> Momma and sisters kept the commercials going,
> to prove we were married in palaces of soap.
> Who would have guessed that the end
> of those voyages, the agony of steerage
> insults from the Yankees, the tenement rooms
> without windows, like fish cans,
> the penny pinching and fear of the bosses
> would end this way, as well-dressed citizens
> devoted to the disinfection of our carpets,
> as the culminating dream of Grandpa
> (who like to spit on floors while he talked)?

Through poems such as this, Papaleo challenges the Italian/American people to consider what they've given up in exchange for a piece of American success.

*February 1989*

## 2

## An Interview with Joseph Papaleo

Note: This interview was due to go to press during a time when an editorial and stylistic transition occurred with the *Fra Noi*. It was never published as it should have been.

*J*oseph Papaleo, chairman of the writing program at Sarah Lawrence College has held guest professorships in Italy. He studied at Sarah Lawrence College (B.A.), the University of Florence, Italy (Diploma), and Columbia University (M.A.). He is the author of two novels, *All the Comforts* and *Out of Place*; a book of poems, *Picasso at Ninety-One*; and numerous short stories appearing in, among others, *Attenzione, Dial, Epoch, Harper's, New Yorker,* and *Penthouse.* He has translated Eugenio Montale's poetry and Dario Fo's dramas. Papaleo has received grants from the Guggenheim Foundation and the New York State Creative Arts Public Service Award. He has won the Ramapo Poetry award.

❀

Fred Gardaphé: *What's the story of your family's coming to America?*
Joseph Papaleo: My parents were both immigrants, reluctant immigrants. My father was the son of the judge; they were well off in the land they came from, Calabria, my grandfather had an office in Rome. They had no intention of immigrating until my grandfather dropped dead of a heart attack. His wife was a peasant woman and sent all her kids to work; they didn't want to work so they all borrowed money and took off and ended up in America and South America. My father was a fairly successful clothing designer. My brothers and sisters all dropped out of school and went into

the clothing business. He insisted that one of his sons get a university degree because he wanted him to be a lawyer. My mother was a pianist. Her father was a successful baker in Salerno. She was the hot shot of the family. She graduated from the academy in Naples and was giving concerts. When her father suddenly died, she was sent to America to earn money for the family. She lived with my uncle who was driven out of Italy because he was a radical socialist, He had an appliance store in the Bronx. She worked all the time. One of her first jobs was playing piano in the silent movie theaters. She was a very bitter woman, like a Doestoevskian character; she got married very late, to a widower with five children, she was in her forties. By now the people in Italy had died and she didn't have to support them. She had one kid, me. I started drawing and painting. I think that's where I got the idea of art or the pleasure in art. When I got into school the academics weren't appealing. I earned the Bachelor's and Master's at Columbia, then University of Florence where I got another master's degree. Writers were encouraging to me.

F.G.: *And your education?*

J.P.: I was studying writing and painting at Penn State during the war, then I went to Sarah Lawrence after the war; there Robert Fitzgerald, Steven Spender, poet from Wisconsin, and Horace Gregory, made it legitimate for me to be a good student who could have been much better because I was giving all my time to this queer thing called art. I began teaching at Fieldstone Prep school in New York which was started by a group of wealthy and brilliant New York people looking for an education that combined the classes. The Ethical Culture Society, started by Felix Adler, was a kind of religious place, a universalist religion which attracted very wealthy German and Jewish immigrants who came to this country not as immigrants but to open up a branch of Bausch and Lomb; they sponsored a great deal of progressive education. The entire experience was family like.

F.G.: *And when did your writing start?*

J.P.: Shortly after college I started publishing short stories in major magazines. The *New Yorker* took a story when I was twenty-one or twenty-two. *Commentary* and other New York magazines took stories. I was publishing a lot of stories while I was writing in kind of a derivative kind of voice from James Joyce's *Dubliners*. I lucked out because I was writing about a theme that was not known, Italian Americans. I started to imitate that. I think that when you're successful as a young writer, you start to imitate yourself, you say well if that's what they like it must be good. So I started to imitate myself without having an original voice. I published a whole bunch of stories then a novel, *All the Comforts* about Italian American and Jews and materialism — getting rich fast. The people who were the richest, because they were ahead on the immigration ladder, were the Jews, and into their lives comes an Italian/American young man who wants to be a singer, someone who has the toughness of one who hasn't made it. And the book is a contrast of the toughness that goes before you've made it and the softness that comes after. It sold well, maybe because it was about something that people, especially people in the city, could relate to. It came out the same year as Puzo's *The Godfather*. My agent was the agent for *The Godfather*, Jim Street; he told me about Mario Puzo, whom I had heard about from my boss at Fieldstone who also taught a course at New School for Social Research, a writing class in which John Kerouac and Mario Puzo studied. Burt Lenrow says 'you got to meet this guy, he's got diabetes, works on Wall Street.' Then I met Street who told me he was selling this very interesting story. He characterized Puzo as a gambler, who loved to play the horses. He also said that Puzo was so hurt that *A Fortunate Pilgrim,* an earlier novel he wrote, had been taken very seriously, but did not receive any recognition. I received a copy from Harvey Swados the guy who hired me here. He gave it a good review, but back then Italian/American literature didn't mean anything. My second novel, *Out of Place,* was published in 1971 to meager reviews.

F.G.: *What does Italian/American literature mean to you?*

J.P.: Italian/American literature? Well, I have to start by talking about the Jewish American writers. There's Bernard Malamud, Philip Roth, both good writers writing about Jewish themes. There are others as well many of whom I've read. In the 1950s there was a flowering of Jewish writing that was simply terrific. When friends of mine started going into publishing as editors, there were publishers and readers who supported it. American/Jewish organizations were publishing it, like the American Jewish Committee; there were magazines filled with stories about Jewish themes, but there was not even the slightest equivalent in the Italian/American community. There wasn't event a knowledge of other writers. I read di Donato as a young high school student. I like Fante more. We do have a tradition in writing, but no one has delineated it yet, no one else can see it. We get encouragement from Jewish writers. As we look into the identity of Italian Americans as they become assimilated, it becomes more confusing and more difficult to find, at a time when Italian/American identity was really diffusing because it was ignored. My latest writing is an attempt to see whether an Italian identity could be revived. I've been doing short stories, poetry, and a novel, *A Nice*

*Boy,* is unpublished and based on a close friend of mine who is a provincial Italian American, urban, radicalized in 1960s at the University of Illinois. He was arrested at peace demonstration. It follows a traditional Italian into radicalism; his parents reject him, yet they're fiercely loyal Americans with an Italian/American affection.

F.G.: *What was it like being the only Italian American at Sarah Lawrence?*

J.P.: It was great. I was being identified with Rome, glorious art, and all that. When I first came here the place was almost totally WASP; it was so detached from what went on in the streets that they didn't know what Italian American meant. My WASP girlfriend thought I was great. I married one. I like the way they had been around for so long that the cultural element of life was a large part of their time, whereas the people I grew up with were so concerned with survival. But that's changing.

F.G.: *Do you think there's a future for the Italian/American story?*

J.P.: I have argued with editors and publishers telling them that there is an audience now that will buy. As soon as one book hits, we'll all follow. Our writers are getting better. I used the same idea years ago, I had read Joyce, Proust, Stendahl, before I sat down to write, then I found D'Agostino, he was terrific and he didn't read anybody. I recognize that it was another stage. We have even more of the richness to work from, we have two more generations of Italian/American life. We see the past, we know present, and our literature is the key to our continued identification with our heritage. I always wondered why relatively bright Italian Americans I grew up with never read any books. The only thing that ever seemed to make sense as an explanation why these people were not culturally dead was a little notice in something called *Civilization and Renaissance in Italy;* he follows the development of the arts in the Renaissance, when he gets to writing, he shows that the development of the novel never took place, Italians never had a basis for this kind of reading, unlike what happened in Russia, a friend of mind had to have his shoes fixed and realized that reading books was everybody's work. That didn't happen in any Italian family that I ever knew.

F.G.: *Do you see this changing through your students as compared to when you were a student?*

J.P.: Today's students are curious about their past and need to be directed. This country has lost something, I'm sure that the situation we're talking about has lost our novels, Fante always was hurt. But this curiosity began after World War II. The idea of getting back to roots was not in the emotional feeling of people at the time. There was a great feeling in this country that Europe had become a little foreign at the same time as young Italian Americans were discovering it, they would not have voluntarily gone back. One guy I grew up had seen the area of Italy, Campagna, where his family comes form and he was just ecstatic about the beauty however he also had the pain of knowing that friends of his had died there and he associated them as Americans, he looked at those people as slightly hostile foreigners. There was a wave of college students who wished to become expatriates. After a war, people get so sick of the war and they blame the world around them and I wanted to get away, I call it the "By-the-time-I-get-to-Phoenix" syndrome. I went off with a group of people who were looking for the expatriate experience. My family liked it but they didn't make any big thing of it. My mother said she would never go back, her heart had been broken by Italy; not having sufficient social security for my mother's family. This experience was one of exploration of people in intellectual circles; these were people who came back to the U.S. got jobs in colleges, and established the junior year abroad programs.

I lived in Florence for three years with my mother's brother, a customs inspector. I taught American Literature at the University of Naples in 1971 for one year. Since then I've been back a couple of times, mostly on the Amalfi Coast.

But there's a glimmer of hope in my two boys, Joe, who is a chef in an Italian restaurant and William who studied and taught in Italy. William is a painter; he recently sold out a show in Provincetown. He travels to Italy and stays with a cousin.

F.G.: *How do you see Italian/American themes coming through literature?*

J.P.: One day the thought came to me that many people in the suburbs were Italian Americans in position of power who felt totally assimilated. Occasionally I'd meet these people, and if the occasion got to it, there'd be some mention, some code-word of a past, an ethnic past that they all had fresh and clean in them, but buried somewhere so they'd say a few words about things they knew, more than just the first exchange of communication which is gastronomy, the sharing of food knowledge. It's more than that, I don't know where it comes from, but it's cultural.

When you write fiction you don't know quite why you're doing it, you get a glimpse of the meaning as you go on. There's the recalling of a past, but it has no meaning except to suggest that the dream world is the entrance to the repository of all those other things. I'm tired of the irrational way of seeing things. That's why my novel, *A Nice Boy,* maintains a traditional style.

Look we're not boys anymore the use of boy is defined through that. All of these things that echo and drive the character crazy when he wants to do a little bit of radical thinking and action at a time when it's desperately necessary in the country, conscience — sense of moral what is right and wrong behavior, muddled in WASPish literature. What my parents taught me was an ancient morality, which certainly in the U.S. is a grave sin. They said if you have a choice of making a lot of money by being cruel and nasty to another human being, don't make the money, because people come first; the moral value is be kind to your fellow human beings. Life deals us cancer, heart attacks, diseases, don't you add to any one's travails cause they're going to get enough. Another novel I wrote quickly is about an Italian American who runs for governor in New York, before Cuomo. This guy's in the bag to be elected, but gets tied to mafia in the press and never makes it. We need to move out from the shadow of time, and people your age continuing to write, destroying the old stereotype by new truth. But what we're dealing with is the prevalence and the power of the old stereotypes. People come first, don't add to anybody's pain, which is really Anti American the only immortality you will ever know.

F.G.: *How can we renew a sense of Italianness?*

J.P.: We can get it from Italy. I translated Dario Fo for Estelle Parsons and the New York Public Theater. When they go to Italy they do wonderful things, because they bring completely fresh new eyes and a kind of affection, understanding and empathy which is very Italian, it's a wonderful combination. The people who should do the talking are the young Italian Americans, because they are the only ones who can tell the Americans and the Italians where we are now, simply by talking about your consciousness which is something that we simply didn't have. I didn't know this persona existed in me and if it did I didn't know what it was and this discovery is something really. I'm not making it up, exaggerating or romanticizing it and that what has to be heard now, young scholars like you need it. I only need a little shack to finish my last novel. It would be very interesting to see just what the few Italian/American writers in the 1950s and 1960s who were struggling away were doing. We need to know what they were doing. The best way to renew a sense of Italianess is to create histories of what it was so that people can compare what they have to what's been lost.

*February 1989*

# Mining the Past

## Jay Parini

### 1

*The Patch Boys*, Jay Parini's most recent novel, has received the critical attention of the *New York Times* and many other national publications.

Set in the anthracite mining area of Pennsylvania during the summer of 1925, the novel is narrated by Sammy di Cantini who tells his coming-of-age story. Sammy is a bookish boy whose father died in a coal mining accident leaving behind his wife (who has taken to running a weekend speakeasy in the basement) and a family of three boys and a girl. The oldest brother, Vincenzo, carries on the father's work, but also steps in as a union organizer. Another older brother has taken off to New York to make a name for himself as a small-time hoodlum. Sammy's sister, Lucy, runs off with a neighboring Sicilian boy who can flash cash and fancy cars. A younger brother, Gino, is entering pubescence with an appetite for whatever he can stuff into his face.

Di Cantini is a narrator that reminds us of John Fante's Arturo Bandini. This self-mocking, self-doubting boy struggles to come to terms with his relationships to his family, friends and society. The ironic tone of the writing rings once again of Fante's style. However, here is where the similarities with Fante end and the reminders of another classic Italian/American author begin. The political consciousness of the narrator reminds us of Pietro di Donato's character, Paul, of *Christ in Concrete*. The mine setting becomes for *Patch Boys* what the construction sight was in di Donato's novel: the background for the conflict of capitalistic greed vs. family need. Slowly di Cantini's family falls victim to the corporate world. And as with di Donato's Paul, we are left with the belief that Sammy's sensitivity and great awareness will enable him to transcend life in the Patch and make something of himself.

Parini is above all a poet and this novel is filled with all the poetry that prose can take without giving in to verse. Parini's eye is tuned to the detail that gives us the telling image without hyper-description and it comes to us in a narrative that is lyrically sound and rhythmically alive as evidenced in the passage where he describes his train ride into New York City.

> The subway came rattling through the dark, stopped, and I got on facing backward. Across from me, on the yellow wicker seat, a beautiful lady faced me with her ankles crossed and her broad hat tipped sideways. She had a ruby mouth that puckered up. In the next seat, a tall man twirled a toothpick in his teeth, his hat pulled forward over his brow. I noticed his fancy leather brogues and the overstuffed briefcase beside him. I cleared my throat loud to attract their attention, then tipped my Panama to each in turn. They did not respond so I felt relieved when we arrived at Fourth Street, my stop.

## Fact and Fiction

Though the novel presents a feeling for the autobiographical, Parini insists that it is a work of fiction. "Fiction," he says, "is a translation, a transmutation, from reality. It is not a mirror held up to life."

Although Parini draws his characters from his life, he adds qualities and dimensions to them that he can't be sure are actual. "To create this novel, I've had to imagine everything. It's based on what I knew from the 1950s and 1960s, so it's kind of an imaginative working backward to try and reconstruct my family's past. There was a lot I got from talking to my family and reading newspapers and local journals from the time period. I was working from a day by day account by local reporters. I spent months doing research before I began to write. I think if you're going to create historical fiction you have to be accurate."

Parini's father comes from a large Italian Catholic family and worked as an insurance salesman before converting to Protestantism. He became so engrossed in his conversion that he was ordained a Baptist minister. Parini's mother is of British descent. Her family settled in America in the early 1700s. "My father having married a non-Italian, a Protestant, and having turned Protestant himself was something of a 'black sheep' in his family. My father's mother has always been a profound influence on me. She is the woman described in the novel [Mrs. di Cantini]. She was from Savona, just north of Genoa. She spoke and read newspapers in Italian and she lived until only a couple of years ago." Parini's grandfather, Octavio, emigrated from Rome and had been a miner. One of Jay's uncles, Gene Parini, was killed in a 1966 mining accident on Jay's high school graduation day.

The first of his family to be formally educated, Parini graduated in 1970 from Lafayette College, in Pennsylvania and spent his junior year abroad at the University of St. Andrews in Scotland, where he later returned to earn a Ph.D. in English Literature. "It was the 1960s. I was fed up with being in America and I wanted to get out of the country. Because I was a student of English literature I was naturally drawn to the British Isles," he says. He remained in Scotland for seven years. "I used Scotland as a base for traveling frequently to France and Italy and everywhere else. I visited the region where my grandparents came from, but never made contact with any relatives because my grandmother had cut herself off completely from her relatives. I'm really an example of an Italian who has been cut off from my roots. There hasn't been much in the way of contact.

"I think of *The Patch Boys* as an act of recovery for me. I'm recovering my ethnic background. Nobody meeting me would ever remotely think of me as an Italo-American because I have a British Ph. D. and I've taught in Ivy League schools. So many times people have told me that they haven't even noticed that my name was Italian. It's not that I hide it; I'm proud of it. It's more a question of people not identifying me as an Italian American."

Parini admits to speaking broken Italian. The Italian in the novel comes from remembering his grandmother's speech, from his academic education in the language and from his frequent trips to Italy. "My Italian is academically right and not the Italian that say my grandmother would speak."

# A Poet First

Parini's first publication *Singing in Time* was a book of poetry published in 1974 by J.W.B. Laing, a local Scottish bookseller. Parini refers to it as, "an apprentice book of poems."

"They're very simple, sensuous and image centered, very much like my current poetry. I haven't changed that much. They're very imitative and in each poem you can see that I was writing after either a Frost, a Wordsworth or a Yeats poem. I was twenty-four years old and learning my craft. I was heavily under the influence of Alastair Reid, a local Scottish poet of great note, who was for a long time a contributor to the *New Yorker* and a writer who has continually affected me."

In 1975 Parini took a position at Dartmouth College in New Hampshire and published a critical study based on his Ph.D. dissertation: *Theodore Roethke: An American Romantic*. *Modern Language Studies* has referred to this book as: "The standard work on Roethke, and a major contribution to modern poetry studies." Five years later Parini's first novel, *The Love Run,* was published.

"I found myself writing longer and longer poems," he says. "There was this urge to tell stories, to make a narrative. I've never really liked long poems, so I thought I'd try my hand at writing fiction. *The Love Run* is essentially the Greek myth of Daphne and Apollo retold in modern dress."

This novel is currently being made into a film by Alan Ladd Company for which Parini contributed the screenplay.

# New Family

In 1981, Parini married Devon Jersild, a writer and a feminist. They have two boys: Will, age four and Oliver, age one. Devon is a writer who has published many book reviews, essays and poems. She is currently working on a novel. The two of them have balanced the work of raising their children and writing so well that they decided to share their strategies with the public by creating a book entitled *Shared Parenting,* a "how-to" book which will be a mix of personal testimony and research based on their interviews of 100 couples on the subject of joint responsibility. They expect this book to be published sometime in the next year. In 1982 Parini moved on to Middlebury College (home of the famed Breadloaf Writer's Conference) where he is currently Director of the Creative Writing Program and a writer-in-residence.

Parini's about as versatile as a writer can be. From screenplays to book reviews, fiction, poetry, journalism, academic, and popular criticism and textbooks (Prentice Hall has recently published his textbook on poetry), he has found an audience in every market he's tried. His most recent book of poetry, *Anthracite Country* sold 5000 copies, a best seller as far as books of poetry go. It is currently out of print, but Parini looks forward to a resurrection in a few years by Holt.

"I've tried to vary my writing. I'm against this compartmentalization that artists are placed in," says Parini. He has had his hand in a variety of literary fields. He is a frequent contributor to magazines such as the *Hudson Review* and has published poems in the *New Yorker* and *Atlantic.* He is also a reviewer for *U.S.A. Today* and has published in many national periodicals. This coming September, the publication of his third book of poetry, *Town Life,* which includes many poems set in Amalfi, Italy, where he and his family have spent time. He looks forward to someday living on his own patch of land in Italy.

## 2

*O*nce upon a time, back in 1892 when Italians from the south of Italy were coming to America in increasing numbers, Christopher Columbus, was the symbol which united diverse ethnic groups. In *America Discovers Columbus,* Claudia Bushman tells of New York City's mammoth five-day celebration honoring the four-hundredth anniversary of Columbus' voyage which featured a parade in which ethnic organizations were able to combine their ethnic and American identities under the banner of Columbus, the first immigrant.

A year later, Chicago followed suit with the World Columbian Exposition designed to showcase American progress in the arts and sciences.

Columbus' service as an American symbol has always been a constant and only recently challenged. As the heroic explorer involved in the founding myth of America, he became one of the few, if not the only, acceptable model for Italian Americans. To Italian immigrants, like the writer Constantine Panunzio, *Columbo* served as one of the few models for their own American experience. No wonder then that Italians would come to identify with the one Italian this country paid public homage to. In the 1960s, while Italian Americans were beginning to organize public presentations of their political agenda, Columbus Day, under the guidance of Illinois Congressman Frank Annunzio, became a national holiday and the one day of the year Italian Americans could publicly represent their pride in their heritage.

During the next thirty years the dominant American culture began listening to the minority groups whose voices had been socially and politically suppressed. Speaking turned to action and listening turned to inclusion. As the face of America changed, so did the interpretation of its traditional symbols. Flags were burned, the Statue of Liberty tarnished, Ellis Island deteriorated and the skeletons in Columbus' closet were exposed. Now, in 1992, the attempts to redefine Columbus as man, as myth, have surfaced in a record number of films and books.

The problem with Columbus today is whose story are we to believe when all the stories are potentially believable.

Author Jay Parini, who has been accused of following the flood of Columbus bashers, attempts to have his say about Columbus in his latest novel. *Bay of Arrows* takes its title from the location in the Dominican Republic where Columbus met his first resistance through the Taino Indians. In this novel, and out of history, the *Bay* becomes a metaphor for the self-discovery of Christopher "call me Geno" Genovese, a middle-aged English professor/poet who leaves the academic grove of a New England college for the "new world" of a tropical paradise. The move is the result of Geno's being awarded a tax-free grant for over half a million dollars by a foundation designed to foster the creativity of geniuses.

Parini sets Geno up as Columbus' 20th century reincarnation. He's got Columbus' red hair, his lust, and his fever for the gold that can be gained through the purchase of penny stocks in Latin American goldmines. But Geno is a family man whose goal is to break away from his job to write poetry and to move his kids to a world without television.

> If they could only live somewhere — on some planet in outer space, if necessary — where TV was still not known. It sickened him to see James or Milo sitting there with the switcher in hand, channel surfing (though he neglected to remember that they'd dumped them in front of the yawning screen since they were old enough to sit still unattended).

The novel also takes up a retelling of Columbus' story through alternate chapters. This is an ambitious juxtaposition that while cleverly conceived, is not always successfully executed and at times seems too gimmicky. Nevertheless, the result is a good read, primarily because of Parini's extraordinary talent with prose.

Perhaps what this novel does, and does better than most of the quincentennial products, is remind us that Columbus was a human being, and like most of us he had good sides and bad sides. His bad sides happen to have been extremely bad. But he was an idealist. At least he told himself that he was doing what he did for religious reasons. He wanted to make Spain rich enough to finance another crusade to the Holy Land. The concept of saving Jerusalem from the heathens still obsessed a lot of people at the time.

Like Columbus, Geno is self-absorbed and, given the opportunity, takes what he needs in spite of its effects on others. This is dramatized through his affair with a student and his use of Haitian natives as workers to build his tropical home. Parini adds an appendix to the novel, which dramatizes a trial of Columbus in heaven. This might have better served the novel at its opening, for it sets up the idea that the story of Columbus is replayed every time an idealist attempts to reach a seemingly impossible goal. Found guilty, Columbus is sent back to earth and has 500 years to redeem himself. If nothing more, this novel accurately reflects contemporary thought during a time when truth is relative and history is studied more like fiction.

While Parini's fourth novel is a lesser effort than his two earlier novels, *The Patch Boys* and *The Last Station*, it is certainly worth more than much of what has been produced during this strange year of the quintcentennial, a year which Native/American leader James Yellowbank asks to be the year that Americans discover America — a request that *Bay of Arrows* certainly begins to accommodate.

*April 1987 / December 1992*

# Not Patriarchal Poetry

## Gianna Patriarca

*Italian Women and Other Tragedies,* Gianna Patriarca's first book of poetry, is an exciting and promising debut for this young poet. A native of Ceprano, Frosinone, Italy, Patriarca left Italy in 1960, with her mother and sister, to join her father who had immigrated to Toronto in 1956. She recounts this experience in the poem "Returning," and reminds us that immigration stories form the basis for Italian/North American culture.

The nearly fifty poems collected here serve as poignant meditations on the plight of women in Italian and Italian/Canadian culture. While covering a wide range of subjects, they speak most eloquently and effectively of the dilemma of women caught up in the clash of two opposing worldviews. That Patriarca has written these poems is a testament to her ability to overcome the obstacles of a cultural past in which women were choked silent. But she has not emerged from that struggle free of scars.

Patriarca's lyrical poetry follows the Greek tradition of the tragic lyric in terms of content, but the style is straight talk that sings with beauty and power. There's no evidence of a poem straining to be poetic, as most first collections usually reveal. Patriarca also avoids even the taint of nostalgia that often accompanies early poetic expression.

Even-handed in her portrayals of both victims and villians, she captures a sense of justice through her artistic rendering of experiences. You never get the feeling that you are comfortably excluded from the terror she creates. Through simple diction, she opens the door to all readers to enter into both the horror and the happiness of being a woman of Italian descent.

The title poem, "Italian Women," sets up the tradition from which she has emerged:

> these are the women
> who were born to give birth
> they breathe only
> leftover air
> and speak only
> when deeper voices
> have fallen asleep.

In a world defined by men, the Italian woman has been crowded out of her own identity through the demands placed on her. While the writing of this poem demonstrates that Patriarca has overcome the repression of her kind, it reminds us of the tragic outcome of her ancestral figures who

> wrap their souls
> around their children
> and serve their own hearts
> in a meal they never
> share.

Many of the poems celebrate relationships both good and bad. The first poems concern the troublesome interaction between father and daughter. Through line breaks and discrete twists of the tongue, Patriarca creates an irony that is rare in the realistic world of emerging Italian/North American women's writing. In "My Birth," she begins:

> my father is a great martyr
> he has forgiven me everything
> even my female birth.

This poem criticizes a culture in which a woman is traditionally valued by how well she makes her bed and lies in it. For men who gain their identity by what their women produce, she reminds us that the difference between being born a male or a female can lead a father to

> mourn the loss of his own
> immortality
> when his wife produces a daughter.

In "Daughters," Patriarca sets up a drama in which the unmarried daughter is subject to the perceptions and of her father and becomes a victing of his his verbal abuse and physical attacks:

> my father called me a whore
> and my mother cried
> a young Italian woman's
> claim to prostitution
> is any activity past
> the midnight hour.

While those poems that come from her own lived experience may resonate deeply in the lives of their readers, the ones that surround the theme of immigration are especially strong in their ability to bring us into the lives of those women whose silent suffering gained voices only for the ears of other women. In "Paesaggi" she shows us how different the experience of immigration is for a woman whose sense of time is measured in terms of children and grandchildren.

The Italian versions of the poems "May" and "The Old Man" are superior to their English translations and do not reflect the linguistic artistry of the other poems. Aside from this minor disappointment, Patriarca has succeeded in taking autobiographical experiences and making them speak to and for so many of us.

While most tragedies end in disappointment and death, this collection ends with the triumphant lyric "For Gia at Bedtime" about the poet's daughter who has become

> my prayer
> the greatest poem of my life.

It is certain that many of the tragedies in the poet's life as a woman will not be repeated in the next generation. And this collection, while documenting the tragic past, will help us all to understand those tragedies while we learn to avoid them in the future.

# Legend Fails as Fiction

## Mario Puzo

$\mathscr{I}$miss the power of Puzo. The force he used to forge such fiction as *Dark Arena, The Fortunate Pilgrim, The Godfather,* and yes, *Fools Die,* is missing in his latest work, *The Sicilian.*

In the writing of *The Godfather,* the reader can feel the action, because the writer locks into a character's point of view. Not so with *The Sicilian,* where the establishment of a character's point of view is not depicted fully enough for the reader to enter what John Gardner's called, "the fictional dream."

In spite of this weak writing, there is a story here worth reading. If anything, the novel reads like a folktale. It is skimpy in the detail. It contains interesting, even bizarre characters who are brought to life and then left without much to do on their own; they are more like puppets than people.

Perhaps the folktale feeling of this novel is the result of drawing on the true-life legend of Salvatore Giuliano. Set in a transitional period of Sicilian history, 1943-1950, *The Sicilian* tells the Robin Hood-like story of Giuliano who rises from the peasant class to challenge the powers that be. Giuliano fights both the ancient traditions of the Mafia and the post World War II Italian democratic government.

A good folk tale makes up for its brevity and sketchy vision by being fast paced, oral and amusing. *The Sicilian* is amusing, but its pace is too slow and its language not very natural. Puzo is at his best in the narrative, when he's giving the history of the island of Sicily and its people. One gets the feeling the storyteller knows what he is talking about and would maybe have done better by writing a non-fiction account of the same material.

The trouble comes when the author is developing a scene with setting and dialogue. I get the feeling that the words I am reading have been translated stiffly from Italian, losing image and flow in the process. I get no sense of voice and of the individuality of each character. Men and women, Sicilians and Italians, may think differently, but they don't sound different when Puzo lets us listen to them.

I'm certain that the buyers of *The Sicilian* will carry the book home thinking: "Finally, more Mafia stories from the man who made them worth reading." And they will be right. The tales of trust and treachery are all here, but they are not presented in the manner we have come to expect from Puzo. At the very beginning we are reunited with Michael Corleone and those who might have forgotten what he looked like will have to imagine Al Pacino; those who have never seen the film won't see Michael Corleone at all.

This seems to be a book designed to reach the fifteen million plus who bought *The Godfather*. Why else would the framing device — Michael Corleone's task to bring *The Sicilian*, Turi Giuliano, back to America — be used? The device is not necessary to the story and takes up room that would have been better spent depicting the real Sicilians, whom the novel seems to want to be about.

This sketchy writing reads more like a screenplay. No doubt this novel has strong cinematic potential. But for a novel, it lacks the concentration of the writer's vision and listening. Perhaps it is the result of having an audience made ready by earlier successes, or a result of the screenwriting that Puzo has been doing. Whatever the reason is I have the feeling that the writing will not be the focus of the negative criticism that will come to this work.

Once again Italian Americans will rise up in protest at yet another stereotypical depiction of Italians and Sicilians. Those protests will come from those who confuse fiction and fact. Such critics should turn their attention to other Italian/American writers who are depicting the mafia-free lives of Italian Americans. Puzo's latest work is clearly labeled *novel*. He is telling a story. There are other stories being told (see the work of John Fante, Pietro di Donato and many other Italian/American writers.) It's just that Puzo's gets all the glitter. And in *The Sicilian*, it is the story, and not the writing, that deserves the gold.

*March 1985*

# New Generation, New Definitions

## Diane Raptosh

## 1

$\mathcal{D}$iane Raptosh is a poet and a teacher and one of the many examples of an Italian/American voice that is not identified as distinctly ethnic. One of three children born into a Czech/Italian family, she grew up in Nebraska and Idaho where a strong ethnic identity is hard to come by. Yet, as some of her poetry demonstrates, she has been strongly affected by her Italian background.

"My grandfather left Palermo by himself and looked for work in America. He found a job at the Ford plant and then later returned to Sicily and brought the family back. My mother was three years old when they came to America and whatever memory she has of life there is based on return visits and invention."

Diane's parents met in Detroit, married and headed west. Her father worked in a furniture factory and wanted to start his own company in a non-urban area, so they moved to Nampa, Idaho. "In Idaho we were isolated from my mother's side of the family," she says. "They were always having get-togethers. My mother wanted to get away from all that. That was the old way, the stuff of an older culture. She and my father were moving west and the American mindset changes the further west it goes."

Raptosh would make it a point to visit Detroit as much as she could. "It was always important to do that. Whenever we'd go to Detroit, there was always somebody's birthday and always huge numbers of family members around, which didn't happen in Idaho. This togetherness represented something different to me. It is only now that I can realize the extent to which my mother wanted to sever herself from her ethnicity, and this was conveyed to me obliquely.

"Because my grandparents spoke Italian, my mother felt stigmatized; she was embarrassed when she would have boys over because her parents would be arguing in Italian. She wanted to move away from that. She has become a perfect westerner. She doesn't speak a word of Italian and she does not want to remember. I think that's why it's so important for me to remember."

The two primary tools of any writer are imagination and memory, both of which Raptosh feels are essential to her work. "Nobody seems to want to do the work of remembering anymore because it reminds us we've inherited certain sins and certain blessings. And it's especially the sins that we're most worried about. It seems peculiarly American to sever yourself from everything. You do it by stepping into the new country, then moving from the area, which can become like a mini-version of the old country, then do, as my mother did, move further west."

Raptosh attended the University of Michigan so that she could be closer to her grandparents. Her grandfather died while she was finishing her M.F.A. in poetry. Her grandmother, the subject of "Emanuela in the New World Garden," lives in Detroit.

The poem combines what Raptosh sees as two of her primary interests; the theme of the frontier and the role of women on the frontier. "I'm interested in Italian/American women and trying to position them on the frontier. I think it has to do with the whole movement of my relatives. Both sets of grandparents came to the New Worlds and moved from older neighborhoods to even newer areas, west."

Raptosh feels that the person who might be in the best position to express *Italianità* is one of a second or third generation, a person who is once-removed from the fact of being Italian. This can happen, she says, through the distance of a generation. "Because being Italian hasn't directly affected my life so that I have to keep moving away from it, as my mother did, my tendency is to move toward it because it's mysterious enough and unknown so that it draws me toward it. My mother, now in her fifties, would probably say that her being Italian is more important to her and perhaps in five or ten years it will be even more important."

This distance that Raptosh speaks of creates a perspective that has enabled many of the younger Italian/American writers to reach larger audiences with their stories, something earlier writers had trouble doing. Her work has appeared in the *Michigan Quarterly Review,* the *Kansas Quarterly,* the *MacGuffin,* and the *Blue Ox Review.*

2

*In Just West of Now,* Diane Raptosh gives voice to the experience of the American West. Many of the poems in this, her first collection, reveal the tension between the American and ethnic cultures which have shaped her identity.

Her mother's father left Palermo by himself and looked for work in America. After finding a job at the Ford plant in Michigan, he returned to Sicily and brought the family back. Her parents met in Detroit, married and moved west to Nampa, Idaho where there were no Italian neighborhoods. It didn't take long for Raptosh to realize that there was something different in her childhood home. "I think it was the hot blood which rose up most noticeably in my mother," she says. "She's very affectionate, demonstrative, and outspoken, traits which clashed with those typical of the west which include remaining aloof and silent. Out here it's important to be self-sustaining and to rarely reveal what's going on inside you. If you've ever been to Idaho you know it's very homogenous; there's very little room for anyone to behave differently from the neighbors." When her grandparents would visit from Detroit they'd bring suitcases full of provolone and pastas unavailable in Idaho. Periodically her family would visit Detroit to attend large family celebrations. These ethnic infusions helped sustain Diane's sense of ethnicity which she explores in her poetry.

*Just West of Now* appears just after Raptosh's six year eastern odyssey during which she earned her M.F.A. in poetry at the University of Michigan under the guidance of Alice Fulton. Raptosh then taught a few years at Columbia College in Chicago where she also worked in the Black Music Research Center. Many of the poems in this collection were previously published in major journals and anthologies during these years before her return to the West. Significantly, the book is evenly divided into two sections, "Place Names" and "Blood Ties," each containing fourteen poems. Many of the poems in the first section deal with the effect the west has had on her own life and the lives of others. "Transcriptions, Rancho Paradise Motor Park" characterizes this effect. In this poem Raptosh captures the voices of those who had a place, sold it, then run around in mobile homes so that every place becomes theirs. These voices embody a western dream of moving around until you arrive at where and to whom you are supposed to be, but the irony is that they never arrive there.

"Concetta Addresses the Cardinal" reflects the poems of the second half which reveals Raptosh's interest in her ethnicity. In this poem she imagines her mother's meditation on her Sicilian upbringing:

> I was born Cardinale. Raised as one
> the likes of you when my dad tore off that last
> bird sound from our soft last name like it was
> stale bread.

In "Casting Hand Shadows" Raptosh, in typical Italian fashion, talks with her hands and creates a series of short poetic scenes which calls for audience participation as we're directed to cast images of subjects like "Grandpa":

> Old Italian men are easy. Leave
> a space between middle and ring
> finger of left hand for his
> eye. You can achieve
> ninety-three years of Roman
> nose in the curve
> of an index
> finger joint.
> You enjoy looking up
> at him — more animated
> than he ever was, he looks down, at your life.

Raptosh finds the blood ties to her ancestral culture are stronger through the women in her family who figure in nine of the poems in "Blood Ties."

"I think it is easier for the daughter to look to the grandmother for ways of being and for different kind of eccentricities to adopt," says Raptosh, "because the mother/daughter relationship is riddled with ambiguities which remain unresolved until you grow older and begin a very different type of relationship with your mother."

A few years ago Raptosh returned to the western home of her childhood and is currently Visiting Professor of English at Albertson College of Idaho. As she explains: "I was pulled back by the myth of place, and myths disappoint less often than actualities. I returned without expectations of going back to the past and now plan to stay here and continue teaching and writing."

While the poetry in *Just West of Now* is colored by the longing that comes from being distant from the subject, Raptosh says her newest work treats subjects more squarely, more straight on. She is currently at work on her next book of poetry which she says is written less from memory.

*June 1987 / February 1993*

# Literary Missionary

## Giose Rimanelli

$\mathcal{I}$n 1935, a ten-year-old native of Molise, Italy entered a Catholic seminary in Puglia with the intention of becoming a missionary. Five years later he left. And though he may have lost his reasons for being a missionary of God, Giose Rimanelli has in many ways become a missionary of literature. His first novel, *Trio al piccione* (1950), was a fictionalized autobiographical account of his early years in Molise and his experiences during the Second World War. This novel was translated into English by Ben Johnson as *The Day of the Lion* and published by Random House in 1954. This novel received critical praise and became a best seller in America. Reissued in 1992 in Italy, *Tiro* became an instant bestseller and reignited interest in Rimanelli's life's work.

In the late 1950s, after a few more books, Rimanelli came to America to give a lecture at the Library of Congress after which he was invited to teach and travel throughout the North and South America. He decided to remain in the U.S.A. where he continued to write poetry and fiction, publishing all his work, except for some academic work, in Italian. Rimanelli had keen insights into the plight of the Italian American long before he ever became one. The Italian living in North America served as a regular subject for his writing. In *Una posizione sociale* (1959), he recounts the life of the Italian living in New Orleans in the early 1900s and examines the lynching of thirteen Italians. In 1966 he collected, edited and introduced *Modern Canadian Stories*. *Tragica America* (1968) contains his reflections of his first years in the United States.

Seven years later he gave us a greater insight into the literature of Italy through *Italian Literature: Roots and Branches*. Now a Professor Emeritus of SUNY-Albany, Rimanelli continues writing his fiction in Italian and publishing it primarily in Italy. Early in the 1970s he wrote his first novel in English entitled *Benedetta in Guysterland,* published by Guernica Editions in Canada. The first question that comes to the reader is why this novel was not published until 1993. After all, when it was written, Rimanelli was an internationally acclaimed writer who had published seven very successful books in Italy that had been translated into eight languages. He was already a well-known journalist and cultural critic. Since 1961 he had been a tenured professor in American universities such as Yale, promoted on the merits of his writing, and not by virtue of his academic credentials. So why didn't he publish this novel right after it was written?

The answer to this question lies in the fact that Rimanelli did not write it for publishing; he did not write it for money; he wrote it for love, for love of literature and for his American friends whose responses he has included in the Appendix. *Benedetta*, according to Rimanelli, was simply an experiment in English, his first response to the demands of starting over again, from scratch, as a writer with a new language, a man of the world with a new toy. Yet while the language was new, his knowledge of world literature and his knowledge of America was not.

While the emphasis of most Italian/American fiction has been the Italian/American experience, most authors have been unable to reach a distance from the subject that would enable them to gain the perspectives necessary to renew the story of Italian life in America. What Mario Puzo romanticized in *The Godfather* (1969), what Gay Talese historicized in *Honor Thy Father* (1971), Giose Rimanelli has parodied in *Benedetta*, and through parody he has gone beyond the Italian/American subject by, above all, writing a book about literature.

Benedetta's story incorporates America's obsessive fascination with the Mafia, sex, and violence. *Benedetta* tells the story of America's flirtatious relationship with Italy and debunks the traditional stereotype of the Italian/American gangster, through the love story of Clara "Benedetta Ashfield" and the real-life *mafioso* Joe Adonis. The result is a vital socio-political parody that shows that sex and violence are in fact displacements of each other.

*Benedetta in Guysterland,* written in Albany, New York, in 1970 and published twenty-three years later in Montreal, Canada, the birthplace of the author's mother, is a novel that reaches beyond its own time, regardless of its subject, and gives to Italian/American culture a needed and long awaited presence in American literature.

*June 1993*

# *Romano Cuts a* Bella Figura

## Rose Romano

$\mathcal{R}$ose Romano, a poet, editor, and freelance typesetter, has undertaken a pioneer literary project by launching *La bella figura,* a literary journal devoted entirely to writing by Italian/American women. The first issue, entitled *Omertà,* features poetry, short fiction, and reviews from both well known and first time published writers. Maria Mazziotti Gillan (*Winter Light*) and Rachel Guido deVries (*An Arc of Light*) are perhaps two of the better known writers featured in the debut issue.

Romano started the journal after literary magazines began publishing work in which she was using, what she calls "this ethnically unspecified presumed to be WASP persona." When she started writing about being Italian American all of a sudden nobody wanted to publish her work. "So I decided to start my own magazine. I was sure there must be somebody else in this country with that problem."

As a young child in Brooklyn, Romano says she didn't realize her Sicilian/Neapolitan American family was any different from others. "I thought everybody had spaghetti and meatballs for Sunday dinner," she says. "I had some kind of awareness of my Italian heritage, especially before my grandmother died, but I didn't realize there was anything unique to being Italian. And I think this is the same for most Italian Americans: we feel that we're American and there's nothing special about us, we don't have any real culture."

Romano tells of getting mixed messages about her *Italianità.* "I was told it was good to be Italian and I should be proud of myself, yet there were times when if you did something obviously Italian, like use an Italian word or gesture, it seemed embarrassing, especially if you were outside the house. If I did something bad or stupid my grandmother would warn my

father that if he didn't do something about it, I'd end up American."
Romano joins Italian/American women such as Helen Barolini, who have
taken the wheel when it comes to directing the promotional drive of
Italian/American writers. However, there's a great deal of work that needs
to be done as far as promoting her work.

"Even in the feminist movement, Italian/American women are not
taken seriously," she says. "We're not considered real; we're Europeans, and
Europeans run the world; it seems that no matter where we go we get it for
being something; you're never the right thing." Her editorial board, which
she calls *Comari*, includes Lucia Chiavola Birnbaum, Elaine Nole, Camille
Paglia, and Flavia Rando. The audience for *La bella figura,* according to
Romano, is "anybody and everybody who is interested, though she says
they largest segment is the "third generation, those in their thirties."

"Now it's like we're American enough that we can afford to be Italian.
We're not foreigners anymore." Romano gets defensive when presented
with the prevailing notion that Italian Americans don't read? "I wouldn't be
surprised percentage wise if Italian Americans don't make up a large reading public, but then again, the little bit that is written about us is usually
written by someone else and it makes no sense to us . . . That's where I got
a poem, 'Sicilian Ways.' I kept reading the white, male historians who were
describing Italian/American women as wimps who keep their mouths shut,
listen to men and do what they're told; all that had nothing to do with what
I grew up with, so why read that stuff."

Romano prints 300 copies of *La bella figura* and sends it out to over
100 subscribers. She does all the soliciting, editing, typesetting and promotion herself. The fall issue, entitled *La Famiglia* has recently been published.
Future issues planned include: winter, open theme: deadline October 1;
spring, immigrants: deadline January 1; summer; the second generation:
deadline April 1; fall, 1989, the third generation: deadline July 1; and
winter, 1989, open theme: deadline October 1, 1989.

Response to the new journal has been good. "People are excited," says
Romano. "I'm pleased and disappointed. Most of the subscribers are Ital-
ian/American women. I wish someone else would be interested in it."
Romano would like someday to go to Naples. After seeing it on television
via the Pavrotti special, she recalls that the street scenes and everything
looked familiar: "The people, the way they moved, the gestures and everything; it was all something I could relate to. I feel I would know the
language and am convinced that somewhere in my brain I can speak Nea-

politan. I just want to go there for six months and get it back. I'd like to go to a place where everybody's Italian."

Romano came to writing by reading. Her mother, who died when Romano was young, taught her how to write her name when she was five and Romano calls that experience, "one of the most exciting things in my life. I started writing novels when I was eight and poetry at fourteen; writing is something I've always done." Romano represents the avant-garde of an Italian/American cultural consciousness that is ready to explode. The heroes of our parents' generation were the Italian Americans who made it into popular culture, those who were able to capture the attention of all Americans; who will be the heroes for the college educated generation? Will they will be the high culture figures? We are just beginning to have those examples in our libraries, schools, and educational institutions. Rose raises the challenge with a line from one of her poems, "Today Italians await and their children don't even know who they are."

*October 1988*

# Holidays on Paper

## Lisa Ruffolo

> *This is the paradox: Italian/American women are
> the core of their families and they are the ones
> who have most subordinated themselves to the
> well-being of the total entity. Family above self.
> But, being at the heart of things, it is they who,
> breaking the silence imposed on them by family
> loyalty, are best suited to make literary use of the
> material implicit in family struggles. What pro-
> vides the thematic material is, ironically, the
> greatest obstacle to the writing. For that old sanc-
> tion of omertà both defies creativity and insti-
> gates it.*
>
> Helen Barolini,
> from Introduction to *The Dream Book*

$\mathcal{L}$isa Ruffolo is a young American author of Italian descent, who with her
first book has captured both prizes and critical acclaim. Ruffolo is one of
the strong voices who refuse to submit themselves to the stereotype of the
silent but nurturing Italian/American women.

Raised in Glendale, Wisconsin, just north of Milwaukee, her talents
for story telling surfaced early in life when in 4th grade she won a "Biggest
Liar's" contest. Ruffolo graduated from high school in 1974. She began
school at the small Cardinal Stritch College in her neighborhood. A year
later she went on to study English and Creative Writing at the University of
Wisconsin in Madison. Under Kelly Cherry, she began developing her
fiction.

After earning her Bachelor's degree from Madison, Ruffolo went off
to Europe. The first of her family to return to the Italian homeland of her

grandparents, Lisa recalls feeling a strong connection to Italy. "My parents are second-generation Italian Americans and though they didn't hide their background, they never did much to promote it," she says. Her father's side hails from Calabria and her mother's from Lucca. Her parents' families settled in Kenosha, Wisconsin, near the American Motors plant. Her father taught music in Whitefish Bay until his recent retirement and her mother ran her own business out of their home. Lisa is the second born in a family of five which includes two brothers and two sisters.

Upon her return from Europe, Lisa applied and was accepted to several Master's of Fine Arts programs in Creative Writing. She chose to pursue her M.F.A. at Johns Hopkins University in order to work with the acclaimed novelist and story writer John Barth. Under Barth's direction, Ruffolo completed a collection of stories, two of which ("Candy" and "Commercials") are contained in her first book.

"Although these two stories don't fit exactly into the theme that most of the stories in *Holidays* revolve around, my publisher, C.W. Truesdale, encouraged me to include them," says Ruffolo.

*Holidays*, Ruffolo's first book, is a collection of short stories written around the theme of family stresses and strains which more often than not surface during holidays. John Barth has high praise for this collection in his comment for the book's jacket which reads: "Here is a new writer well worth reading. Ruffolo's stories are poignant, well finished American realism. More than one in this collection — 'Commercials,' for example, and 'Candy' — deserve to be anthologized."

Upon completion of her M.F.A., Ruffolo taught English in private secondary schools in Vermont and Michigan, experiences which she drew on for stories included in *Holidays*. In an earlier form, *Holidays* was submitted for the 1985 Minnesota Voices Project Literary awards. "Though I wasn't a prize winner that year," says Ruffolo, "Bill Truesdale returned the manuscript to me with much encouragement to rewrite and resubmit for 1986." After some hard work, Ruffolo captured the 1986 prize which included publication and distribution. Jeanne McCulloch, a reviewer for the *New York Times*, referred to *Holidays* as a "notable debut." The title story was awarded first place in the UNICO national literary contest. That was not the first time that this young writer was honored by UNICO. In 1974 she was awarded a college scholarship by UNICO International.

Currently Ruffolo is a principal in The Software Resource, a firm specializing in writing computer user manuals. She is co-founder of this firm that evolved from doing freelance work in the area. Ruffolo also teaches creative writing at Edgewood College in Madison and last year taught in the University of Wisconsin's fiction program.

*October 1987*

# Bye Bye America. Hello Sicily

## Nat Scammacca

*N*at Scammacca was born in Brooklyn in 1924. He received his B.A. in literature and philosophy from Long Island University and his M.A. in education from New York University. During World War II he and his twin brother Saverio were commissioned officers in the U.S. Army Air Force, serving as pilots over the Himalayas in the India-Burma-China theater. Their many drop missions of vital supplies, troops and intelligence personnel earned them a number of medals, including the Distinguished Flying Cross and the Bronze Star.

Following the war, Nat traveled to Europe with brief residencies in Paris and Barcelona and eventually decided to seek out his origins in Italy; there he studied at the University of Perugia and was graduated. Afterwards he visited New York for a brief period, earning his living as a social worker for the Italian Board of Guardians. He then returned to Sicily to stay. His maternal grandparents left Western Sicily because of the Mafia.

"Grandmother, Giuseppina Lampasona, escaped from an old, ugly mafia boss in Santa Ninfa, who wanted her, notwithstanding the fact that she found him dangerous," says Scammacca. His grandfather, Saverio Catalano, a blacksmith, left the mountain of Eryn, sacred to Aphrodite, to escape the local mafia in Marsala, where he had set up his shop. In Brooklyn, New York, Nat's grandfather Saverio worked his whole life as a blacksmith for the same firm. Scammacca tells that his grandfather was very strong and once beat up a big German worker with one hand tied behind his back, winning a keg of beer that he shared with his fellow workers. Saverio worked on the George Washington Statue in Washington and was trapped overnight inside the horse because the others had forgotten he was working inside. President Wilson complimented him for his dedication.

Scammacca attributes his own interest in story telling to his grandfather's stories. "Grandpa Saverio would always tell us stories about Sicily, describing the orange groves and blossoms and would take us children to listen to 'Piccolo Pete,' who would play Sicilian songs on his *friscalettu*, and then stop and tell us wonderful myths about Sicily and its people. The strongest man in Brooklyn was a Sicilian giant who once picked up the end of a trolley, placing it back onto the trolley tracks. This story we liked best of all." As a child, Nat's father returned to Sicily several times with his mother and sisters. He became a barber like his father, Ignazio Scammacca, while studying law at night at Northeastern University in Boston.

"Because my mother wanted to return to live with her family in Brooklyn, my father, already a practicing lawyer in Massachusetts, had to return to law school in New York, and supported his family by barbering, an occupation he detested. Finally he set up a new law practice in Ridgewook, Brooklyn." His parents spoke Sicilian in whispers, he says, so that their children would not learn the idiom. When he later decided to remain in Italy, Scammacca had to study Italian at the Universita per Stranieri in Perugia. "Our American school teachers did everything to make us ashamed of our Sicilian heritage, so there was an enormous void of any cultural background. We were taught to aspire only to an English heritage and not the rich Sicilian culture."

## Leaving America

"It took me two decades to give up America and two families. The remorse is still great; tears come to my eyes for what I have had to give up. I supply myself with ideological excuses for my choices and destiny. Like Odysseus, I had to return to Sicily if life had any meaning at all. My father was very disappointed. He died at forty-seven years of age, without seeing his grandchildren Arleen and Glen. Scammacca says he had practically no encouragement in pursuing an academic/ artistic career.

"I had to express myself, especially in poetry or the bubble would burst, a very interesting life and imagination did the rest. Being an extremist, sacrificing two families and a whole country to literature, placing myself in awkward situations produced the content for my poetry and prose."

# *Antigruppo*

Deeply affected by the disparities of life in the land of his forefathers, Nat with other Sicilian poets, conceived of the *Antigruppo*, a group against groups, against the fascisti, the mafia, the privileged establishment which in his view collaborated to suppress the common man and his essential creative force. The 1960s and 1970s became explosive decades in Italian literature and resulted in the development of the formalistic avant-garde in Sicily with the *scuola di Palermo* (Gruppo 63) which proposed linguistic transgressions of the most radical, neo-experimentalism imaginable. The Antigruppo, the new ideological avant-garde, emerged like a tidal wave and struck at all the traditional institutions, including literature and in particular, poetry.

The intellectual, bombarded by the new poetics and activities of the Antigruppo, was forced to examine his role as poet and writer in the society of today and tomorrow. "The concept of Antigruppo (that which is against self contained, closed and isolated group structures and relationships) was at first polemically proposed to mean: 'The need to transgress every monopoly of cultural poor in the name of liberty (art and poetry) which can only be guaranteed through the cultural freedom and participation and direct democracy ideally expressed in the small city state, especially the ones that originally existed in Sicily and southern Italy.' "

The Sicilian Antigruppo, conscientiously embraced this concept, adapting it to the historical reality of the island by making it the subject and means of a particular transgression that is directed toward calling up the most vital forces of artistic creativity in Sicily and at the same time, awakening those dormant, yet politically vital forces, getting workers and farmers to recite their own poetry in public squares at the end of Antigruppo poetry readings, to cooperate in common democratic battles until the antiquated structures of the Sicilian establishment crumble on all ethical, political, and cultural levels.

The battle, conducted above all at the grassroots levels of an underground nature, uses pamphlets, mural poetry, poetical manifestos, recitals in working places, meetings in *la casa del popolo*, recreational centers for the common people, and the assembly halls of ARCI, finds its total expression in the *summa* testimonial of the two anthologies of poetry: *Antigrupppo 73* compiled by Sicily's greatest poet from Mount Etna, Santo Calì, and *Antigruppo 75* and "A Possible Poetics for an Antigruppo" compiled by Nat

Scammacca. The Antigruppo represents a new Sicily, not of the Mafia, the land owners, and their ally, the Church — but that of common workers, farmers and students which insists on the complete participation of every-one in the artistic activities of society instead of a passive submission to the large newspaper, magazine, radio and television media.

"The Antigruppo encourages out-of-the-way places to reach out and come into contact with other local and artistic peripheries in the world, so as to force the monopolizing cultural centers to relinquish to the rim areas a part of the great means of expression. Let the wheel turn, but let us remember the rim is as important as the hub. It is the work that must continue. In fact, after my deal, years will pass and I will be forgotten, but poetry will survive and be remembered. To the devil with the universal and the impersonal. It is our fallibility, our imperfections that perhaps for this reason create one poetry."

## *Trapani Nuova*

Now as editor of the voice of the Antigruppo, the *Terza pagina*, of the regional weekly *Trapani Nuova*, Scammacca is the acknowledged leader of the movement and has been responsible for generating a remarkable series of populist poetry events and publishing milestones, expressions of the literary artistic magnificence that survives and is nurtured in Sicily. "Our movement is chronicled in the weekly, *Trapani Nuova*," says Scammacca, "and through the books we publish through the Cooperativa Editrice Anti-gruppo. This is the way we strengthen the recollection of our forgotten past heritage: both in America and Southern Italy. Southern Italo-Americans are proud to learn who they are and to identify with Mediterranean culture. By maintaining cultural ties, we can give the lost cultural past and identity back to southern Italo Americans This goes toward making our people happy — they want to hear about their ancient forefathers and not just about the recent ones who only ate garlic submissively. They are proud to learn how great southern Italians once were; they do not always want to hear the stories, the history and the glory of other peoples. The southern Italo American glorifies in his own past myths and legends and that these are proving to be historical through recent archeological finds of the more attentive and scholarly research of names, proto history and the memory of peoples in the Mediterranean."

Scammacca now lives in Trapani with his wife and their two children and grandchildren. He is Professor Emeritus at the British College in Palermo and devotes his time completely to the publishing efforts of the Antigruppo. The author of hundreds of poems, stories and articles, his most recent work can be found in a collection of short stories *Bye Bye America: Memories of a Sicilian American* and a novel entitled *Due Mondi.*

*January 1988*

# The Gift of One's Self

## Gaetano Talese

*F*or nearly thirty years the writing of Gay Talese has been a mirror of American life. Whether the subject was *The New York Times* in *The Kingdom and the Power*, the mafia in *Honor Thy Father*, or sexuality and the First Amendment in *Thy Neighbor's Wife*, Gay Talese's best-selling books have reflected American experiences. Up until now, those experiences were not his own.

In *Unto the Sons*, his latest book, Talese has turned the mirror onto himself. In the process, he also captures images of the forces of history that have shaped modern Italy and America and those who have contributed the making of a man named Gay Talese. *Unto the Sons* represents the biggest risk Talese has taken yet in career as one of America's most successful and innovative writers. That risk, however, has led him to his greatest subject yet: the Italian/American experience.

Talese is certainly not the first to write about Italian America. His predecessors, such as Jerre Mangione, Helen Barolini, Angelo Pellegrini, and Dorothy Bryant, have established a formidable Italian/American presence in American culture. However, with *Unto the Sons*, Talese has reached audiences who have been virtually untouched by these authors. Talese's success is due in part to the advantages of name recognition for having creating best sellers in the past, and to an unprecedented nation-wide marketing campaign, for a non-mafia related book. This campaign brought Talese around the country and into the homes of millions of Americans through media interviews.

But there's more to this book than Talese's name and a publisher's heavy investment in promotion. In many ways, Talese has spent an entire life preparing for this book. And its success is a result of applying the skills he honed on his earlier works to a most personal subject. What's remarkable about Talese's presentation of the Italian/American experience is the skillful and imaginative way he uses his own life as a stepping stone into a past that has shaped two nations.

Ten years of research and writing have enabled him to weave the fabric of his book with threads of oral tradition as recalled personally and through interviews, history, myth, and autobiography. The result is a style that breaks down the wall between fiction and non-fiction. His retelling of ancient myths, of St. Paola di Francesco's miracles, and accounts of the evil eye, are combined with excerpts taken right out of his Uncle Antonio Cristiani's diary, interviews of living relatives and research from a number of written sources.

What Talese didn't experience himself, he reconstructs using the techniques of fiction writing so that what we have in this book is fictional autobiography. This is a far more challenging project than the usual autobiographical fiction that has been the staple fare offered by Italian/American writers.

"The ambitions for this book," says Talese, "were to write as imaginatively as I would if I were writing a novel, but not write a novel, to write personally, but not necessarily write a traditional autobiography. I wanted to do something different, something that was a blend of history, a history that I thought had to and should be written because I didn't read it all in one book of the American Italian experience." In doing this, Talese has produced a book that Italian Americans, whether they know it or not, have been waiting for.

Talese shows us that the best way to take control of our own image is to know our past, to interpret it and to write about it. He says that the lesson of this book is that it is important to know our history. Only in this way can we challenge and replace the shallow caricatures that others have created out of our cultural materials. *Unto the Sons* is a well-crafted chronicle of a man making sense of his past. In the process of learning this past, he rediscovers the "old country" of our parents' and grandparents' and reclaims an identity with Italian culture.

The early chapters focus on Talese's youth, as an "olive skinned" kid in a "freckled-face" Ocean City, New Jersey during World War II. This section introduces the conflict that second-generation Italian Americans know all too well: "There were many times when I wished that I had been born into a different family, a plain and simple family of impeccable American credentials — a no-secrets, nonwhispering, no-enemy-soldiers family that never received mail from POW camps, or prayed to a painting of an ugly monk, or ate Italian bread with pungent cheese."

From there we move into his father's story in Maida, a village in the toe of the Italian boot, and onto his father's immigration to America. The story then shifts back to his great-grandparents. Towards the end of this volume, Talese becomes a character, like the others in his own book. The book ends by circling back to the opening, a move that prepares us for the sequel that Talese says will follow his personal history from college, (the only one he could get into), through his stint in the 3rd Armor Division in Germany, where he served as public information officer for Creighton W. Abrams.

*Unto the Sons* opens in a first person point of view, as a traditional autobiography, then shifts almost imperceptibly into third person where it stays even through the author's own birth and childhood. By remaining in this point of view, Talese reminds us that we are not who or what we were in our past. He also reminds us that our representation of that past is, in fact, a "fiction" in the true sense of the word: a conscious construction, susceptible to interpretation and revision.

Throughout *Sons* there are profiles of historical figures such as Garibaldi, Napoleon, and Mussolini, that, while connecting his family's stories to the larger fabric of history, serve as vehicles for exploring and criticizing the Italian character. Talese's interpretation destroys the stereotypes of the cowardly Italian soldier, and explains why Italians, "individualistic in the extreme," never organized into a strong socio-political force in America. He explores old world notions of fatalism, and then recreates the lives of those immigrants who defied *destino* to renew their lives in America.

Here and there Talese injects the history of Italy, from pre-Christian times, through various foreign invasions and occupations by the Spanish, an experience which led to the creation of the phrase *non ti spagnare* (don't be afraid), the French, and the English. All these invasions forced upon native Italians the fear of outsiders that exists even to this day. Talese presents the evolution of independent city states, the rise of the republic through the *Risorgimento,* Italy's entrance into the modern world and the modern world's entrance into the *Sleepy Hollow* world of Maida.

Like the various autobiographical writings of Jerre Mangione, Talese's story, transcends his self to create a group biography. But groups, as we know, are made up of individuals, and individual's lives are affected by others. That's why we have so many characters in this book. Each character, in his or her own way, has contributed to the identity of the man we know as Gay Talese. Through his recounting the pasts of these many characters, Talese shows us how we are created out of the stories we are told and recreated by the stories that we tell.

This book represents the first public response of Talese's three trips to Italy. The first visit, which lasted less than a day, was as an American soldier stationed in Germany during the 1950s. "I felt I had to get out of there," says Talese. "My curiosity had brought me here, but it was too much for me. I couldn't communicate with my own grandmother or uncles. They welcomed me as a lost hero, and all I wanted was to get away from all those arms around me.

"As an American Italian, I didn't want to be Italian, but, if that was the case why did I go there to begin with. No one forced me. Back then there were two guys operating inside me. I wasn't ready for it." A few years later Talese accompanied his father on a trip back to Maida, and then didn't return again until he decided to work on this book.

While the reviews of this book have been, for the most part quite positive, much of what he's been criticized for is precisely what makes it Italian/American. Critics have complained about the amount of space Talese gives to Richard Mattison, the man who made a fortune making asbestos, the manufacturing of which "murdered" Talese's namesake grandfather Gaetano. But what these critics do not realize is that Mattison is the antagonist of this immigration epic.

Talese has also been attacked for his emphasis on the stories of his male ancestors. But it is a well known fact, in Italian/American culture, the women are central to men's ability to do what they do. Talese demonstrates this through his stories of "white widows," the wives left behind by immigrating "birds of passage." Further evidence of Talese's respect for the power women have comes through the story of Talese's mother Catherine's taking over her husband's business while her husband broods over the conflicts his native and adopted countries face during World War II.

Along with critical success, *Unto the Sons* achieved popular approval as evidenced by its long stay on *The New York Times* bestseller list. However, the real success of this book lies in wait, far beyond any material success it has already achieved. "My dream for this book is that it will start, in a public way, an awareness in the larger America of American Italian writers; if this book is sufficiently successful it will shake publishers into the realization there is something about the American Italian experience that is worth publishing because there is an audience out there; in the past, there was no belief that there was an audience; there is one now."

Talese is planning to devote what looks like the rest of his life to this subject. He hopes that this book and its sequels will attract younger Italian/American writers to join him in telling the stories of America's Italians. *Unto the Sons* is a gift, given by a man to his people. Will it be accepted, or will it, like so many other gifts presented to Italian America by its artists, fall into the mainstream where it will not be completely appreciated. Talese is not only rewriting history, he is making it by writing this book. And in the process he is calling for a response. If we, who have settled comfortably into other's perceptions of us, rise up and lend our voices to his, his success could be ours as well.

*May 1992*

# Off the Streets: The New Intellectual

## Anthony Julian Tamburri

*P*rofessor and literary critic Anthony Tamburri is representative of the up and coming Italian/American intelligentsia. Born in working class, ethnic community of Stamford, Connecticut, Tamburri worked his way through college because, "someone told me I could do better; that I could go to work with a tie on," and so he did.

Tamburri, a collegiate gymnast, attended Southern Connecticut State College out of a desire to teach Physical Education. "Because it was a crowded field," he says, "they suggested I choose something else; and so I picked Italian, intending to change to P.E. later on." That change never came.

After graduating with a Bachelor of Science degree in Education, with a major in Italian, he went on to earn a Master's Degree at Middlebury, and taught high school for one year before going on to earn his Ph.D. in Italian at University of California at Berkeley. His decision to devote his life to the study of Italian language and literature stems from an enjoyment that he says is combined with, "a sense of discovery of my roots." Tamburri traces his ancestral lineage to Faeto, Foggia, on his mother's side, and to Settefrati, Frosinone on his father's side. "All the time I was studying Italian, I was also verifying the stories, the anecdotes, the fables and myths that had been created during my childhood in the kitchens and dining rooms during the holidays."

After teaching college at Smith, Middlebury, and Auburn, Tamburri took a position at Purdue University where is currently tenured as Associate Professor. A turning point in his career came in 1982 when he was asked to participate in an Italian/American seminar at the Modern Languages Association conference. "It was my first real contact with literature of the

Italian/American experience; however, this interest remained undeveloped until 1987, after I had completed a book on the Italian Futurist writer Aldo Palazzeschi." That's when he presented a paper at the 20th-century Literature Conference at the University of Louisville. "That work, along with the papers presented by Paolo Giordano and Fred Gardaphé, became the basis for developing the anthology, *From the Margin*, which led to the journal *VIA*, which, I'm finding out, is leading to other projects in Italian/American culture."

One of those other projects is his recently published, *To Hyphenate or Not to Hyphenate*. "The scope of this study is two-fold," says Tamburri, "to draw out pertinent questions regarding any literature we consider ethnic, and to develop a theoretical model for the basis of future studies of mine in Italian/American culture and for any "Other" literature or art."

His latest book is only a small contribution to what he calls, "The Italian/American project." "Criticism of a culture must develop from within as well as from without. This doesn't mean you have to be Italian/American to criticize Italian/American artists.

"We have arrived at a point in the development of our culture where we need needed to bring the works of Italian/American artists to national audiences and professional scholarly organizations. And this is the job of critics and scholars. We are planning both more studies and books, but while we are writing them we also need to find audiences. Italian/Americans should support the literature created by Italian Americans by subscribing to the four or five major national forums, *Fra Noi*, *VIA*, *Italian Americana*, *La bella figura*, and *Il caffé*." All of them together cost less than 100 dollars per year."

Tamburri also believes Italian/Americans need a physical meeting place, and it is his dream to someday have an institute designed to foster the exploration, analysis and evaluation of Italian and Italian/American culture. "There are fine institutes devoted to our political and sociological agendas, but I believe we need one dedicated to the arts. This is of utmost importance in our project of propagating alternative images outside Italian/America. Such a place would help us to become more sophisticated consumers of the culture produced by Italian/Americans. Italian America has superseded the *pergola*, the plastic grapes hanging, red and white table clothes, that's only one piece of the mosaic we can call Italian America, which like the larger American culture, is constantly changing and evolving like a kaleidoscope. Through education, we might begin to realize that a film like *Good-Fellas* is not necessarily a negative films of Italian Americana, it might show a negative aspect of Italian America, but films like this are important contributions to the general representation of Italian Americans."

## To Hyphenate or Not To Hyphenate

In this essay, Anthony Tamburri not only offers an explanation of our use of the hyphen, he challenges it and proposes that something be done about it. *To Hyphenate or Not to Hyphenate: The Italian/American Writer — An "Other" American Writer* questions the arbitrary construction of rules, rules which most of us take for granted. In that questioning he reveals how they contribute to the distance our society has created among its cultures. Rules and standards, Tamburri tells us, when examined closely, reveal prejudices and the socio-cultural mechanisms which produce them.

This discussion is substantive in its own right, but it is also, and perhaps more importantly, symbolic of the great need our society has to reconcile the marginalization of minority cultures. Tamburri, seeing literature as "a mirror of society in which it was conceived, created and perceived," tells us that one of the goals of ethnic literature is to "dislodge and debunk the negative stereotypes." This, he tells us, requires that we employ a comparative process in our analyses of literary and cultural products. It's the critic/theorist's job to validate literature, and in this essay, Tamburri advances the validation, not only of Italian/American literature, but the literatures of all minority cultures.

Tamburri has both the expertise and the experience for this task. His previous work on the early 20th-century Italian avant-garde, in the many essays he's published and most recently in his book Of Saltimbanchi and Incendiari: *Aldo Palazzeschi and Avant-Gardism in Italy*, serves him well in his theorizing about Italian/American literature. After a very careful introduction to the goals of the book and the problems he is attempting to solve, Tamburri proceeds to a discussion of Italian/American literature, presenting a case for its existence and in the process, validating its legitimacy. Much of this section has been taken from the Introduction of *From the Margin*, of which Tamburri is a contributing co-editor. However, in this context, the material takes on a new, and different life. Tamburri's writing serves as a vital challenge to sociologist Richard Alba's notion of the *Twilight of Ethnicity*. Tamburri makes a strong case for the renewal of ethnicity. Italian/American ethnicity, he tells us, is not dying, but being revised and re-invented by today's artists.

As he examines the marginalizing process and its effects, Tamburri comes to the conclusion that Italian/American writers are re-covering as they discover their pasts and add it to their self-identities. From here, he moves into a discussion of the hyphen. Using a paradigm set up by Daniel Aaron in his essay "The Hyphenate Writer and American Letters," Tamburri presents the evolutionary stages that occur within an author as well as among generations. We've always known that we were different, but in our struggle to assimilate we have forgotten just what being Italian American means. Tamburri reminds us as he uses the tools provided by postmodern literary and cultural theory to dissemble the mechanism of viewing texts that had previously kept Italian/American literature invisible.

Tamburri sees the hyphen as one tool that mainstream culture has used to maintain the distance between "American Literature" and "Ethnic/American Literature." The hyphen, Tamburri suggests, has a "disjunctive" and not a "conjunctive" function. It's a colonizing sign, a tattoo of otherness etched into the face of texts created by members of minority cultures. It separates with the effect of maintaining that separation. So why don't we just get rid of it? As some have done. However, Tamburri's too slick for that anarchic stunt. By turning it up 45 degrees into a slash, the result is that it shortens the gap between the words while maintaining the rule.

While his argument is geared for an academic audience versed in semiotics and postmodern theory, Tamburri manages to tone down the jargon so that you don't need to have a Ph.D. to figure out what he's saying. Perhaps the only problem we have here is in the evidence Tamburri provides for his case; in this slim volume we're given with just a hint of the possibilities of what could happen when we apply his theory. His conclusion, confusing to those without much postmodern theoretical study, is really more of a challenge than any attempt to have a final, definitive word on the subject. This is the first major suggestion of a way of reading Italian/American writers since Rose Basile Green's sociological categories. With this work, Tamburri has offered a tool that needs to be applied to writing by Americans of Italian descent. His work can also help us examine the works of Martin Scorsese, Francis Ford Coppola and other Italian/American artists.

*October 1991*

# An "Amazing" Debut

## Bill Tonelli

*In* The Amazing Story of the Tonelli Family in America, Esquire senior editor Bill Tonelli takes off in a rented Buick out of South Philly in search of Americans who share his last name. His inspiration and direction are supplied by a piece of junkmail many of us have received and most of us have ignored — that postcard that says if you act quickly you can have the story of your family name and a list of all Americans sharing it for a pre-publication price of $29.95. I threw mine away. Tonelli actually sent for it, and what happens after he received it is all documented in a wonderfully funny, yet serious commentary on ethnicity and self identity in America.

The story starts in 1984, with his receipt of *The Amazing Story of the Tonelli Family in America*. "Reading it," he writes, "had the same effect as staring at a map . . . capable of sucking you into a dream state." The experience stayed dreamlike in his mind for years until he gets the idea to use the book as a travel guide for his first trans-America voyage. But before he hits the road he sends a cover letter with a survey out to those listed in the book. The returns are exciting, and for each response he places pins on a map of America "I'm in a constant state of wonder as the nation I imagined becomes real, as I slit envelopes sealed by Tonelli tongues and Tonelli spit, and read Tonelli thoughts, written with Tonelli pens, in Tonelli hands."

The focus of Tonelli's quest for a "Tonelli Nation" turns a vacation into an odyssey. In the course of traveling to Tonelli homes — in the country, in the city and in public institutions like prisons, the author meets with those whose relationship to their Italian heritage varies greatly. For the most part, he finds normal American individuals and families who have drifted as far in spirit from their Italian heritage as their immigrant ancestors have in body from their homelands.

For some, there's still pizza or tortellini night and holidays when the whole family comes together. For others, there's the solitude of a federal penitentiary or an isolated Alaskan log cabin, where Italian identities are hard to come by. What Tonelli does with all these experiences is create a mixture of television's *Funny Home Videos* and Jack Kerouac's *On the Road*.

This is Tonelli's first book, but in reading it one wonders where this guy's been. His in-your-face style combines street smarts with book learning that record his epiphanies in a lively voice. He's part journalist, part philosopher, part comic, and all writer. There's something in here for everyone.

He combines fact and feeling into a witty, often comic, accounts of the decline of Italian/American ethnicity. But there's irony in Tonelli's experience. The less he sees others identifying with Italian/American culture, the stronger his own identity becomes. One question we're left with is how have his visits affected those Tonellis who had not, or rarely, thought of their Italianness before he landed in their lives. Like a Paul Revere of ethnicity, he might have actually reignited a sense of identity in some of those he visited.

Tonelli comes to the conclusion that "Ethnicity equals history; History equals memory; America equals amnesia." But underscoring his lament of the end of Italian identity in Americans of the third, fourth and fifth generation, is the realization and reminder that ethnicity is in us and that to learn about others is to learn about the self. While some might read this as a philosophical swan song for Italian Americaness, I see it as one of the great stories that dying or changing cultures offer as a way of connecting past to present, old country to new, and self to other.

While he might have led himself to a cultural crossroads where the future of an ethnic identity depends on the past, you can bet, that after this trip, there's few people more aware of what it means to be Italian in America than Bill Tonelli. Rumor has it he's not done investigating all this. I heard he's studying Italian and preparing for a trip to the old country. I wouldn't be surprised if right now he was conjugating verbs, declining nouns, and planning a trip to Italy as a sequel to this innovative exploration of ethnicity.

*June 1994*

# Bensonhurst and Beyond

## Marianna DeMarco Torgovnick

$\mathcal{N}$ourished by stories in the oral tradition of her immigrant ancestors, Marianna De Marco Torgovnick documents her personal and professional journey towards American assimilation in *Crossing Ocean Parkway: Readings by an Italian American Daughter*. "What I tell here," she writes, "is different from the story of arrival. It is the story of assimilation — one that Italian Americans of my generation are uniquely prepared to tell, and that females need to tell most of all."

Torgovnick, a professor of English at Duke University, is the author of three other critical studies. Her most recent, *Gone Primitive: Savage Intellects, Modern Lives*, is an important look at the way Western civilization has created and viewed versions of the "primitive" to separate self and other. In *Crossing Ocean Parkway*, she continues using interdisciplinary approaches to cultural critique, but shifts the focus of earlier critical gazes to examine her own relationship to Italian and American cultures through eight essays and an epilogue.

The opening essay, "On Being White, Female, and Born in Bensonhurst," selected for *Best American Essays 1991*, was written in response to the 1989 murder of Yusuf Hawkins. The killing occurred in her old neighborhood, and as soon as she hears the news she plans to write about it, but hesitation sets in as she thinks about what her family and their neighbors might say if they see it. The essay deftly juxtaposes the sense of success and freedom that she gains by leaving Bensonhurst with the "choking and nutritive power" of being reminded of her roots. Torgovnick captures the ambivalence that any successful intellectual refugee from the "old neighborhood" faces when looking back to the road that led away from home.

The title essay, "Crossing Ocean Parkway," continues this examination of the past as she tells us about her marriage to a man who lives on the Jewish side of Ocean Parkway. Sparked by the racial murders in Crown Heights, this essay tracks Torgovnick's evolution as an intellectual.

> I had convinced myself already that Italian Americans did not value girls and especially girls who were good at the kinds of things I liked — reading, thinking, and writing . . . I had many fantasies about life outside of Bensonhurst, in "the city" and beyond, fantasies of the most "American" kind, about upward mobility in a feminine key.

One step on her way out of Bensonhurst is marrying into a Jewish/American family.

"Slasher Stories" is a very personal reaction to a very public reality of the portrayal of women as helpless victims of male rage. Woven into her criticism of popular and high cultural depictions of violence against women, is a poignant account of her early experience as a mother of a child born with what would prove to be a fatal heart defect. Without drowning in self pity, Torgovnick ably presents her experiences while challenging the reader to help her find a way to transcend traditional stereotypes of men and women.

In "The College Way," Torgovnick recalls the experience of taking a job as an assistant professor in a small, wealthy New England college town where she begins to learn what it takes to assimilate and the toll that assimilation enacts. She "learned to eat meals using silverware from the outside in," "not to curse in the matter-of-fact way New Yorkers do," and that this was a world in which she would never feel comfortable. While she would try to adjust her behavior, she could do little to change the way others perceived her. After losing her child and being denied tenure, she and her husband move on.

In the last four essays, Torgovnick's personal life takes a back seat to the subjects of her criticism. However, it becomes obvious, especially after reading the earlier essays, that criticism really can be a form of autobiography. "Dr. Dolittle and the Acquisitive Life," explores the evolution of the Dr. Dolittle books and its relationship to the maturation of her consciousness.

In "The Paglia Principle," she presents a balanced critique of the critical pose struck by the now infamous Camille Paglia. In the last two essays, "*The Godfather* as the World's Most Typical Novel" and "The Politics of the *We*," she examines the socio-historical constructions of Italian/American literature and the point-of-view (re)presented by critics such as Lionel Trilling. While she appropriately identifies herself with the developing literary tradition of Italian/American culture, Torgovnick's sense of the evolution of that tradition — like the sense conveyed by Gay Talese's infamous *New York Times Book Review* essay, "Where are the Italian American Novelists?" (March 14, 1993) — is hindered by her unfamiliarity with the hundreds of writers (both female and male) who have paved the way.

To say "For Italian American culture there is virtually only Puzo's *The Fortunate Pilgrim*" is a violation of the critic's responsibility to be informed. She's on target when she says, "writing as an Italian American woman means an awareness of paradox: reading, thinking, writing, finding a voice," but her argument is weakened when she follows that with, "imping onto a tradition of active intellectual life which has no branch marked Italian American and female." While Torgovnick has much to learn about Italian/American literature, she has much to teach us all about what it means to be an Italian/American female intellectual who has broken a stereotypical mold to become a major voice in American cultural criticism.

*December 1994*

# At Bat for Bart

## Anthony Valerio

*W*hen he was a kid, Anthony Valerio was a troublemaker and one form of punishment was to watch other kids play. Little did he know that this exile from activity would be training for a career as a writer. He started writing when he was visiting Italy in his early twenties. One day he sat on a curb and began simply by describing what he saw. "I had to be in another country, feeling lonely, isolated from my neighborhood," he says. "I realized that what was important was not that I was writing, but that I was a witness and not a participant."

With no creative writing courses available Valerio needed to find a way to apprentice himself to the writing trade. He showed his first story, which was about Mussolini and his mistress, to an editor who then put him to work answering phones. Eventually he was trained as a copy-editor, which he says is "practically a dead skill now."

During the following ten years he threw away almost everything he wrote. "I felt no need to publish everything I wrote," he says. One of the first stories he sent out was "The Sky Jacker," and it was accepted by the *Paris Review.* Today Valerio writes full-time; he has taught creative writing workshops at New York University and Rutgers, but he's stopped teaching because he felt he was drifting too far from his root as a practitioner. Valerio's three books to date all deal with Italian and Italian/American subjects. He says he first became aware of his subject area as he was teaching young writers to become aware of exploring and mining their own terrain. "I was conscious that there was a huge hole in the extant literature of Italy and Italian America.

"I first knew myself as an Italian, when on his deathbed, my paternal grandfather Antonio Valerio grabbed my shirt, pulled me down to him and said, 'Now you're me.'" Both sets of Valerio's grandparents immigrated from Naples and Sicily, during the early 20th century. From Naples, Valerio says he gained the sweet part of his nature, and from Sicily he says he gets the hardworking and disciplined side. While there was no identifiable Italian/American audience for his work, he did publish *The Mediterranean Runs through Brooklyn* in 1982, and a few years later *Valentino and the Great Italians,* 1986, to critical acclaim; however, both achieved little commercial success. "I was aware of the secret code of silence, *omertà*," he says, "and I knew it had to be broken; I also knew that it wouldn't be done without exacting a price."

At fifty-one, Valerio feels he's just hitting his stride as a writer. What is helping him now is a sense of camaraderie with other Italian/American writers, something that was lacking during the early part of his career. "Now that we're meeting at readings and conferences," he says, "there's an openness, a sense of sharing that is comforting; it's not as strong as I would like it to be, but we're just beginning to create our own academics, and critics, and writers. I am more inspired now that I know there are brothers and sisters who are reading me. Before I felt I was all alone in this territory."

His most recent publication is *A Life of A. Bartlett Giamatti,* a subject he was considering for *The Great Italians,* but, as he says, he "had no way of understanding or reconciling a man who at thirty-nine became the youngest president of Yale and who later became the president of baseball's National League. The night Giamatti died I went to the library and read all his academic work. And it was at this point that I was able to see him as a subject. I learned that Giamatti's vision was one that I shared."

Valerio is now at work on a book on Garibaldi which will be the first in American history. He says it took him six years just to find the form which combines approaches in his earlier books and his Giamatti book. "Writers are workers who can't be blinded by their subjects, as were so many of the early biographers of Columbus. We have a tendency to find our stars in the sky and remain content with gazing at them from a distance. This is not going to be the case with my approach to Garibaldi; I'm going to examine him up close."

*Bart: The Life of A. Bartlett Giamatti by Him and about Him*, is Anthony Valerio's third book. While it seems to be so entirely different from his first two, *Bart* is actually one step ahead of them both. His earlier books were full of well developed personal connections between the author and his Italian and Italian/American subjects, a posture which both enlivened the narrative and enchanted the reader. In this book, Valerio steps back from the microphone and lets a variety of other voices tell the story.

After a brief introduction, Valerio disappears and we are left to experience Giamatti from a variety of perspectives: Giamatti's own, his friends, family, students, professional colleagues, and critics. Valerio's research took him through Giamatti's books: *The Earthly Paradise and the Renaissance Epic, Exile and Change in Renaissance Literature, Play of Double Senses: Spenser's Faerie Queen,* and *A Free and Ordered Space: The Real World of the University.* He juxtaposes excerpts from these books with excerpts from Giamatti's writings on sports. Interspersed are illustrations from Renaissance art and classic baseball photography. By avoiding the usual mediating narrative, Valerio does a great service both to Giamatti and to the reader. The effort results is a classy and fitting tribute to a true 20th-century renaissance man.

We find out through selections from articles and interviews the necessary biographical statistics. Born in 1938, Giamatti was named after grandfathers Angelo Giammattei, an Italian immigrant on his father's side, and Bartlett Walton a Harvard graduate. Giamatti's father Valentine, a Phi Beta Kappa graduate of Yale, Ph.D. from Harvard, became an authority on Dante and was an enormous influence on Giamatti: "I adored him, I think I learned all my real lessons from my father . . . He was the first person to introduce me to literature and he gave me to understand that the academic world, while it's never a perfect world . . . , is one where there are real aspirations and ideals."

Giamatti applied these lessons to the game of baseball; we learn his love for the sport came not as a player, but as an observer and an organizer. He never played ball, but worked as a team manager. His understanding of the deeper levels of baseball most probably stem from his great ability to abstract from this experience and connect his observations to philosophical truths he came to learn through his study of literature.

One gets the sense from reading this book that there is more to baseball than playing it or being a fan in the stands. There are rewards to studying life and the games we play, and we learn that Giamatti was one person who knew how to balance analysis and enjoyment. Valerio's narrative control is invisible; in fact, the author, in true *maestro* fashion, makes no sound during the performance. Yet, when we step back from the book, we can't but realize that his work is what made these many disparate parts come together so smoothly. While the larger structure of the book moves chronologically from Giamatti's early life to death at an early age, the segments of each chapter transcend any typical chronological flow, reminding us that life is composed of the uncontrolled connections between past, present and future, between Giamatti's lives as Renaissance scholar, Yale President, President of the National League and Commissioner of Baseball. Valerio's success with this book lies in his ability to connect the ideal and the real; the Renaissance garden and the baseball diamond, high art and popular culture, and in the process he creates a synthesis of a whole life.

With *Bart*, Valerio has given much more than he might receive. It's the kind of book you can pick up at any time and read it through, or flip back and forth. It's a beautiful gift, one of those rare publications that will easily cross the boundaries of high and popular culture. It is not only handsomely produced, it is also thoughtfully constructed by a master who in his search for A. Bartlett Giamatti, has found a way for us to get a better look at the many lives that make up the life of one man.

In *Valentino and the Great Italians, According to Anthony Valerio*, we learn that while we might make history, history also makes us. In this collection of twenty-two essays, primarily portraits of famous, infamous and newly crowned heroes, Anthony Valerio elevates regular Joes and Josephines, as easily (and as wittily) as he levels the stature of such household names as Enrico Caruso, Frank Sinatra, and Joe DiMaggio. What is wonderful about all this literary play is that Valerio creates new myths by demystifying the old.

This is the second time around for *Valentino*. First published in 1986 by a press that soon went out of business, *Valentino* opened to critical acclaim. However, for years the only way to get the book was through a library or out of Valerio's closet. Now Antonio D'Alfonso of Guernica Editions makes this gem available in a paperback edition that should be required reading for everyone who's ever listened to Frank Sinatra, eaten pizza or sipped an imported wine.

Like many great artists, Valerio was way ahead of his time. His writing is intelligent, irreverent, and always entertaining. Who else could begin an essay on Christopher Columbus with: "My experience as sea is confined to the baths my mother gave me," and get away with admitting to familial lust. His style is a unique blend of ironic irreverence that actually sacralizes the mundane. There's no doubt that the Philp Roth of Italian/American literature is here. While Valerio's one writer who can make you cry and laugh in the same sentence, he also makes you think.

There's a strong thread of autobiography that runs through each essay, and his personal reactions to the great, and not-so-great, Italians, have a way of connecting to our own lives in ways only a truly gifted writer can do. By exploring both the Italians who have achieved greatness and those whose lives might have remained unknown had he not chosen them as subjects, Valerio speaks of and for the earlier generations of Italian Americans who consumed popular culture while it consumed them. But more importantly, he creates a literary art that transcends the confines of Little Italies.

This is all must reading for even those most knowledgable in Italian and Italian/American culture. In "Pietro Laclacca," Valerio finds that Caruso can be a way of connecting science and the arts as he looks for links between the old country and the old neighborhood. There's no better essay on Garibaldi, or his comrade-wife Anita, than what Valerio has produced in this collection. You'll laugh and cry with "The DiGeorgio Girls" and "Boys," see a side of stars like Valentino, Caruso, Mona Lisa, Mario Cuomo, and Lee Iacocca that have never been known.

While there may have been no identifiable Italian/American audience for his earlier books, Valerio has continued to write and with the publication of *Valentino and the Great Italians* may finally reach the audience that is ready for him.

*December 1991 / August 1994*

# The Future of Columbus

## Robert Viscusi

*C*ould Columbus have a future after the bashing and thrashing he under-
went last year? This is a question that poet Robert Viscusi confronts with
his long poem, *An Oration Upon the Most Recent Death of Christopher
Columbus.*

First delivered on Columbus Day 1992 in New York City, and again in
Washington, D.C. at the annual conference of the American Italian Historical Association, *An Oration* began to attract an audience because the poem
speaks to the many different perspectives by which Columbus can be
viewed. "It's the kind of poem that lives on after you've heard it," said one
listener. "It's one of those poems you want to have in your hands, cause you
know there's a lot to it," said another. Because of such responses, "An
Oration" became the first volume of "VIA Folios," a new publication series
launched by the journal *Voices in Italian Americana.*

Viscusi, better known as one of the foremost critics of Italian/Ameri-
can literature and culture, and Director of the Wolfe Humanities Institute at
Brooklyn College, has produced a landmark poem in the history of Italian
Americana. The poem is written in thirty-three stanzas composed in a
variety of poetic styles including free verse, the sonnet, and blank verse. For
those familiar with the poetry of the Beats, *An Oration* could be read as an
Italian/American "Howl," that monumental epic of Allen Ginsberg which
spoke for a whole generation. With this poem, Viscusi speaks of and for
many generations and offers an explanation of how and why Italian Americans clung to Columbus in their efforts to be accepted as Americans. He
also speaks to the difficulty of clinging to the traditional notion of Columbus as we move into the next century.

The poem opens with the narrator's discovery of Columbus.

## The Future of Columbus

> i found christopher columbus hiding in the ash tray
> what are you doing there if you please?
> no one smokes, he said, leave me alone!

From here the poet suggests that we can learn to live without Columbus just like we have learned to travel without St. Christopher, the desanctified hero of the highways and airways. The poet then wonders if Garibaldi might replace our fallen heroes.

> the fact is columbus day will go the way of the dinosaur
> along with everything else
> meanwhile what about garibaldi
> who was fighting for the poor of italy
> but after the revolution
> lived to see the rich steal italy
> and starve the poor
> selling them to labor gangs in suez
> shipping them to new york to dig subways
> in return for cheap american grain
> they brought back in the empty ships

In a playful and artful fashion, the poet examines the evolution Columbus as a figure of American culture who once represented the "freedom of inquiry" and the advance of science over superstition, but who has become useless in our postmodern age. Yet, Viscusi shows us how we can put Columbus to good use, to tell our history, to map our future, and to explain the Italian/American presence in American culture.

*October 1993*

# A Jack of All Trades

## Justin Vitiello

## 1

*F*or Justin Vitiello, writing and reading are the ways to bridge the gap between the streets and the academy, between the oral and literary traditions of Italian and American culture. Born in Queens, New York, and raised outside the city in Nutley, New Jersey, Vitiello says a wild and potentially destructive adolescence was tamed by his parents and his education.

Italian on his father's side, Vitiello's grandfather was an anarchist and pacifist who emigrated from a small town called Boscoreale, at the foot of Mt. Vesuvius in Italy in 1901. On his mother's side he's German. He was raised primarily in the Neapolitan tradition except that, "We were not allowed to speak Italian at home; we were supposed to be American." To make sure this would happen, his parents sent him and his siblings to the best schools. For Justin, it was Brown University in Rhode Island.

"By getting out of the neighborhood, I came to understand it better. Once you go to a place like Brown, where there was some discrimination against Italian Americans — we were considered dummies and genetically criminal — you're going to get cosmopolitanized. But you can live the tension between what you become (the intellectual) and what you were (a street kid)."

After graduation Vitiello was awarded a Fulbright fellowship to Spain where he continued his study of the Spanish language and culture. "My father wanted me to learn Spanish so that I could become an engineer. His idea of becoming professional was tied to science." But Vitiello had different plans.

In 1964 he began graduate studies in Spanish at the University of Michigan where came to study Italian through the Spanish Renaissance. In 1973 he earned his Ph.D. and was hired to teach comparative literature in an experimental Residential College program which he left protesting the school's "loss of founding ideals." For a while he worked for minimum wage in a Vermont furniture factory. A year later he was hired in Italian at Temple University in Philadelphia were he has since taught Italian, humanities and Italian Americana. Between 1977 and 1979 he headed Temple's Rome program. During that period he worked with Danilo Dolci, the Italian poet and non-violent reformer. Besides assisting in Dolci's Sicilian peasant reform movement, Vitiello also translated Dolci's poetry and later set up a multi-disciplinary summer study program in Trapetto. He soon became head of the American "Friends of Danilo Dolci." In 1984 he began applying Dolci's ideas to help foster peace and social justice in south Philadelphia.

"In an effort to promote our own cultures we found local Italian and Black talent which we hoped to foster through an Italo/Afro American carnival in the basement of a local church. Some of the older people in our organization didn't like the idea of working with blacks. Unfortunately, Dolci listened to these people and pulled out his support." During a 1987 sabbatical, Vitiello returned to Trapetto and began studying immigration/emigration through oral history. When listening their stories he realized that they were telling their history through folk narrative, "They saw their lives as types of 'Odysseys' and I wanted to record their history from their point of view, a perspective usually left out of history books." These oral histories and his analysis of them resulted in a book which is currently circulating publishers. His most recent publication is *Vanzetti's Fish Cart,* a collection of poems started twenty-five years ago which he describes as the result of his "wanting to get back to the spoken voice."

Vitiello has contributed much to the promotion of Italian/American culture. He has published poems, short stories, and essays on Italian, Italian/American and American culture, and is currently working on poetic travel books on Spain and Sicily and on a new book of poetry entitled *Subway Home*, in which he interweaves self-reflection as an Italian American with the social reality of Queens. Vitiello believes that the time has come for a greater appreciation of Italian/American literature. "Books like *The Dream Book* and *From the Margin* have called attention to a body of literature that has for too long been unknown. Most of us come from peasant culture which was rejected or simply left behind during the immigrant experience. Up until recently our people didn't read. A lot of them traded the storytelling for television — the destroyer of literary tradition. Another factor was the importance for us to become doctors and lawyers; these were the reasons to go on to school. But now we've got our writers and a great body of readers; no matter what they've studied in college, they read, and it's up to us to give them something to read."

# 2

# Vanzetti's Fish Cart

*I*n 1989, Justin Vitiello published "Il carro del pesce di Vanzetti," his first book of poetry in Italian. Published by Corpo 10, Italy's equivalent of America's City Lights Books, to enthusiastic critical response. *Il carro* contained the same poems in this English language edition. Because Vitiello composes in both languages (and has translated the likes of Danilo Dolci, Gaspara Stampa and Michelangelo), it's unfortunate that we can't get these two publications together to present a single bilingual edition so that we'd could better come to know the dual nature of this Italian/American writer.

*Vanzetti's Fish Cart* contains thirty-two poems which, when read from beginning to end, form a spiraling journey from self which gains its identity from family, to portraits of others, and finally to a new level of self-reflection. Vitiello's geography bridges the space between "Little Italy" ghettoes, to ancestral villages and the wide open lands of strangers in between.

What's exciting about Vitiello's poetry is the way he weaves a personal tapestry from the threads of the various cultures he's lived in and studied. America, Italy, and Spain all figure into his work. And while to the more well versed readers, some of the influences may seem too strong, Vitiello counters the likes of Theocritus in "journey," Lorca in "death called me to the door," Pound in "attic" and Williams in "all angels are created equal" with strong doses of southern Italian and Italian/American oral tradition.

Years of studying oral culture and collecting oral histories have paid off in such gems as "why Volpe cant change his skin" and "with a crossbow we divided" — pure Studs Terkel in verse. Vitiello has an ear for the poetry in other's voices and an eye for getting it down onto the page. Adroitly mining both sides of his Italian/American psyche, Vitiello bridges both quite smoothly through his mixture of diction. Those who wish to preserve the memory of the immigrant grandparent in verse portraits would do well to read "survivor" before even attempting it. Here Vitiello shows his poetic skills, balancing his phrasing so well that his poem neither falls into sentimental nostalgia nor slips into pompous glorification of the past. He connects present to past and memory to myth so well that its hard to tell them apart, and impossible to believe we're not listening to the original voice.

Vitiello's collection contains a variety of poetic forms, relying mainly on stanzaic lyrics and longer prosaic travel narratives (some of which read as dramatic scenes). "January 12, 1977" is a prime example of the drama that Vitiello can create. In the form of a monologue spoken to a dead father, the poet captures so well the struggle between parent and child and the realization that while death may halt the interaction, it doesn't lessen the impact:

> *basta così*, knowing death surprised you as you would have it while you were still glutted with work, and that the services, so arranged, are a compromise we both accept, I can curse in silence and see that our pact of contrary friendship is sealed.

The collection's "Prologue" presents an Eskimo version of Plato's "Allegory of the Cave," in which a returning traveler tells his villagers all the wonders of his voyage to America only to be banished and later killed. Too often this is the plight of the Italian/American writer who has left Little Italy, returned with something to say, and is ignored, or even worse, dismissed as an "intellectual." Let's hope this is not a prophecy, for what Vitiello has to tell us, in this book that shortens the distance between the streets and the schools, is something we all need to hear.

## 3

*Sicily Within, Supplement IV of Arba Sicula*, a journal of Sicilian folklore and literature, is the account of Justin Vitiello's love affair with Sicily that began in the late 1970s and continues to this day. Through travelogue-type journalism, poetry, memoirs and imaginative narrative, and crisp dialogue,

Vitiello recreates his nine year journey from tourist to near native of this island that is as time filled as it is timeless.

> In Sicily you are nowhere but the dead center of the Mediterranean. To cultivate the art of doing nothing. Now. Here. In silence. Or just extemporizing. Transported in to past of future as if always present.

Vitiello, a veteran translator of Italian and Sicilian works, presents a view of Sicily rarely seen by travelers. He steps back often and gives the spotlight to the locals like Toto, his guide through Trapetto, Zu Sariddu, who at 91 "has won the respect of a tribal sage. And whenever experts invade the Jato Valley to study progress in developing areas, he is there, short and curved like a Bronze Age hoe, with a trunk slung close to the furrows," and Gino Orlando, an itinerant ghetto barber who serves as Vitiello's guide through Palermo. *Sicily Within* is a treat served up by a pro.

# 4

# Joe the Confessor

*Confessions of a Joe Rock* is Vitiello's response to Daniel DeFoe's *Moll Flanders*. Set up as a manuscript received by a professor from a New Jersey student, *Confessions* is the hilarious tale of a half Italian/half Puerto Rican/American street kid who heads west in search of an education, carrying with him the story of Joe Rock. Rock, the alter-ego of most second- and third-generation Italian/American male intellectuals, grew up tough: "Some folks say childhood is magic. You know what my three wishes was? End it, get out, never go back." Set in the 1960s, *Confessions* is filled with all the sex, drugs, and rock and roll of the period, and tells it all without that nasty aftertaste of nostalgia that has flattened much of what's been written about those days. Vitiello, a poet at heart, goes wild with this coming of age story of a guy whose a cross between a wiseguy and a Huckleberry Finn.

# 5

$\mathscr{A}$s a novelist, poet, translator, scholar and critic, Justin Vitiello has contributed much to the promotion of Sicilian, Italian and Italian/American culture. While not of Sicilian ancestry, he's Italian on his father's side and German on his mother's, he has proven himself to be one of its most dedicated students. His poetic travel narrative, entitled *Sicily Within,* published in 1992 by *Arba Sicula,* was early evidence that for Vitiello Sicily was more than an interesting place on a map.

In 1987 Vitiello returned to Trapetto, Sicily, and began studying the village's emigration through oral history. These oral histories and his analysis of them resulted in his latest publication: *Poetics and Literature of the Sicilian Diaspora.*

This reading of Sicily through the people of the village of Trapetto connects the contemporary to the classic, the scientific to the mythic and preserves what makes Sicily continue to be a major crossroads of world cultures. In this latest effort to bridge cultures, he has brought all his skills to bear on making the connection between the oral and literary traditions of Sicilian culture. This volume is a testament to solid scholarship that presents keen insights to humanity and displays Vitiello's tremendous talents as a writer.

What we have here is one book made up of a number of books. His presentation of the developments in oral history, research and interpretation, provides an excellent survey of the field, useful to amateur and professional alike. Vitiello uses his knowledge of anthropology, history, sociology, political science, linguistics, folklore studies, and literary criticism to create a truly interdisciplinary approach to his subject. Throughout this scholarship Vitiello weaves a narrative that renders the entire experience in the best tradition of travel writing.

Using fiction and poetry, he captures insights that seldom find their way into traditional scholarship. The train ride south and Vitiello's conversations with native Sicilians sets up a dialectic that recalls Elio Vittorini's In Sicilia. His presentation of the oral histories, without any scholarly or analytical interruption, enables the reader to listen to these people, the way our guide did, and to draw our own conclusions. The result is a most interesting and never-before-done ethnographic account of Sicilian culture as told by those who know it best because they have made it.

At $100, *Poetics and Literature* might not be in most readers' price range; however, it is a must for all libraries and is certainly worth owning for those doing research on the Sicilian diaspora. Vitiello has provided us all with a valuable resource that is a pleasure to read and a major foundation for future studies.

*January 1991/January 1992/August 1992/December 1993*

# Bibliography

Alfonsi, Ferdinando. *Poesia Italo-Americana: Saggi e testi. Italian American Poetry: Essays and Texts*. Catanzaro: Carello Editore, 1991.

Ancona, Vincenzo. *Malidittu la lingua (Damned Language): Poetry and Miniatures*. Bilingual, trans. Gaetano Cipolla. (With two audio cassettes). Brooklyn, NY Legas, 1990.

Ardizzone, Tony. *The Evening News*. Athens, GA: University of Georgia Press, 1986.

——————. *Heart of the Order*. New York: Henry Holt & Co, 1986.

——————. *Larabi's Ox*. Minneapolis: Milkweed Editions, 1992.

Barolini, Helen. Ed. *The Dream Book*. New York: Shocken Books, 1985.

Bernardi, Adria. *House with Names: The Immigrants of Highwood, Illinois*. Urbana, IL: University of Illinois Press, 1990.

Birnbaum, Lucia Chiavola. *Black Madonnas: Feminism, Religion and Politics in Italy Boston*: Northeastern Univesity Press, 1993.

——————. *Liberazione della donna: Feminism in Italy*. Middletown, CT: Wesleyan University Press, 1986.

Bona, Mary Jo. Ed. *The Voices We Carry: Recent Italian/American Women's Fiction*. Toronto/New York: Guernica Editions, 1994.

Bryant, Dorothy Calvetti. *Anita, Anita*. Berkeley, CA: Ata Books, 1993.

Bush, Mary. *A Place of Light*. New York: William Morrow, 1991.

Calcagno, Anne. *Pray for Yourself*. Evanston, IL: Tri-Quarterly Books, 1993.

Carrera, Alessandro. *The Perfect Bride/La sposa perfetta*. Houston: The Thorn Books, 1991.

Cipolla, Gaetano, trans. *The Poetry of Nino Martoglio*. Brooklyn: Legas, 1993.

Cuomo, George. *Trial by Water*. New York: Random House, 1993.

D'Alfonso, Antonio. *The Other Shore*. Montreal/Toronto/ New York: Guernica Editions, 1988.

——————. *Panick Love*. Toronto/New York: Guernica Editions, 1992.

DeRosa, Tina. *Paper Fish*. Chicago: The Wine Press, 1980.

DiBartolomeo, Albert. *Fool's Gold*. New York: St. Martin's Press, 1992.

——————. *The Vespers Tapes*. New York: The Walker Co, 1991.

Di Donato, Pietro. *Christ in Concrete*. New York: Signet, 1993.

——————. *Immigrant Saint: The Life of Mother Cabrini*. New York: St. Martin's Press, 1991.

DiStasi, Lawrence. Ed. *The Big Book of Italian American Culture* (Formerly titled *Dream Streets*). New York: Harper Collins, 1992.

Fante, John. *1933 Was a Bad Year*. Santa Rosa, CA: Black Sparrow Press, 1985.

——————. *West of Rome*. Santa Rosa, CA: Black Sparrow Press, 1986.

Gillan, Maria Mazziotti. *The Weather of Old Seasons*. Merrick, NY: Cross-Cultural Communications, 1989.

——————. *Taking Back My Name*. San Francisco: malafemmina press, 1991.

Hendin, Josephine Gattuso. *The Right Thing to Do*. Boston: David Godine, 1988.

La Puma, Salvatore. *The Boys of Bensonhurst*. Athens, GA: University of Georgia Press, 1987.

——————. *Teaching Angels to Fly*. New York: W.W. Norton & Company, 1992.

——————. *A Time for Wedding Cake*. New York: W.W. Norton, 1991.

La Sorte, Michael. *La Merica: Images of the Italian Greenhorn*. Phildelphia: Temple University Press, 1986.

Lentricchia, Frank. *The Edge of Night: A Confession*. New York: Random House, 1994.

Lloyd, Susan Caperna. *No Pictures in My Grave: A Spiritual Journey in Sicily*. San Francisco: Mercury House, 1992.

Malpezzi, Frances and William M. Clements. *Italian-American Folklore*. Little Rock, Arkansas: August House, Inc.,1992.

Manes, Rose Tavino. *Prima Vera*. Ft. Lauderdale, FL: Ashley Books, 1991.

Manfredi, Renee. *Where Love Leaves Us*. Iowa City, IA: University of Iowa Press, 1994.

Mangione, Jerre. *A Passion for Sicilians:The World around Danilo Dolci*. New Brunswick, N.J. Transaction Books, 1985.

Mangione, Jerre and Ben Morreale. *La Storia*. New York: Harper-Collins, 1992.

Marzani, Carl. *The Education of a Reluctant Radical: Growing Up American, Book 2*. New York: Topical Books, 1993.

——————. *The Education of a Reluctant Radical: Roman Childhood, Book 1*. New York: Topical Books, 1992.

——————. *The Education of a Reluctant Radical: Spain, Munich and Dying Empires,*Book 3. New York: Topical Books, 1994.

Maso, Carole. *Ava*. Normal, IL: Dalkey Archive Press, 1993.

Mathias, Elizabeth, and Richard Raspa. *Italian Folktales: The Verbal Art of an Immigrant Woman*. Detroit: Wayne State University Press, 1985.

Morreale, Ben. *A Few Virtuous Men*. Plattsburg, NY: Tundra Books, 1973.

——————. *Monday Tuesday, Never Come Sunday*. Plattsburg, NY: tundra Books, 1977.

——————. *The Seventh Saracen*. London: Victor Gollancz, Ltd, 1959.

Napoli, Joseph. *A Dying Cadence: Memories of a Sicilian Chidhood*. W. Bethesda, MD: Marna Press, 1986.

Parini, Jay. *Bay of Arrows* New York: Henry & Co., 1992.

——————. *The Patch Boys*. New York: Holt, 1986.

Patriarca, Gianna. *Italian Women and Other Tragedies*. Toronto/New York: Guernica, 1994.

Puzo, Mario. *The Sicilian*. New York: Linden Press, 1984.

Raptosh, Diane. *Just West of Now*. Toronto/New York: Guernica Editions, 1993.

Rimanelli, Giose. *Benedetta in Guysterland*. Toronto/New York: Guernica Editions, 1993.

Ruffolo, Lisa. *Holidays*. St. Paul, M.N.: New Rivers Press, 1987.

Scammacca, Nat. *Bye Bye America: Memories of a Sicilian-American*. Merrick, NY: Cross-Cultural Communications, 1986.

Silesky, Barry. *Ferlinghetti: the artist in his time*. New York: Warner Books, 1990.

Talese, Gay. *Unto the Sons*. New York: Alfred A. Knopf, 1992.

Tamburri, Anthony Julian. *To Hyphenate or Not to Hyphenate: The Italian/American Writer: An "Other" American*. Montreal/Toronto/New York: Guernica Editions, 1991.

Tonelli, Bill. *The Amazing Story of the Tonelli Family in America*. New York: Addison-Wesley Publishing Co., 1994.

Torgovnick, Marianna DeMarco, *Crossing Ocean Parkway: Readings by an Italian American Daughter*. Chicago: University of Chicago Press, 1994.

Valerio, Anthony. *Bart, A Life of A. Bartlett Giamatti: By Him and About Him*. New York: Harcourt, Brace and Jovanovich, 1991.

———. *Valentino and the Great Italians, According to Anthony Valerio*. Toronto/New York: Guernica Editions, 1994.

Viscusi, Robert. *An Oration Upon the Most Recent Death of Christopher Columbus*. W. Lafayette, IN: VIA Folios, 1993.

Vitiello, Justin. *Confessions of A Joe Rock*. Franklin Lakes, NJ: Lincoln Springs, 1992.

———. *Poetics and Literature of the Sicilian Diaspora: Studies in Oral History and Story-Telling*. Lewiston, N.Y.: The Edwin Mellen Press, 1993.

———. *Vanzetti's Fish Cart*. Lewiston, N.Y.: The Mellen Poetry Press, 1991.

———. *Sicily Within*. Jamaica, NY: Arba Sicula, 1992.

# The Guernica Essay Series

Anselmi, William, and Gouliamos, Kosta, Editors. *Mediating Culture*. 1994
Anselmi, William, and Gouliamos, Kosta. *Elusive Margins*. 1997.
Arnopoulos, Paris. *Sociopolitics: Political Development in Postmodern Societies*. 1994
Arnopoulos, Paris. *Cosmopolitics: Public Policy of Outer Space*. 1997.
Beaudet, Pierre. Editor. *Under the Boardwalk in Quebec City*. 1990
Chamberland, Paul. *The Courage of Poetry*. 1987
Chiellino, Gino. *Fremde: A Discourse of the Foreign*. 1994.
Chion, Michel. *The Films of Jacques Tati*. 1996
D'Alfonso, Antonio. *In Italics: In Defense of Ethnicity*. 1996.
Del Negro, Giovanna. *Looking through My Mother's Eyes*. 1997
Doré, Jean. *For Montreal*. 1986
Gambino, Richard. *Blood of My Blood: The Dilemma of the Italian-Americans*. 1996.
Gardaphé, Fred. *Dagoes Read: Tradition and the Italian/American Writer*. 1996.
Gualtieri, Antonio R. *Conscience and Coercion: Ahmadi Muslims and Orthodoxy in Pakinstan*. 1989
Gualtieri, Antonio R. *Search for Meaning: Exploring Religions of the World*. 1991
Loriggio, Francesco, Editor. *Social Pluralism and Literary History: The Literature of Italian Immigration*. 1996.
Minni, C.D. and Foschi Ciampolini, Anna. Editors. *Writers in Transition*. 1990
Melfi, Mary, Editor. *Painting Moments: Art, AIDS, and Nick Palazzo*. 1997.
O'Meara, John. *Otherworldly Hamlet*. 1991
O'Meara, John. *Othello's Sacrifice: Essays on Shakespeare and Romantic Tradition*. 1996.
Perin, Roberto and Sturino, Franc. *Arrangiarsi: The Italian Immigration Experience in Canada*. 1989
Pivato, Joseph. *Echo: Essays on Other Literatures*. 1994.
Pivato, Joseph. Editor. *Contrasts: Comparative Essays on Italian-Canadian Writing*. 1985
Royer, Jean. *Interviews to Literature*. 1996.
Tamburri, Anthony J. *To Hyphenate or Not to Hyphenate*. 1991
Tuzi, Marino. *The Power of Allegiances*. 1997.
Verdicchio, Pasquale. *Devils in Paradise*. 1997.